# Women and Social Work

# Women and Social Work
## Narrative Approaches

**Judith Milner**
**Consultant Editor: Jo Campling**

palgrave

First published 2001 by
PALGRAVE
Houndmills, Basingstoke, Hampshire RG21 6XS and
175 Fifth Avenue, New York, N.Y. 10010
Companies and representatives throughout the world

PALGRAVE is the new global academic imprint of
St. Martin's Press LLC Scholarly and Reference Division and
Palgrave Publishers Ltd (formerly Macmillan Press Ltd).

ISBN 0–333–92245–x paperback

This book is printed on paper suitable for recycling and
made from fully managed and sustained forest sources.

A catalogue record for this book is available
from the British Library.

10   9   8   7   6   5   4   3   2   1
10   09  08  07  06  05  04  03  02  01

Printed in Malaysia

*To N. C. who, quite unknowingly, provided me with the motivation to write this book*

# Contents

# Preface

Practising feminist social work is far from straightforward. Not only are the knowledge base and organisational structures of social work based largely on men's ways of understanding and managing women as wives and mothers but women service users frequently resist the feminist insights of their social workers. During a brief break from my post as a senior lecturer in social work at the University of Huddersfield in 1991 to work as a child protection practitioner, I found myself increasing women's responsibility-taking for every aspect of family life and failing to include men in the social work endeavour (Milner, 1993a; 1993b; 1996) – despite my expressed feminist intentions. A lengthy rethink of ways in which women service users could be empowered to gain meaningful control over their lives led to a developing interest in applying solution-focused and narrative therapy to statutory social work practice. The offer of an early retirement package by the university then gave me an opportunity to return to practice and I accepted a post as a mentor to a 'failing' children's home and sessional work on the Northorpe Hall Trust counselling scheme for young people who have experienced violence. Determined to 'do better' as a feminist practitioner, I began slowly and methodically to use a solution-focused approach, listening very carefully to young people and women's concerns and preferred solutions.

What happened over the next three years was a realisation that while my years of 'expert' knowledge explained young people and women's general circumstances, it told me very little about their specific concerns and competencies. My hypotheses often turned out to be completely wrong; my ideas about possible solutions had usually been tried and failed, and service users had much better ideas. The realisation that service users' knowledge, what Turnell and Edwards (1999) call 'local knowledge', was more important than my 'professional knowledge' meant that I gave up many cherished theories and ideas. I learnt so much about service users' successes under conditions of adversity and creativity in solution finding that I was as delighted as they were when they answered a regularly asked solution-focused question: did you know this about yourself? Working with people to find their preferred solutions is a joyous way of working that avoids becoming stuck and burn-out. It is a genuinely anti-oppressive way of operating; one which helped me figure out how to *do* feminist social work, although I prefer to call this a womanly approach. Womens' solutions turn out to be both complex and subtle; as they have to be if women and young people are to create larger spaces for themselves at the same time as maintaining their relationships with the men in their lives.

This book is an account of how I developed the confidence to incorporate ideas from narrative therapy into my work. In focusing on how women can begin to take only reasonable and achievable responsibility for relationships, it is essentially a book for women. However, when women start taking less responsibility, then men have to begin taking more. So, men have crept into this book too and I have discovered that men often have similar needs to women. I offer the stories of people's success in this book as an invitation to the reader to (re)discover the often neglected potential of service users to find solutions to all manner of problems when they are consulted as experts in their own lives.

# Acknowledgements

There are many marvellous people to whom I owe thanks for opportunities, ideas, critical comments on earlier drafts and enthusiastic support:

**Northorpe Hall Trust**
Dorothy Jessop for managing me and saying no as well as yes but supporting me either way.

Nick Lofthouse for creating the best networking room I have experienced; and the fashion advice. Joan Blakey for making my job a lot easier by providing a warm welcome to all the young people and their families who come nervously for sessions. Molly Pratt, who not only is the best therapist I know but also makes a mean chocolate cake. Rayner Jessop and Tony Pratt for sound common sense, practical support and unfailing good humour.

**St James's University Hospital**
Dilys Antoniades, who not only knows more about 'confusion' than anyone I have ever met but also sorted out mine. Rosemary Cheshire for critical comments. Ruth Crowther for demonstrating just how bedside interviewing should be done. Sonia Hennigan for helping me understand the complexities for people undergoing transplant surgery. Chris Wood, for providing the challenge to work with chronically ill people and supporting me whilst I attempted it. Marie Gallagher for being supportive, not least for guiding me through the vagaries of the computer system. Margaret Nichols for being supportive and helpful without ever being obvious; a real mover and shaker.

**The University of Huddersfield**
Christine Horrocks for writing 'you can't say that!' and 'where are the messy cases?'all over earlier drafts. Nancy Kelly for saying the same things, only more tactfully. Neither of them for taking me to see the film *Sleepy Hollow*.

And not forgetting all the opportunities, advice and support from Jo Campling; my supervisor, Patrick O'Byrne; staff and residents at Woodlands Children's Home; Phil Tomlinson of Kirklees SSD;

Dave Basker of North Lincolnshire SSD; and Fran Richards at Armley Gaol. I also (grudgingly) offer thanks to my dachsund, Rosie, who tolerated my strange working hours in the writing of this book with less good humour than usual. She much prefers meeting the people who gave me permission to share their stories of hope and provided me with the creative solutions described in this book. I extend my warmest appreciation of their courage and abilities and hope that you, too, will be cheered by their stories and inspired to discover similar expertise in all the service users you meet.

# 1

# Combining narrative and solution-focused approaches

## What are solution-focused and narrative approaches to social work?

Narrative and solution-focused therapies are based on the simple idea that it is not only not necessary to understand a problem to arrive at its solution but it is also more profitable for both social workers and their service users to concentrate on competencies rather than deficits. The therapy is, therefore, future-oriented instead of being preoccupied with the past, emphasises human resources rather than risks, and studies success instead of failure. As these are aspects of their lives in which service users are most interested, it has much to offer social workers as a means of engaging service users in a cooperative endeavour.

It is not, however, a simplistic emphasis on discovering positives. Although a solution-focused approach, for example, is based on the notion that all problems have exceptions, times when the problem could have occurred but somehow did not, it involves a rigorous search for these exceptions. Exceptions to problems may be very small, unrecognised, or even discounted by service users so a high degree of communication skill is required if they are to be identified, and then developed, in order to construct a picture of a possible future without the problem. For example, the only time that Bridget had felt free from her depression was when she was 'away' on holiday abroad. This was not an experience she could repeat regularly but careful listening to the words she used to describe what 'being away' was like revealed the significance of being near water to her being less oppressed by dark thoughts. She could then identify smaller occasions when the depression was less, such as walking along a river bank, and increase this coping strategy by taking up swimming, arranging trips to the seaside, and buying a fish tank for her home. At no point was 'depression' analysed so, in the sense that it grows out of detailed observations, a solution-focused approach is said

1

to be atheoretical (de Shazer, 1988), although it is based on ideas from social constructionism. It seeks always to find the service user's unique way of cooperating with the social work enterprise, whether the service user is voluntarily seeking help or is a mandated service user.

Narrative approaches also depend on listening skills as they are aimed at providing options for the telling and retelling of preferred stories of people's lives (*their* solutions) by deconstructing dominant cultural stories, particularly those which marginalise and oppress service users. Based on poststructural ideas, narrative therapy challenges people's beliefs that a problem speaks their identity, a 'totalising' effect which conflates the person with the problem. It seeks to separate the person from the problem and develop a sense of incongruency between the two which opens up new possibilities for responsibility taking and accountability. The most significant difference between solution-focused and narrative approaches is the more explicit acknowledgment of power issues in the latter.

Both approaches can be combined in social work practice as they share common ideas about the uniqueness of individuals, are interested in present and future functioning rather than past failure, and relinquish social worker expertise in the understanding of problems in favour of influencing service users in the construction of their own competencies. They cannot be combined with more traditional approaches to social work practice in some sort of 'add-on' way in certain cases as an entirely different philosophy and set of principles is involved, based on a fundamentally different way of understanding the nature of people.

The basic philosophy of both narrative and solution-focused approaches is that people are experts in their own lives, even though this expertise may have been undermined by the structural inequalities which affect many service users' lives; and traditional ways of explaining human behaviour, which are often unreliable (Dryden & Fletham, 1994). If this expertise is validated in conversations, initiated by the worker in an atmosphere of respectful uncertainty, service users will then be empowered to find their own solutions to their problems and take responsibility for their own behaviour. This philosophy leads to a very simple set of principles: if it ain't broke, don't fix it; if it works, do more of it; and, if it doesn't work, do something different. These principles also apply to you, the reader. If your existing method of working works for you and service users are happy with the outcomes, then do more of it. If, however, you find yourself 'stuck' with service users, or in conflict with them, then do something different: consider adopting a combined solution-focused/narrative approach to your work. It offers a much more cooperative way of working, measurable outcomes, and a rediscovery of your communication skills. A word of caution, though: you will have to give up much of your existing knowledge about the nature of people. Social work has long been preoccupied with people's problems and the answers to them, so adopting a combined approach demands a radical rethink of social work practice.

## Incompatibilities between traditional and narrative approaches to social work

The main difficulty in explaining narrative and solution-focused approaches is that people tend to recognise what seems familiar rather than what is different. For social workers, the most obviously familiar characteristic of the new approaches is the emphasis on the uniqueness of individuals. But we have always individualised our service users, comes the cry, as they remember the basic tenets of social work practice expounded by Biestek (1957) and Mary Richmond (1917, 1922) or the teaching of person-centred counselling on a more recent training course. Additionally they are insulted by the very idea that they may not be treating people as unique individuals, despite the very real tensions this creates between care and control for the social worker concerned with agency function (for an excellent discussion of this, see Horne, 1990).

However, this is to neglect the context in which individualisation takes place. Lacking a knowledge base of its own, social work – in its inception – borrowed freely from other 'people' professional knowledge; most notably, psychiatry and psychology. These were both based on a medical model and, therefore, rooted in pathology. Social work not only adopted what Harrison (1995) refers to as the 'forensic gaze' but also accepted the white, male psychological discourse about what is considered normal and pathological (for a fuller discussion, see Milner & O'Byrne, 1998). Thus Mary Richmond (1917) and, later, Florence Hollis (1964) identified two central themes for social work: that clients and their problems have to be individualised and that successful casework requires careful diagnosis. Pyschosocial casework, underpinned by Freudian theorising, thus became the dominant activity of social work with social problems recast as individual, or family, pathology.

The 'problem' with this is that individualisation *and* diagnosis is a contradiction in terms; it not being possible to reconcile individual differences within a diagnostic process which categorises and homogenises many individuals. Thus the psychosocial caseworker, unlike the psychotherapist with voluntary clients, quickly finds herself in conflict with her service users whose own stories do not match the expert diagnoses – although most service users are too powerless to protest other than passively. To accommodate the different explanations of problems, maintain professional credibility, retain the role of expert, and ignore power elements such as structural inequalities, psychosocial workers are obliged to recast the service user as 'mistaken'. Attributions of denial and resistance to service users lead social workers to value insight and intuition, which also hinders individualisation; 'totalising' service users within a pathologising discourse is neither emphatic nor individualising. Even where it provides a compelling explanation for why a problem occurred in the first place, it has little to offer the service user in terms of current and future functioning. The disillusioned service user's passive resistance to these sorts of explanations for their behaviour is therefore interpreted in terms of resistance, transference, and denial. Only the psychosocial caseworker can remain in 'reality' (for a fuller discussion, see Barber, 1991).

In terms of outcomes, pyschosocial casework has a poor track record with service users; witness a whole range of studies such as Mayer and Timms's classic *The Client Speaks* (1970) to more recent research (Packman *et al.*, 1986; Challis & Davies, 1986; Sinclair *et al.*, 1995), but it remains the most common form of social work activity. O'Hanlon (1993) refers to this as the 'first wave' of social work practice. It not only remains the favoured approach but its psychological discourse has become so embedded in popular consciousness that we all use it to explain and regulate our lives. Ingleby (1985) refers to this as a total institution without walls but, more simply, the psychologising of the family has elevated mother-blaming to the heights of a national sport. Practically every defined element of 'normality': good enough parenting, emotional well-being, social harmony, etc., can thus be explained in terms of family, rather than social, functioning.

In contrast to this, there emerged a 'second wave', also from psychology, which abandoned the pathological approach in favour of problem solving in which existing individual and family solutions to problems were viewed as making the problem worse (O'Hanlon, 1993). The influence of cognitive/behavioural psychology was strong here, leading initially to task-centred casework and, later, to family therapy (Miller, 1997a). In both instances the worker remained the expert in people's lives, prescribing ways in which the problems could be solved; and framing the problems within a psychological discourse. There may not have been the same emphasis on resistance and denial but there remained the tendency to categorise and repair deficits. In both 'waves' of social work practice,

FIGURE 1.1   *Summary of the main differences between traditional and narrative approaches*

| Traditional casework | Narrative and solution-focused approaches |
|---|---|
| conversations for true explanation | conversations accepting people's experiences |
| seeking to understand problems | searching for solutions |
| searching for causes | searching for competencies away from the problem |
| a focus on history | a focus on what the person wants to talk about |
| a focus on emotions | a focus on behaviour |
| diagnosis, categorisation | searching for difference |
| pathologising | identifying uniqueness |
| mending deficits | broadening competencies |
| insight and inference | respectful uncertainty |
| blame | reasonable responsibility taking |
| denial and resistance | searching for unique ways of cooperating |
| worker is the expert | service user is the expert, worker is influential |

there is a preoccupation with 'why?' and an assumption that solutions cannot possibly be found until it is known why problems exist in the first place. This is echoed by service users who, not infrequently, ask 'why me?' This is not unexpected; many service users having adopted a negative attributional style in which they discount their successes as luck and blame themselves for their failures – in converse to the more usual 'self-seeking' attributional style. This focuses the social work effort on conversations for 'true' explanations of the causes of problems, on past history, the making of inferences, and the development of hypotheses (Milner & O'Byrne, 1998).

The 'third wave', narrative and solution-focused approaches, ignores the 'why?' question on the grounds that it is unhelpful, unfruitful, and unnecessary. As dominant psychological explanations are now an integral part of popular culture, we cannot all be suffering from lack of insight into our problems; it is simply that insight does not lead directly to problem resolution: 'What clients often lack is the knowledge and skills required to act differently'. (Culley, 1991, p. 51). Answers to 'why?' are limited to dominant cultural discourses which lack the capacity to provide explanations on the simple grounds that these discourses exist to silence the voices that are inconvenient to the status quo (Barber, 1991; White, 1995). When asked which would be better for them, to know 'why?' or to find a solution to a problem, service users usually opt for the latter (O'Hanlon & Weiner-Davis, 1989). Social workers, by nature of their training, find it difficult to relinquish a preoccupation with underlying reasons but it is, nevertheless, a vital change of attitude needed before a combined solution-focused/narrative approach can be applied to social work practice (see Figure 1.1).

**A case example of how a preoccupation
with 'why?' can hinder progress**

Fourteen-year-old James was referred to the independent counselling project at Northorpe Hall Trust by his school for help in coming to terms with his damaging home circumstances, which his teachers saw as the explanation for his poor attendance, self-harm, inability to maintain eye contact with teachers, and habit of hugging the walls as he walked along the corridor. They attributed this behaviour to physical abuse within the family, hoping that his deficits would be mended through insight, and ascribing their failure to assist James to his denial of the effects of his abusive experiences. In other words, a 'traditional' account of one boy's failure to conform to expected school standards, ascribed to a pathological family; and one which failed to find a solution. The fact that James's social worker agreed with the explanation bolstered the 'expert' view. Regardless of all the hard work, genuine caring, and thoughtful hypothesising which had gone into the case, the professionals were not only 'stuck' but declared themselves desperate: 'we are losing him', the teacher wrote on the referral form.

By resolutely ignoring the 'why?' question and entering into a narrative conversation with James, it was quickly clear that his abusive history was not relevant to his current behaviour. He was mainly concerned about his grandfather's recent ill health, which reminded him how sad he felt when his grandmother died. These preoccupations were affecting his concentration at school; hence he had developed coping mechanisms, although the school saw these as dysfunctional. He commented that 'not looking someone in the eye doesn't mean I'm not listening'. His self-harm consisted of sticking a compass in his arm – 'I do it when I'm bored.'

He felt that he was at least 75 per cent in control of his behaviour and had a supportive friend he turned to to talk about his worries. *His* preferred solution was to make a start by attending school in full uniform, as he considered himself to be capable of doing this and he wagered me a large bag of crisps that he could do so by the end of term (empathy comes in many forms!). In taking this step, he would necessarily resolve the attendance 'problem'. For his second session, James was asked to make a list of his good points so that we could use these in his preferred solutions and the choice of appointment date and time was left to him. James spoke freely throughout the session, maintaining eye contact, and left with a smile on his face. Not having to talk about someone else's explanation of his problem freed him up to be a respected individual.

[Towards the end of the session, James made a point of asking me to keep my notes on him. I offered him a copy of them when typed up and this was accepted. So far, no service user has taken me up on my offer to destroy the verbatim notes I take during each session and they have almost all given me permission to use their stories to help other people. This does not mean that they wish to be gossiped about so I would ask the reader to treat the disguised stories in this book with respect. They are included to illuminate the process of narrative social work and I trust that you will not betray the privileged position in which these unique and intensely personal stories place you.]

The whole session consisted of nothing more than carefully listening to James's unique account of his present life, influencing the conversation only insofar as it focused him away from failure and towards competence and personal responsibility taking. Yet it is not easy to make this shift in talking to people, involving as it does the surrender of cherished ideas about the probable causes of problems (which would be my history – not James's) and worries about superficial therapy and problems going 'underground' (the burden of psychosocial explanations). Making this shift away from traditional therapy is easier if a combined approach is applied systematically as a check against old habits – it really is hard to resist asking 'why?'. This may seem artificial until one's communication skills are rediscovered and resisting being an expert becomes a more comfortable option. The techniques and ideological basis of the two approaches are outlined briefly below as an aid to broadening social worker competence before describing how the approaches can be combined.

## Getting started – solution-focused approaches

Solution-focused therapy originated in the work of the Milwaukee Centre for Brief Therapy, largely pioneered by de Shazer, who researched therapeutic practice to find out what worked and what made a difference (for a detailed account of the intricacies and origins of solution-focused approaches, see Parton & O'Byrne, 2000). He simplified the identified elements into a solution-focused way of talking with service users (de Shazer *et al.*, 1986). At the heart of effective practice is the notion of exceptions. All problems, however entrenched, have exceptions and it is within these exceptions that the seeds of solutions lie. Identifying what a person is doing or thinking differently that alleviates the problem is the task of the worker, who initiates a therapeutic conversation which not only identifies goals but engenders hope that the goals will be realised. Although the emphasis is on the behaviour and thoughts present during the exceptions to the problem, this does not mean that emotion is ignored. It would be heartless to ignore emotion and there is no reason why tears and laughter should be excluded from the conversation. It is simply that the focus is not primarily on emotion; instead the worker will ask questions that reveal how the emotion is manifested in behaviour, i.e. how do you do sadness? how would I know you were happier? when you are calm, what are you doing? Everything the service user says is taken at face value; it is that person's reality and how they make meaning of it so, although respectful challenges can be made about individual responsibility taking, no interpretations are offered.

Solution-focused talk has been criticised as a mechanical and artificial way of holding a therapeutic conversation but the set formula approach is actually helpful to the solution-focused worker who is just starting out, as it helps her to maintain a future orientation and avoid asking the 'why question'. Turnell and Lipchik (1999) suggest that it helps the service user feel better understood and is, therefore, fundamentally empathic. As will be seen by the illustrations used here, and later in the book, there is ample scope to exercise social work skills in communicating with people in trouble. The first session is outlined in some detail because if it is done carefully, there frequently is no need to hold a second session. Indeed, where agencies run a formal appointment system in which the person is asked to note what changes happen between the making and keeping of the first appointment, the service user will often find the solution to their problem in this space. This is what solution-focused workers call pre-session change and is based on the premise that change is constant but that people do not mention it unless asked (de Shazer, 1988). Asking also increases service users' sense of self-agency; the will to do or be something that has such a major role in resilience processes (Gilgun, 1999).

The first session has three phases: the service user's assessment of the problem, identifying any exceptions to the problem and progress in resolving it; a message which summarises thoughts on solutions and possible strengths which can be used; and tasks to be undertaken before the second session. There is also the preliminary phase of scene-setting; making introductions which establish a solution-focused orientation and encourage service users to develop self-agency.

### The preliminary phase

Service users are likely to have extensive experience of welfare professionals attempting to help them run their lives and this may well have engendered feelings of failure which can be extreme: 'The Welfare arrived and never left. Once these people get a smell of you, they sink their teeth into the soft unsuspecting placenta of your life. They squeezed our spirits within moments of extinction' (Perry, 1997, p. 30). When self-esteem is low, it is difficult for service users to use criticism constructively, therefore it is worth the time and effort to introduce yourself carefully to set the tone for a solution-focused approach which emphasises the importance you accord to their assessment of their problem. You will have your own preferred style but some useful areas to cover on a first meeting include:

Explain who you are, handing over your agency information pack at this point. I tell people a little bit about my approach to work with them, outlining my understanding of the nature of people, i.e. my faith in people discovering their own solutions to their problems through finding out what is going right and how they can do more of this, therefore I will be talking more about where they are going than where they have been. I usually add that this means that they don't have to talk about problems if they don't want to but, equally, they can if they want to. I explain that I am rather tactless and it would be helpful to me if they could say something like 'pass' if I ask a question they don't want to answer instead of looking at their feet and hoping I will change the subject, or tell me an untruth. A 'pass' is just as revealing as a longer answer, especially if you have asked a question about continuing substance abuse. I also explain the limits of confidentiality and explain why I am taking notes; what will happen to these, what access they have to them, and who will supervise my work. As this has involved me talking non-stop, I then ask for comments before asking fun questions which enable me to remind them of the 'pass' convention in order to establish honest communication and openness about power issues.

It is important to check out the referral details at this point. The referral is the beginning of the case file and once something is written down it gains authority. As White and Epston (1990) suggest, the invention of the case file enables individuals to be captured and fixed in writing; writing which will become diagnostic rather than simply factual and which may not reflect the service user's assessment of their problem. Sometimes there are factual inaccuracies but mostly the referral is simply someone else's assessment of what is wrong and is phrased in terms which fit the agency referral criteria rather than reflect the service user's reality. This is particularly true of inter-agency referrals which have the covert aim of obtaining access to limited resources. In my counselling role, I experimented with not reading the referrals until after the first session and this was most revealing; on most occasions, the referrer's assessment bore absolutely no relation at all to the service user's assessment; and not knowing what the 'problem' was supposed to be helped me to listen more carefully.

A study of case records found that 'categorisation of people is endemic in local government and has great significance for those "ordered, ranked or timetabled"' (Prince, 1996, p. 10) so it is important to alter the referral form where necessary and change any words which tend to pathologise the service user. For example, when I read out James's referral to him, he asked what 'lethargic' meant. When I explained this, he explained his 'lethargic' behaviour in a way that made complete sense to both of us. Similarly, Melanie's referral consisted of a five-page report, listing three different psychiatric diagnoses: one psychiatrist had labelled her as having a depressive illness, another said she suffered from conduct disorder, and a third considered that her problems stemmed from an anxious attachment to her mother. Melanie explained that she never bothered to read reports on herself – 'they're all rubbish, I bin them'. I agreed to bin this referral report and start again. When I asked her how she would describe herself, she said 'my trouble is that when I haven't got the support I need, I fuck up'. This term much more accurately described her behaviour and proved useful throughout our sessions. Her problem was already constructed, what was necessary was to discover a solution in which her 'fuck-ups' became smaller and safer. Writing down what the service user says communicates to them that what they say is important and helps you to establish them as experts in their own lives by checking the accuracy of your notes and comments with questions such as 'have I got this right?'

Having cleared the ground in this way, I then ask the service user what they expect to happen in this session for it to have been worthwhile them giving up the time to see me. This is not only respectful but helps to establish clear goals at an early stage. It is particularly important with service users whose goals may be completely unacceptable or unattainable. For example, nineteen-year-old Laura said that she wanted to learn how to handle her partner's temper so that he wouldn't need to hit her. I responded that, as a woman worker, I didn't see it as my job to help her become a better-balanced battered woman. On another occasion, Shaun's expectation of me was that I would write a report for the court which outlined the damaging effects of his abusive childhood experiences in the hope that he would escape a prison sentence for fraud. Clarification of goals at this point meant that we were able to establish how I could help him work out what he could do to deal with what were two separate issues. Empowering the service user at this early stage to become experts in their own lives encourages personal responsibility taking.

### *The problem-assessment phase – taking a history which reduces helplessness and feelings of failure*

Your time and skills are expensive and need to be focused on 'stuck' problems rather than ordinary problems, so beware of using your interviewing skills to elicit disclosures which are not the focus of your intervention and which emphasise the overwhelming nature of problems. Dolan (1998a) argues that talking too much about the past encourages the service user to remain in a victim role and that even developing a survivor identity concentrates too much on the original trauma, therefore the work should enable the service user's present to become more vivid than the past so that they can recover the ability to imagine a positive future. Helping the service user to orient to the present can be encouraged by a number of history-taking exercises, all of which kindle hope and indicate what a first step to a positive future would involve. These include:

### *Scaled questions*

These can relate to any area of human functioning but an initial one usually uses some index of current self-concept or happiness. For example, in the case of the former you might ask, 'think of the best person you could be and give that person 100 points. Now tell me how many points you would give yourself these days.' In the case of the latter, you could draw a line with 0 representing the blackest of depression and 100 as complete bliss. Most people without serious problems would rank themselves at about 70 but service users vary enormously, the majority saying 'somewhere in the middle', and this is then followed up with a question asking them whether they are at the 49 or 51 side of the middle. The numbers mean nothing in themselves but position the person on their own continuum of goal achievement. This scaled question is then followed up with another; usually, 'on a scale of 1–10, how satisfied are you with this score?' The answer to the second question gives you some indication of their willingness to make changes to their lives; the possibility that they may be very dissatisfied but have little control over their lives; or enjoying their misery. Christopher, for example, told me that when he was high on the happiness scale, he was low on the satisfaction scale and vice versa. It was hard to resist making inferences about his psychiatric state but teasing out what he meant by this proved that this was how he maintained some semblance of control over his life – not letting people know how he felt – a competence which we could use.

Having gained an idea of where the service user positions themselves, you then ask what they will be doing differently when they are higher on the scale. This is often expressed in emotional terms such as 'I would be happier.' This is converted into actual behaviour by such questions as 'how would I know you were happier?' 'What would you be doing that made you smile more?' 'How do you do happiness?' 'What's the highest you have ever been and what were you doing then?' These questions ask nothing about the problem but open the door to finding exceptions – in which lie the seeds of solutions. They also clarify for the service user what change is within their control, especially when followed up with 'how did you do that?' – a question which highlights competence. The voluntary service user is more likely to answer these questions in terms of their own behaviour and the mandated service user in terms of the social worker's behaviour. In the latter case, you ask what they will be doing differently when the social worker no longer needs to be visiting; for example, 'what would you be doing differently that would make social services know that your children were safe?'

When exceptions have been identified, scaled questions can be used to identify motivation and ability to make changes. For example, you can ask 'what are the chances on a scale of 1–10 that you can do this again?', or you can ask them to rate themselves on both ability and motivation scales. Depending on their ratings, you will know on which element to concentrate. It is not unusual to find that ability is rated more highly than motivation (for example, I have a high ability to stop smoking but a low motivation) so then you start a search for exceptions to low motivation.

For the social worker experienced in interviewing, these questions often seem so highly formulaic that they stultify a therapeutic conversation but they do not need to be asked in a mechanical way. I often use extremes of scales to inject some fun into the conversation and remove some of the heat of 'failed' perceptions. For example, when scaling a boy's delinquent behaviour, I set 0 as 'an angel' and 100 as a 'triple axe-murderer' or when asking a woman about her mothering ability, I set 0 as 'Rosemary West' and 100 as 'Mother Teresa'. This helps the service user to engage with me and discourages over-optimistic responses. When asking someone to rate themselves on a truthfulness scale, you provide an opportunity to query any answer they give you and remind them of your 'pass' convention, although they usually are painfully honest about their lying and express amusement at your queries. It is also possible to use scaling questions to break down distinctions between those family members who are complaining and those who are complained about. Here you give each family member a card and ask them to scale both their estimation of the severity of the problem and other's estimates. You then ask them to guess what everyone else has written before asking people to read out their own scores. This can be great fun for families as well as an eye-opener about previously unrecognised strengths but be well prepared – it can be complicated to explain and do. It is also useful when dealing with 'complained about' behaviour to rate self-esteem as well; parents are often stunned by how low their child's self-esteem is and unaware of how their criticism has contributed to this.

When service users rate themselves at the bottom of a scale (sometimes they even go into minus points), you can ask them how they have managed to keep going when they have felt so low. Exceptions can be hard to find with people who have no memory of ever being happy or feeling in control of their lives but, here, a version of the 'miracle question' will usually illuminate some difference that can be used.

*The miracle question*

This asks the service user to describe life in which a miracle has happened and goals were reached overnight whilst the person was asleep: 'Because you were asleep, you do not yet know that it has happened so what is the first thing you would notice that would tell you?' The morning after the miracle is constructed more easily because service users can describe what they want without having to concern themselves with the problem and traditional assumptions that the solution has to be connected with understanding or eliminating the problem. As service users not infrequently say that they would have won the lottery, you always ask 'another question', i.e. 'What would you be doing differently if you had more money?' and 'Can any of this start before the money comes?' as well as lots of 'and what else would be happening?' to elicit as clear and detailed a picture as possible. For example, Ian said that he would be coming downstairs with a smile on his face and that his brother would not be teasing him at breakfast. His mother promptly intervened with the comment, 'If you come downstairs with a smile on your face, I will tell your brother to stop teasing you.' This was sufficient for them to devise and operationalise their own solution to the problem without the need for further sessions other than one to report that things 'are going fine now'. This was despite the referral indicating long-standing, serious problems.

de Shazer uses the miracle question as his initial enquiry but many solution-focused workers use a variation on it. Berg and Reuss (1998), for example, find that a reversed miracle question – the 'nightmare scenario' – is useful in work with people with chronic alcohol problems; while Dolan (1991) has devised a 'wise woman scenario' for women who have experienced sexual abuse. Here she asks them to consult an older and wiser self to envisage not only what a problem-free future looks like but also to identify how it happened. I adapt this for younger service users by asking them to take a journey to visit themselves in the future via the car in the Michael J. Fox film, *Back to the Future*. I ask them to describe the older self in great detail and then ask the older self for advice. Another variation of this, particularly useful with people who have little sense of a future, is to ask them to describe their wildest dreams. These may not be realistically attainable but they do open up the service user's preferred goals, whether any of it is happening at the moment, or where the first step needs to be taken.

These two sorts of questions are sufficient to complete the service user's assessment of the problem, identify exceptions, and set goals; then follows a summarising phase of the session – *before* any tasks are suggested.

### *Message on thoughts about possible solutions and strengths which can be used*

Many solution-focused therapists take a break at this time to talk over the session with a consulting team which has been viewing the session, identify strengths and provide a commentary on progress to date. You are unlikely to have this luxury of on-the-spot consultation but it is still possible to create this sort of space to summarise and check your perceptions. Simply say something like: 'let's stop for a moment and check where we're up to ... [look back through your notes] ... now, when you're busy, the problem isn't so bad. And when you're busy, you're ... ? [make a note of what the person says] ... and this is what you are doing when things are going well ... and these are the good things about you [rewrite them] ... quite a list, isn't it? Are there any other strengths you have that I can add to this list ...?' and so on. Some service users have so got into the habit of running themselves down that they might find it difficult to identify good things about themselves and you will need to give them a starter – it doesn't matter how small a thing it is as long as it is a competence from which they can work. Sometimes a person's life has been so hard that the only compliment you can offer is about their endurance or their concentration in the current session.

The main thing about this part of the session is that you are high-lighting exceptions and progress; remaining future-oriented; setting the scene for broadening competence; and encouraging the service user to see that they can have control over life events. On writing your notes up later, you will probably have more ideas on this part of the session and these can be written down and posted to the service user – it is no bad thing to make service users' successes visible in this way.

### Setting tasks/homework

#### The standard F1 task

de Shazer sets different sorts of tasks, depending on how the session has developed. In the worst scenario where the situation is so vague that it has not been possible to identify any goals, he recommends that the service user be asked to do nothing more than make a list of what they do *not* want to change about their lives. I usually allocate myself a task at this point: I will put my mind to the situation when I read through my notes and consult with my supervisor. I also add that if I come up with any possibilities, I will write to the service user. This helps the service user engage with the therapeutic effort as well as giving me some space for second thoughts.

#### Pretend tasks

Where the goals are clear but there are no exceptions, a pretend task is set. For example, the service user is asked to pretend that the miracle has occurred on alternate days and study what happens. Usually, they are advised not to tell the person who is complaining about their behav-iour which day is which but ask them to see if they can work this out.

As it is impossible to pretend behaviour, it gives the person space in which to try out possibilities without pressure and there is usually some change before the next session.

*Prediction tasks*

Where there are exceptions but the service user insists that they are accidental – not unusual in someone who feels they lack control over their lives – they are asked to make a prediction each night about what will happen the next day. The following evening, they are asked to check whether or not their predictions were accurate. However infrequently their predictions are accurate, this does lead to them realising that they are in control of their behaviour to some extent. Prediction tasks are particularly useful for people who ascribe their behaviour to impulsiveness.

*Straightforward tasks*

Where it has been possible to identify deliberate exceptions to the problem, you merely advocate that they do 'more of the same'. The skill here is in identifying the detail so that these exceptions can become more frequent – how did they do it once, is anyone else needed to help, etc.? There is also the possibility here to emphasise the service user's existing ability to solve the problem, thus broadening their competencies.

**The second session**

This follows a set pattern in that the first question is always a version of 'what's better?' You are presuming that change always happens. Where success is reported, then the session is devoted to getting as much detail as possible about the change; particularly, 'How did you do that?' so that the person can 'do more of it'. Solution-focused workers often call this 'cheering on change' although it is important not to get too enthusiastic about very minor improvements – service users feel patronised if you are happy with such slight improvement in their lives. It is essential to ask them how satisfied they are with the improvement before launching into 'cheering' mode. Service users (particularly children) often have high aspirations for themselves and it is not our job to lower these.

Often service users will report that nothing is better. In part this is because they are accustomed to telling their problems rather than their successes. de Shazer recommends that you listen to the problem story without showing much interest in it but I think this can appear rather unfeeling so always allow the person full scope to talk about disasters. I do not, however, then look for answers to these but ask for a detailed account of what happened on any one day to search for small exceptions. For example, Pam reported that things were worse at her second session, giving a well-rehearsed story of an overdose attempt, so I puzzled over how she managed not to kill herself. She was intrigued by this question and exceptions appeared as she worked out the answer to the question. It is rare to find that there are no exceptions (in which case the message is 'What can you do differently, then?'), and these can be developed along the lines of the first session. Usually, if you have taken sufficient time to identify exceptions and how they happened, then the person has sufficient 'lift-off' to get on with their own problem resolution.

### *Termination*

This is simple; the service user will report that they feel sufficiently in control of their life and they do not need your help any more so you merely offer the opportunity of a follow-up session, should they want one. James, for example, reported at the second session – some three weeks after the first one – that he had gone to school successfully, people had noticed a change in him, and he was happy with his life. Sometimes people are unsure of their progress or move the goal posts, in which case you can ask, 'How will you know that you don't need any more help?' This enables them to identify how their goals can be measured and evaluated. For mandated service users, these measures will include other people's perceptions as well, usually to do with issues of safety.

### **Getting started – narrative approaches**

Narrative therapy originated in the work of White and Epston at the Dulwich Centre in Adelaide. It challenges people's beliefs that the problem speaks of their identity, i.e. 'He is an eneuretic.' The person's experience of the problem is explored by means of conversations which provide an account of how the problem has influenced the person and what influences the person can exert on the problem. Traditional psychotherapeutic concepts are reconstructed in narrative therapy: interpretation is how service users can make meaning of their lives rather than be entered into stories by others; and resistance is the way in which they can resist the influence of the problem on their lives. The worker relinquishes the role of expert in people's lives but remains

FIGURE 1.2  *Formal systems of analysis and narrative analysis*

| Formal (theoretical) systems of analysis | Narrative analysis |
|---|---|
| establishes global accounts of life and universal accounts of human nature that construct naturalised and essentialist notions of the self | brings forth the contradictory experiences of subjectivity, and denaturalised notions of a self that is multi-sited |
| produces flat 'monographic' descriptions of life which attempt to render events predictable | speaks of a multi-storied conception of life |
| seeks the general so as not to be misled by the unique | seeks the unique so as not be misled by the general |
| champions the norm and renders the unexpected invisible | enshrines the unexpected and deconstructs the norm |
| informs studies in the reproduction and transmission of dominant notions of self and of culture | provides opportunities to seize upon the unique in the reworking of dominant notions and practices of self and of culture |

*Source*:  White (1999).

influential in the questions asked to challenge unhelpful stories. For example, by asking a service user if they can change the ending of a recurring nightmare, you are being influential. By asking what would be a good ending for them, you are handing the expertise for solution-finding over to them. As in solution-focused approaches, solutions are constructed in narrative, what Furman and Ahola (1992) refer to as solution talk as opposed to problem talk, but narrative approaches are very much more interested in power issues. Where solution-focused approaches are grounded in constructivism, narrative ones are located firmly in poststructuralism; for example, White (1999) identifies the differences between traditional approaches based on rationalist theory and those based on narrative analysis (see Figure 1.2).

Narrative conversations are, therefore, much more fluid than solution-focused ones, although there remain key elements which are used to deconstruct problems before moving on the constructing solutions. The preliminary phase of the conversation is similar, especially the explicit acknowledgment of one's own values and the limitations of one's own understanding of human behaviour. This is followed by questions aimed at challenging dominant cultural stories about the problem, identifying unique outcomes and externalising problems; although not necessarily in that order. As a new story develops, the worker then attempts to strengthen it – what narrative therapists refer to as 'thickening the counterplot' (Freeman *et al.*, 1997).

### Deconstructing problem-saturated stories

By stories, narrative therapists mean the ways in which we make sense of our lives; the frameworks we use to interpret experiences. White (1995) argues that there isn't a single story of life which is free of ambiguity and contradiction and that can handle all the contingencies of life. These ambiguities, contradictions and contingencies stretch our meaning-making resources; especially when there are dominant cultural stories about particular sorts of behaviour. These stories tend to concentrate on identifying the average sort of behaviour in any given situation – or the behaviour seen as desirable by the most powerful group of people – with the norm becoming elevated to a desirable 'normality'. This means that people who are not 'average' become storied as abnormal; what White (1995) refers to as being entered into a story, a story in which they are defined as lacking in some way. Consider this agony aunt reply to a letter in which the writer tells of how she broke free from an unhealthy relationship with her mother after counselling:

> Your letter upset me, because I get so many letters from heart-broken parents who believe that counsellors have taken away their children. The fact that you feel good doesn't mean anything. Adultery feels good at first – otherwise nobody would bother with it. Whatever you blame your mother for, you must surely recognise that she must now be devastated. Real maturity is being able to relate to people without being controlled by them. So please make contact with her as soon as you can. (*Daily Telegraph*, 18.6.1999, p. 21)

This illustrates a dominant cultural story of family life in which mothers naturally love their children and are loved by them. When children are unloved, they can only make sense of their lives by seeing themselves as unlovable, imperfect and to be blamed. Solutions sought within this dominant story only sends them back for more hurt and misery. A dominant story developed by a powerful group – white, middle-class men – is one of self-possession, self-actualisation and self-containment in which individuality becomes a culturally preferred way of being. Psychology has added meaning to this culturally preferred way of being by explaining how it best comes about. For example, the psychology of attachment suggests that sensitive mothers provide children with a secure base from which to develop individuality and to which they can return at times of need. While this story has considerable explanatory power, it does require that someone loses out on individuality in order to remain still at the centre and provide the secure base – usually a mother. Thus mothers are entered into a story which contains contradictions if they, too, have hopes to develop individuality.

Psychiatry also provides dominant stories of culturally undesirable ways of being. For example, Melanie's referral form listed three different explanations of her behaviour: she had been 'diagnosed' as depressed, suffering a conduct disorder and experiencing anxious attachments, depending on which psychiatrist she had seen. These three stories 'totalised' her misery about being in care and her reactions to it; as well as providing the rationale for sending her to secure accommodation on two occasions. Challenging these dominant stories consisted of asking her what sense they made to her and how *she* would describe her behaviour. The dominant story was further undermined by asking her what influence it exerted on her; for example, how had she come to believe that she couldn't function without support? Dominant stories make others into experts and the storied person as one needing the expert's support and solutions.

Furman and Ahola (1992) comment that psychiatric diagnoses often tell us little about the actual problem but a great deal that we should think about, suggesting that challenges to dominant stories 'leave the door open for clients to decide for themselves whether to accept or reject the various explanations embedded in the story' (p. 90). This means that workers must not press their own alternatives to dominant stories on to service users but, instead, ask questions such as 'Does it really suit you to be dominated by the problem?', 'Given a choice between life with the problem and life free of the problem, which would you choose?', 'Do you want to keep the problem in your life?' Sometimes they do wish to keep at least part of the problem; for example, although a medical diagnosis may 'story' a person in a way which does not fit with their own meaning making, they may well find it comfortable to be so positioned in that it provides a relief from previously unsuccessful struggles against the problem. Similarly people may experience feeling oppressed by a dominant religious story but have no desire at all to break free from it as many other, satisfactory parts of their lives are interwoven with this. Thus challenges take the form of tentatively offering alternative stories and providing the opportunity for the service user to try them on for fit. Narrative therapists use metaphors extensively in this phase of the work and these reflect the worker's as well as the service user's worlds. For example, I sometimes explain my proffered alternative stories to women as being rather like going clothes shopping when we do not know what we are looking for but will recognise it when we see it. As we may try on clothes for colour, shape or fit – or a completely new style – so the alternative stories are hanging on a rail for the service user to pick one out and hold it up against themselves. This frees the service user up to develop a completely new story for themselves; one in which they make their own interpretations of their behaviour.

### *Identifying unique outcomes*

Whereas solution-focused therapists search for exceptions to problems and, therefore, concentrate on problem-free talk, in narrative work deconstruction of the problem takes the form of searching for unique outcomes – times when the service user actively resisted the influence of the problem, a contradiction to the dominant plot (Epston, 1998, p. 11). Here the worker asks questions such as 'What influences led to your enslavement by the problem?', 'What prevented you from resisting it?', 'When there are unique outcomes, what are the implications for the sort of person you are when you refuse to cooperate with the problem's invitations?', 'What does it say about your ability to undermine the problem?' These questions reflect on the qualities of the person rather than their actions and add to the language of resistance and liberation. This involves looking back at the past before going on to the future but it is not a blaming look or a search for deficits – it is empowering in that it develops a sense of the person *not being* the problem but as *being oppressed by it* and sometimes colluding with it. This phase of the conversation usually overlaps with the earlier part described above.

### *Separating the person from the problem*

There are some similarities to solution-focused approaches here in that the worker aims to get to know the person apart from the problem by listing their unique qualities and ideas but the problem is not ignored; in narrative therapy, the problem is the problem, not the person. However, problems can have so much weight that they silence and immobilise people. When a person thinks of a problem as an integral part of their character it is difficult for them to change, i.e. 'I am a bad child', 'I am a heroin addict', 'She is a depressive.' These sorts of problem-saturated stories limit people, especially when the 'expert' solution to their ascribed problem fails to work; leaving nothing but an unsatisfactory label. Separating the person from the problem via an externalising conversation relieves the pressures of blame, defensiveness and failure and frees up the person, and their family, to have a different relationship with the problem – one in which they can bring their resources to bear on the problem rather than the person. As can be seen in the example of James, 'In the space between person and problem, responsibility, choice and personal agency tend to expand' (Freeman *et al.*, 1997, p. 8).

A simple way of externalising the problem is to give the problem a name of its own, one which reflects its unique qualities, and identify the parts of it which are most affecting the service user. For example, Tamara's referral form described her as a depressed and violent girl who had not attended school for eighteen months – conflating the problem with the person. She described her problem as 'being in a mood'. An externalising conversation encouraged her to describe this in more detail and it emerged as a bad mood which was triggered by derogatory remarks of peers and grief at her grandmother's death. It started with a pain in her eye, inability to breathe and then 'it comes bursting out. It's like I explode.' She described it as a Red Devil that was taking over her life, 'like a cancer. I got depressed, then fat and that made me angry and made the pain go away. I needed something that made me happy and relaxed so I started taking drugs' – this latter was not known by her referrers. I invited her to reflect on how the Red Devil influenced her life, the strategies it had used to get an upper hand in her life, its purposes in dominating her life, who stands with the problem and encourages it, and the plans that the problem has already put into action should its dominance be threatened (White, 1999). Through this externalising conversation, Tamara was able to reflect on the sort of relationship she wanted to have with the Red Devil and she decided to be a devious Black Devil who would subvert the Red one. At the next appointment, she reported that she was back to her old devious self, had returned to school, stopped taking drugs, was on better terms with her mother, and had talked to herself: 'I say, what am I doing? It's not like me to have a frown on my face. I went to a party and I didn't care. I wore a red skirt and top, new shoes, bag. I didn't care what people thought. I danced and sang all night.'

### Developing an alternative story

An externalised problem can be viewed as skilled in covering up its attempts to hide its failures to exert influence on the person's life, and these failures (the unique outcomes) are identified to allow the development of an alternative story which has meaning for the person. The new story can be constructed by using narrative questions such as those outlined above or specific techniques; many of which will be familiar to social workers accustomed to direct work with children but easily adaptable for adults too. Talk is not the only medium of narrative work – play, drawing, painting, dough, sand, puppets and masks can all be used, as can literature and writing. Even where people have internalised the problem as an integral part of themselves, they often identify with a character in a book or a person in real life who has suffered and overcome similar oppression. An alternative story can be developed by asking the person to borrow from a life they admire on alternate days. This frees them up further from the problem and allows them space to try out a new story without any pressure to commit themselves fully to it or risk failure.

Similarly, the alternative story may require some further externalisation such as the 'differentiation of self from family of origin' exercise described by Dolan (1998a, p. 126). Here, self-agency is enhanced by asking the person to identify in what ways they are similar to each parent, in what ways they are different and which of these traits they wish to keep. The old story may also be undermined by the use of a 'write, read and burn' exercise in which an unhelpful thought is written down and burnt and then a more positive message written and retained. Where an alternative story is elusive or vague, the person can be asked to write a letter from the future in which they describe a satisfactory life in detail before adding a paragraph on how they did this. No medium in which the service user has ability is ignored, whether this is poetry writing, crafts, an interest in videos, or a hobby.

### Thickening the counterplot

New stories lack the weight and density of old stories, so successes in living a reauthored life are fragile; hence the need to thicken the counterplot. Again there are similarities with solution-focused approaches to broadening competencies by asking in detail how a person 'did that', although a narrative approach attempts to thicken the counterplot by consulting the person as expert. Instead of 'how did you do that?', the person can be asked what advice they would offer to people oppressed by a similar problem and permission is sought to broadcast the news. This information is genuinely useful for the worker but its prime purpose is to help make the new plot weightier by reflecting on what has been successful.

A further way of thickening the counterplot is the telling of alternative stories to other people in the person's life. Questions used here include 'To whom can you tell the story of your decision to fight the problem?', 'Because it is easier to tell the story to people who are willing to believe it, who would be the best person to start with?' (this also increases the person's interactions with supportive as opposed to unsupportive friends), and 'How could the audience be increased?' Telling leads to performing and also enables the person to reflect on solutions and add to them through the circulation of an alternative story. Women, with their tendency to intimate disclosure, respond well to telling other people whilst men's tendencies to self containment mean that they often prefer individual metaphors but both ways of thickening the counterplot reduce dependency on the worker.

### *Termination*

As in solution-focused approaches, termination is initiated by the service user although the narrative worker will check that the person is happy with the alternative story. Again, there are dangers of enthusing about small changes without asking if the progress made is sufficient for the service user. For example, when I asked Tamara if she was pleased with all her progress, she said 'I'm a *bit* pleased.' I was surprised at this tepid reply but asked her what she meant by 'a bit': 'There's so much more I want to be able to do', she replied. A clear sign that your services are no longer required is when the service user thanks you for your help. White (1999) recommends that this should be graciously accepted as it is patronising and dishonest to tell the person that they did it all themselves. You may not have been an expert in their lives but your questions have been influential. In entering into someone's else's reality, you will probably have been changed and influenced too – not least in your increased understanding of human behaviour and the possibilities for resilience and resistance.

### *The second session*

As in solution-focused work, a second session may well not be necessary. If it is, it follows the same format as the first one, forming part of an ongoing narrative conversation. I have found an important factor in speedy solution-finding is the spacing of sessions. Some service users do want to see you each week but this carries a heavy expectation of continuous change; a significant difference between narrative and traditional approaches is that change occurs *between* sessions in the former. Asking someone to reflect on possible ways of reauthoring their lives (or, indeed, carrying out tasks in solution-focused work) demands an enormous effort and takes time. The second session, then, should be scheduled to fit the magnitude of the work to be done in between sessions. You can ask 'How long do you think it will take you to do all these things we have been talking about?' and set the appointment from a joint agreement on this point. Narrative and solution-focused work are often called 'brief therapy' but it takes 'as long as it takes'. This is usually brief in terms of the number of sessions required but it may be spread out over many weeks. I find many service users continue the conversation long after they have ceased official contact with letters and cards, in which they continue to reflect on their satisfaction with the alternative story. This is not only personally rewarding but also provides a useful measure of the effectiveness of the work undertaken for your agency's outcome expectations.

## Combining the approaches

de Shazer's (1988) solution-focused practice is influenced by the philosophies of Wittgenstein and Derrida, the practice of Milton Erikson, and ideas from Buddhism but he prefers to view his position as largely atheoretical in that he considers power to be a *meta-narrative* imposed on us. This is actually a postmodern idea – Lyotard (1984), for example, claims that *meta-narratives* do not help us understand cultural revisions – but de Shazer mostly uses the language of constructivism. The approach is based on the idea that there are no incontrovertible social 'truths', only stories that can be developed through conversations. As language constantly changes and varies within cultures, something always happens. There are some superficial similarities with personal construct therapy but the personal construct therapist remains within traditional approaches by retaining expertise and accepting ideas about transition diagnoses, insight and transference (Fransella & Dalton, 1990).

White and Epston, however, recognise that some social 'truths' have more weight than others; particularly those that are written down and constitute 'official' knowledge. They acknowledge more openly the nature of power, being influenced by the counter-discourses of Foucault, Rorty and Derrida. Despite these influences being largely postmodern, they locate themselves within poststructuralist thought. White (1995, chapter 2), for example, makes a distinction between externalising the problem and externalising the internalised discourse, examining how psychologies and psychotherapies play a significant role in the reproduction of dominant cultural ideas. Epston (1988, chapter 4) is influenced by the sociolinguist Halliday's concept of anti-language and Goffman's primary frameworks. Both take a more overt stance against structural inequalities than de Shazer, seeing narrative therapy as having a role at group, community and cultural levels.

What makes the two approaches combinable is the shared emphasis on the self-reflexivity of postmodernism and the search for meaning making via reconstruction and deconstruction which 'tests the limits of any formal system of meaning by highlighting a text's conflicts and ambiguities. As a form of analysis, deconstruction can therefore function very creatively' (Humm, 1995, p. 111). James's story was elicited by the use of a combined approach. Scaled questions were used to aid goal setting and identify exceptions and progress at the beginning of the first session, particularly questions to do with ability and motivation; whereas narrative approaches were used to thicken the counterplot in the second session. Although James reported: 'Next term I'm going to school all the time ... life's satisfactory, I'm happy with it', he was also asked what advice he would offer to other boys with the same problem (so that he could more easily identify how he did it), who and what helped him (complimentary comments from the referring teacher on his behaviour back at school, support from friends, and rereading his session notes), and how he would cope with any slip-backs (talk things over with his mum and friends, request another appointment if necessary).

However there are potential problems for women in adopting a way of working which is grounded in poststructural or postmodern ideas. Di Stephano (1990) argues that while the rationalist framework – which underpins traditional social work practice – dissolves *she* into *he* as gender differences are collapsed; in postrationalism, '*she* dissolves into a plurality of differences, none of which can be theoretically or politically privileged over others' (p. 77). This, she suggests, makes a feminist politics impossible. However, Humm (1995) argues that the female experience in general is close to postmodernism: 'Women have always been marginal to the social order and frequently had to understand "double" languages – the language of the home and the language of institutions such as school' (p. 130). Whether or not it is indeed necessary to locate narrative and solution-focused approaches to working with women in either poststructuralism or postmodernism is a point which I discuss in Chapter 3, but, first, I intend to examine power issues more generally; particularly the potentially troublesome issue that the new approaches do not always make explicit a value base which has meaning for social work practice in the UK.

## SUMMARY

- It is not necessary to understand the causes of problems in order to arrive at solutions but it is important to recognise that the person is not the problem. Problem-saturated stories can be deconstructed so that people are empowered to control and direct their lives.
- The basic philosophy of solution-focused and narrative approaches is that people are experts in their own lives. Diagnosis and categorisation is therefore avoided.
- Solution-focused and narrative approaches are incompatible with traditional approaches as they are concerned with the *How* of behaviour rather than the *Why*. Cooperation is virtually automatic and the only resistance that is encouraged is resistance to the influence of the problem on the service users' lives.
- Practising a solution-focused approach to social work involves discovering service users' assessments of the problems, identifying any exceptions to problems and progress in resolving them, giving a message summarising thoughts on solutions and possible strengths which can be used, and setting tasks to be undertaken before the next session.
- Practising narrative approaches to social work involves challenging dominant cultural stories about problems, identifying unique outcomes, externalising problems, and strengthening new stories.
- The two approaches can be combined in social work practice despite theoretical differences as they both stress the self-reflexivity of postmodernism. Solution-focused approaches are based on the idea that there are no fixed truths, but narrative approaches accept that some social truths have more weight than others.

# 2

# Values, power and the ethics of influence

## Values in action

It is difficult *not* to be ethical when using a solution-focused approach to social work because of its central emphasis on empowerment, respectful uncertainty and minimum intervention; all of which Korman (1997) suggests open up possibilities for service users rather than the direct influence of traditional approaches which categorise and pathologise. The assumption that the approach is intrinsically anti-oppressive means that there is little in the solution-focused literature that deals explicitly with values although there are important principles which fit with the values laid down in government guidance on how social workers, as service providers, are expected to deliver welfare services to service users. These values were first expressed in legislation in the National Health Service and Community Care Act 1990, which specifies that service users are entitled to a choice of service, in partnership with service providers; be in charge of their own lives; have their needs individually assessed (within cultural and religious sensitivity); and for interventions to be speedy, simple and value for money. The principles of solution-focused work are contrasted with these expectations below, using examples of work undertaken on the Northorpe Hall Trust counselling project for young people who have experienced violence.

### Being in charge of one's own life

In solution-focused work, rather than looking for what is wrong and how to fix it, the worker looks for what is right and how to use it. Competencies are highlighted through the exploration of exceptions and, as service users become able to repeat the successful behaviour, so they gain control over their lives: 'Solution focused therapists' major responsibility ... is to help clients literally talk themselves out of their

28

troubles by encouraging them to describe their lives in new ways' (Miller, 1997b, p. 6).

Mark, a twelve-year-old boy with learning difficulties, was referred by his mother and social worker for assistance with his stealing, lying, kicking, biting, spitting, and temper tantrums, the former complaining that 'Either he goes into care or I'll put him six feet under. His dad won't even be in the same room as him and his sisters are not speaking to him.' She was very dubious about counselling as 'he can't concentrate for more than a few minutes'.

### Getting Mark's assessment of the problem

I asked Mark a number of scaled questions, i.e. 'If 0 is an angel and 10 a devil, where are you on this scale?' He rated himself as a full-blown devil but only 2–3 on the 'best person he could be' scale; 5–6 on the 'stealing' scale; and 10 on the 'dishonesty' scale. We had a laugh about my not being able to believe this last rating – perhaps he might even be more honest but be lying about it! Mum expressed amazement at his truthful answers to the scaled questions – one of her big grumbles was that he would never admit to any misdemeanour – so I used the opportunity to compliment Mark and asked her what his good points were. She listed: doing jobs for people, bit helpful, bit kind, good with his hands, very creative, very imaginative, always on the go. I said that I was going to describe him and he must correct me if I get him wrong; he sounds like a specially talented person who has two parts; that perhaps frustration turns the talented person into the badly behaved one? Mark seized on my explanation which separates the person from the problem (discouraging what White, 1995, refers to as 'totalising') and added detail to it: he saw it as temper rather than frustration – he said it was red, like a bomb exploding and that he had no control over it.

### Finding exceptions

*Me*: How long has the red temper been stopping you from being a good person?
*Mark*: Seven years.
*Me*: Have you ever beaten it?
*Mark*: Yes, at my old school. I was good for five weeks. I got this sticker book and some sweets.
*Me*: Can you remember how you did it?
*Mark*: No.
*Me*: Can Mum remember?

*Mum*: No. Just one day he came home with a good behaviour award and was over the moon. I said keep it up and he did till something snapped and then he went backwards. [This reminded her of a lot of negative things which she started to tell me and Mark responded by asking permission to go off and play in the toy attic. Permission to leave the room at any time is given during the introduction phrase of the session and young people often use it when they are hearing negative things about themselves. While he was out of the room I continued to search for exceptions.]

*Me*: Can you remember any other times when he beat the temper?

*Mum*: Yes. He was good over the holidays when he could play out but I don't like the ones he mixes with. He's got loads of energy. [Mark returned at this point. It was obvious that he was listening at the door and was eager to return as soon as the conversation got onto his good points. He offered to make us a cup of tea; offer accepted. We spent some time examining his temper in detail to get a clue as to how he can beat it.]

### The temper

Mark said it is bad, not nice, swears, stamps, kicks and spits, thumps, throws things. We agreed that it was a grade B temper, verging on grade A. People calling him names got it started but he thought he might go to school with it. He gets up so slowly that the temper gets a head start on him – gets him to clump down the stairs before he has even had breakfast. He takes the temper to school. If the temper wasn't with him, he would walk down the steps in the morning with a big smile on his face. Mum could help him get up without the temper by reminding him to get his things ready the night before. He thought he could change the ending of the temper story. I expressed doubts and suggested an experiment – choose three days in the following week to beat the temper and have three ordinary days but not tell anyone which day is which, and see if the family can guess. Mark liked this idea.

### Commentary

There are probably more exceptions in Mark's life than we discovered in this session which show he has the capacity to behave differently; the problem is that he wasn't clear about how he did it. The externalising and studying of the temper was a way to help him find out how he succeeds so that he can 'do more of it'. This was not a boy who needed to be told what he is doing wrong – with his self-esteem rating at only 2–3, he was not going to be able to accept any criticism.

*Outcome*

Mark's behaviour was radically improved by the second session. Two follow-up sessions were offered to strengthen success and he gained his twelve-year-old silver good behaviour certificate twelve weeks later (see Chapter 5 for details of this).

## Individual assessment of needs (within religious/ cultural sensitivity)

Respecting ethnic, cultural, age or gender differences presents few problems in solution-focused work as the service user is *always* asked to explain their reality, adopting what my supervisor refers to as respectful uncertainty in order to bridge gaps (for a fuller discussion, see Milner & O'Byrne, 1998). This process is further added to by the presence of a reflective team or, where this does not exist, by the way the message on possible solutions is delivered and the space this provides for challenges to assumptions on the part of the worker. Racial similarity of social worker and service user has not been found to be an essential quality, although cultural awareness is a preferable one (Shafi, 1998). Additionally a supervisor of the same gender and ethnicity as the worker can be consulted; what Waldegrave (1985) refers to as 'just therapy'. As it is not possible for young people to have workers similar in age to themselves, they – not the adults in their lives – make the decision to begin counselling; often after a preliminary visit. Also they are given some control over events by putting them in charge of tea-making facilities (thus adults have to wait to be asked by young people if they want a cup of tea) and giving them permission to leave the session for a break at any time of their choosing (with adults being banned from talking about the young person while they are out of the room, unless the talk is complimentary).

Sixteen-year-old Ramzan had been referred by her school (without parental knowledge), following a suicide attempt triggered by unhappiness resulting from emotional and physical abuse on the part of her parents. She had been the subject of a child protection investigation in the past but did not wish social services to be reinvolved as she was dissatisfied with the options provided by the social worker; she did not want to be removed from her home and found that efforts to work with her parents aggravated her difficulties. Her preferred solution was to find ways of tolerating her home situation while she achieved good examination results which would get her to university. She described her problem as difficulty in completing her homework and her suicide attempt coincided with much lower than average school results which threatened to remove her from the top sets.

The intention had been for Ramzan to be seen by an Asian woman counsellor but she knew of me from a white schoolfriend. At the first session she described her parents as thoughtless and cruel. Although she did not locate this in a context of living as an Asian family in a pre-dominantly white community, I remained conscious of the need to be aware of racial and age differences between us. This awareness was translated into action by attending to 'the level of the word', especially as Ramzan accorded a specific meaning to some words. Weingarten (1998) suggests that particular attention is paid to the ways that even the small and the ordinary – simple words, single gestures, minor asides, trivial actions – can provide opportunities for generating new meanings. Ramzan expressed herself well verbally but identified a sec-ondary problem as not always using the most appropriate words in her written work, even though she regularly consulted a thesaurus.

At the third session she reported considerable progress in making some private and peaceful space at home in which to do her homework but remained angry at her parents. She had been keeping a diary – 'it does have some good words in it, words like "retaliate" and "express"' – but her sister had found it. I suggested that she might consider using imaginary names:

*Ramzan*: YES. I'd use names I hate. George, that's what I'll call my father. George ... because it's old-fashioned, strict and stubborn. That's what you get the feeling of. And my mum ... I'm going to have to think about that.
*Me*: What about you?
*Ramzan*: Maria. I like that name. You think everything elegant and smooth.
*Me*: These are all English names you are choosing ...
*Ramzan*: Maria is Asian as well.
*Me*: Is it spelt the same?
*Ramzan*: Yes, but it's pronounced differently. It's *Ma*ria.
*Me*: I think I like that best.

Attending to the small and the ordinary in this case revealed more about *my* assumptions of the possible significance of ethnic issues and allowed me to check these out before joining with Ramzan in her story. Exploring and respecting difference is relatively straightforward in solution-focused work but it is considerably more difficult to challenge racism and sexism on the part of white men and sexism on the part of black men. For example, one young, black man responded to my exploration of our differences by telling me that he preferred to be seen by a woman as he found he got his own way more. Similarly, at one point in twelve-year-old Andrew's work on his temper, his mum took the opportunity of a quiet moment in the kitchen with me to say that she was worried about getting an Asian social worker when the white, male student social worker finished his placement. She admitted that her husband was racist and sexist, although he would tolerate an Afro-Caribbean worker, but did not want to lose the progress made by the good relationship between her husband and the student. I did not see that challenging her husband would have any effect on his racism or sexism but discussed my values with her – and the reality that the team covering her area did have mostly black staff. I am not at all sure to what extent a white service user is entitled to choose a white worker but would have been prepared to discuss the man's racism with the new worker. In the event, the possibility of an Asian worker being allocated the case acted as a spur; the family timed their solving of their problems to coincide with the student's placement ending.

Differences in socioeconomic status and positioning in agency hierarchies also need consideration. For example, during a period when I worked as a mentor for a troubled children's home faced with the possibility of closure if matters did not improve, I arrived at the home one day to find a large young man hurling furniture and pot plants at staff and residents who were 'holed up' in the dining room. I quickly restored order and was feeling mightily pleased with myself until I saw the expressions on staff members' faces. It was much easier for me to exert control as the residents were as aware as everyone else of the precarious nature of the home's continuing existence and my potentially powerful role in this. Neither was I exhausted by a long and difficult night shift or demoralised by the threat of losing my post. Next time I became involved in such a situation at the home, I asked the regular staff what help they required of me before doing anything and their skills were evident once they were supported. It is hard not to be helpful but when this involves unequal access to power, it does not lead to long-lasting solutions.

The principle of *utilisation* (Berg & Miller, 1992) is also used to ensure assessments are *truly* individual. This is not simply a matter of using service users' skills and family/community networks; all resources are utilised: knowledge, motivation, behaviour, ideas, beliefs, myths, hobbies and personal idiosyncrasies, however odd they may seem. The service user is presumed not only to have creative potential but the worker relinquishes the role of expert to become respectfully curious about each service user's individual hopes, desires and dreams.

Elaine, a seventeen-year-old who was accommodated in supported lodgings, was referred by her social worker for assistance with depression and self-harming behaviours resulting from earlier emotional and physical abuse. At the first session it was impossible to discover any strengths. Elaine appeared to have no resources: she was unhappy with her lodgings (which were socially isolated), found her social worker unhelpful, had no family or friends, no hobbies, little interest in the future, no motivation, and was overweight, drinking and in debt. She dismissed any discussion of possible exceptions to her misery, even when asked a 'pessimistic question': 'problems usually have good and bad points. How can you lose the problem but keep it's advantages?'

Life had been so hard for Elaine that she couldn't formulate even the simplest goal so I decided to explore her earlier cherished dreams and hopes to enable her to develop a belief that good things could really happen to her. Adapting a version of the 'letter from the future' exercise (Dolan, 1998a), I asked her to tell me exactly what she would be doing if her wildest dream came true. She thought this rather silly but made a start. I helped by asking questions and enjoying the dream with her: she would be sitting beside a swimming pool, drinking a mint julep. The pool would be in the grounds of Graceland and she would be employed as the secretary of the Elvis Presley fan club. We got into quite a lot of detail about what we would do when I came to visit but then she stopped, saying 'its a waste of time, it won't come true'. I agreed that it wouldn't if she didn't make a start; what was the first small step to making this dream come true? She said that it was too big a dream, there was no point starting, so I helped her story what her life would be like if only part of it came true: 'Stories provide the frames that make it possible for us to interpret our experience, and these acts of interpretation are achievements that we can take an active part in' (White, 1995, p. 15). She decided she would be more than happy if she was part of the Barry Manilow fan club and admitted that she had been a member of both fan clubs at one time and that she had written to ask to meet Barry Manilow on one occasion. At last, exceptions to her story of total failure.

Elaine then discovered some of the skills she already possessed which could be used towards this dream: she had resat her English O level and gained a slightly better mark, she knew the music of both singers well, and she had studied their lives in magazine articles. The first small step she needed to take was, she decided, to find out about word-processing courses so that she could handle the mail when she became secretary of a fan club.

At the next session, Elaine was animated as she told me all her successes: she had enrolled for a course on word processing, had taken a book on Barry Manilow out of the library, had requested a book search at the local bookshop for an out-of-print book of his life, got her television mended so she could watch a programme about Barry Manilow, and begun a novel about her life as a famous fan-club secretary. She was particularly excited about this last success, telling me that she written twenty pages on A4 paper. Thus Elaine was discovered to have lots of resources which could then be used when other difficulties arose in her life. After six sessions she was cheerful and optimistic, well into her course, had joined a creative writing group, insisted her social worker let her spend her birthday money on a bicycle so she could get more exercise and not be dependent on the infrequent bus service from her lodgings, and challenged some decisions at her review (at which it had been suggested she spend less time on her dreams and get herself a job at a local supermarket). This challenging had been difficult but had resulted in a change of social worker so she considered it worth the emotional effort. She gave me permission to use her story with other 'depressed' young women I see and it has proved very useful.

### *Partnership*

In solution-focused terms, this is described as developing cooperation but the emphasis is on the *worker* actively cooperating with service users to discover *their* unique ways of cooperating. The worker does not supply explanations, insights or hypotheses; the service user's story is accepted at face value, although alternative stories may be proffered for evaluation by the service user. Solution-focused work has no concept of resistance, denial, or manipulation; these behaviours are merely the service user's way of letting us know how to help them (de Shazer, 1984). Inevitably, hypotheses about resistance or denial turn out to be little more than insulting ways of describing the service user's strategies for coping, of which the worker does not approve. It is more profitable to stop hypothesising and search for the person's unique way of cooperating.

David was an nine-year-old boy with learning difficulties who witnessed his father's serious violence to his mum some years previously and was now exhibiting the same behaviour – he had violent temper tantrums during which he threatened his mum with weapons, kicked her, attempted to strangle her, shouted and swore. At other times he was abusive to his six-year-old sister, Cathy. A year previously he had been briefly placed with experienced foster parents who found him no problem and his Mum was now asking for him to be accommodated again. She had one other child from an earlier violent relationship with whom there was no contact. She had a new partner by whom she was currently five months pregnant. Social services referred David to the project in the hope of avoiding another care episode. At the first session, David was monosyllabic but made it plain how much he hated his mum. He reported small but significant progress in controlling his temper at the second session; the following conversation took place at the end of that session:

*Me*: We keep coming back to your mum. We can't choose our mums, we have to make do with the ones we've got. How many points out of a hundred would you give your mum on her mothering?

*David*: Sixty.

*Me*: Just above average. That's not bad. What would she be doing if she got 100?

*David*: She wouldn't be nagging me.

Me: How does she do nagging?

*David*: She goes on at me and then I lose my temper and I slap her. Or I get sent to bed.

*Me*: I bet you stamp upstairs and she shouts 'and you can take that expression off your face'?

*David*: [he nods, surprised] Then I stamp as loud as I can and bang the door.

*Me*: How many times does this happen?

*David*: [thinks hard] We had about two, three arguments last week.

*Me*: Good, that's an improvement. So, what were you doing when she wasn't doing nagging?

*David*: [either he misunderstands or he wants to talk about her nagging] Tell her to shut up.

*Me*: Could you tell her to shut up in a polite way?

*David*: There isn't one.

*Me*: How about, 'Could you stop saying that, it's upsetting me?'

*David*: Wouldn't work. She'd just get mad.

*Me*: So, solution time again. Let's think of some solutions to stop your mum getting mad.

*David*: Execute her.

*Me*: Right, that's solution number one. How would you do it?

*David*: Stick a knife in her head.

*Me*: Back or front?

*David*: Front.

*Me*: It might not kill her.

*David*: Hit her with a baseball bat, then.

*Me*: You'd be cleaning blood up for days. Anyway, you can't afford a baseball bat [this refers to an earlier part of the conversation]. I think we need some more solutions.

*David*: I could walk upstairs quietly.

*Me*: Good thinking. Would it work?

*David*: No. She'd come after me and shout ... I could ignore her ...

*Me*: Yes. Good idea. It's worth trying. Can anyone else help you? What about [partner's name]?

*David*: He's allus on her side.

*Me*: If he thought it might help with the rows ... [this refers to an earlier part of the conversation].

*David*: I'll ask him [writes it laboriously on his Post-it].

*Me*: What are the good things your mum does?

*David*: Makes tea ... washes up ...

*Me*: Is that all?

*David*: Yes.

*Me*: What does a good Mum do?

*David*: Look after us.

*Me*: And does she?

*David*: [grudgingly] Yes.

*Me*: You seem pretty mad at your Mum. Do you blame her for everything?

*David*: No. She's only nagged me once this week.

*Me*: That's pretty good. [I attempt to find out what he was doing differently when she is not nagging but he is unable to tell me so I set a pretend task – pretend to be polite one day and do it for real the next, see if anyone notices any difference – but he doesn't understand what I mean. He is also visibly tiring with the effort of concentrating for an hour so I summarise his progress and remind him of his tasks; to do more of the same to avoid rows – as agreed at the first session]. So, do you want to come back next week and tell me how you get on?

*David*: Yes.

*Me*: Actually, you've made a lot of progress. Pretty sneaky of you!

*David*: [grinning like a Cheshire cat] Skill. It's skill.

*Commentary*

Although David had a poor relationship with his mother, it was important to focus on what was working and not get into theories of mothering. I slipped up when I asked him if he blamed his mum for everything but he rescued me by returning to 'nagging'. Asking for detail about how she 'does nagging' helped identify exceptions and enabled me to check out any possible child protection issues. The use of reflexive verbs and gerunds helped separate David and his mum from the problem (White, 1995).

*Outcome*

Progress in this case was interrupted by the discovery that mum's partner was a Schedule One offender. Mum's pregnancy was a difficult one and both David and Cathy were accommodated briefly. Fortunately the Family Support Team workers became involved as mum was by now not wanting either of her children accommodated and the team was able to continue working with David with a good outcome. Cathy's behaviour deteriorated and she was referred to me with suspicions that her increasingly aggressive behaviour indicated that she had been sexually abused by mum's partner. I saw mum and Cathy on six occasions and Cathy's behaviour improved markedly.

### Choice

Solutions are co-constructed as the worker helps the service user reauthor their lives (Epston & White, 1992). Any tasks suggested are voluntary, and to be discontinued if they do not work or the service user comes up with a better idea (which they frequently do); the central philosophy of solution-focused work being: if it works, do more of it; if it doesn't work, don't do it again, do something different. This ensures that the service user has both choice and control over their preferred solutions.

Stephanie was a 24-year-old woman, whose four children were subject to interim care orders, two of whom were in foster care. She had a history of care herself and social services were concerned about her failure to come to terms with her experiences of sexual abuse, despite several referrals to psychiatrists and psychologists. At the first session she was preoccupied with her intense feelings of despair about her life in general. She was unable to either eat or sleep and chose these as the starting point of therapy.

After a detailed analysis of her current (non)-eating and sleeping patterns, and the few exceptions we could find, she decided on the following strategies:

1   She will not eat during the day, but after putting the children to bed she will prepare a proper supper for herself. If she doesn't want to eat it, she will leave it.

2   After the children fall asleep, she will have a short, hot bath to wash away her bad thoughts about herself.
3   She will then have a longer, warm bath with nice-smelling things and pamper herself, think good thoughts.
4   She will drink some hot chocolate and go to bed.
5   If any parts of this plan don't work, she will do something different.

Stephanie arrived at the next session smartly dressed and looking more cheerful. She had not managed to eat supper the first night but found the bath sequence soothing. However, on going to bed, she found her eldest daughter in it. Rather than get in with her daughter as she had done in the past, she went into her daughter's bed. Both of them had their best night's sleep in weeks. She then changed the bedtime routine for all the family, with the result that they were all eating and sleeping better. Because Stephanie had choice and control over her solutions (particularly important to her in view of the control exerted over her by social services), she was able to choose the issues she wanted to work on at each session. This control meant that during a difficult episode when her violent ex-partner moved back in with her, she was able to discuss her (temporary) return to drink and drug misuse, and the child protection issues this raised, as that session's topics. Her chosen solution was to report herself to social services. At a later stage she volunteered that she was ready to work on her sexual abuse experiences.

### *Speedy and simple interventions with value for money*

Keeping it simple and working from the 'bottom up' is an important principle in solution-focused work; de Shazer's (1988) maxim of 'simplify!' being central. The orientation is on successful functioning in the present and future, and preventing the past from oppressing this functioning, with a ripple effect stemming from small change in one area. Because of this, the approach is not only speedy and simple but also least invasive. As service users decide when they have satisfactorily reached their goals (providing that they are neither illegal nor harmful), they are in charge of termination. In the examples of James and Tamara it can be seen that they terminated counselling as soon as they had reached their goals. As their solutions worked swiftly for them, there was no need to dwell painfully and lengthily on their past failures and miseries. Swift problem resolution is by no means atypical as the following 'value-for-money' analysis shows.

The Northorpe Hall Trust counselling project aims to provide flexible services for children and young people within tight budget limits.

An important feature of the project is a speedy response to referrals within a short-term structure of six to eight, hour-long sessions. All non-urgent referrals are seen within a fortnight at most, at times to suit their commitments, and urgent referrals within 24 hours but the appointments may well be staggered over several weeks. Of the first 52 service users I saw who have successfully achieved their goals, eight needed only one session. The overall average was 4.5 sessions. Only five referrals took longer than six sessions and these included a group of three sisters and their mother, while another three included separate meetings with family support workers.

In the same period, there were also three one-off sessions where the outcome was not known; a one-off session where the young person did not engage as it became clear that she had been coerced into attending by her mother; and seven inappropriate referrals which did not progress past the first session (e.g. referred to the police child protection unit with the young person's permission). There were also nine service users who only partly met their goals, each requiring six sessions. No service user with learning difficulties achieved their goals in under four sessions and the looked-after young people all required the maximum number of sessions, mainly because their preferred plans for their futures were restricted by the existence of child care plans with which they did not agree and much time was spent on examining this issue.

## Limitations of the antioppressive nature of solution-focused approaches

I chose the examples above from the early stages of my attempts to adopt a systematic approach to using a solution-focused approach for two reasons. First, this was a rewarding period of work in which I became confident of the ethical nature of the approach and, equally, that it was not superficial in it's effects. It did genuinely open up new possibilities of change for service users which, had I not been attending to their unique ways of cooperating, would have limited their choices. Dryden and Fletham (1994) review the research on counselling, concluding that 'clients prefer to be given full information, to have matters explained to them, and to be consulted as equals' (p. 5). Second, a period of reflection caused me to realise that these possibilities were still limited to progress at the personal and psychological dimension of antioppressive work. For example, David and Cathy's home life improved markedly but their future was still severely circumscribed by their mum's social reality. Although she was enjoying her 'mothering' more, she remained socially isolated, short of money, grieving for yet another failed relationship, and in poor health.

Similarly, Mark was re-referred to the project some months later following a disclosure of attempted sexual abuse by a neighbour. I could discover no reason why Mark should have further sessions; he had realised the danger he was in and had reported it immediately. As he said, 'I'm still proud of myself. I'm not doing any of that stuff no more and I'm doing right good at school.' The referring social worker was concerned that Mark was unsupervised and was suggesting that Mark become involved in personal safety work or that his mum give up her job, which entailed unsocial hours, to supervise her children more closely. Mark's father, who the social worker found uncooperative, was unemployed and spent most of his time in bed. My earlier sessions with Mark and his mum had not revealed the fact that mum had struggled to fit his appointments with me around her job demands.

Although I could rationalise my neglect of these issues in terms of the project offering only brief counselling for specific problems, I was appalled that I was, once again, focusing on mothers and children and ignoring both the influence of the men in their lives – something I have examined in my previous practice at length (Milner, 1993a; 1993b; 1996) – and the cultural and structural dimensions of inequality and powerlessness (Thompson, 1993). There is a very real danger that in rejecting the notion of social 'truth', the reality that some 'truths' have more power than others is disregarded. As Law and Madigan (1994) point out, 'the idea that power doesn't exist tends to be quite popular among middle-class white persons. However, it seems not so popular an idea among the poor, the oppressed and the marginalised' (p. 3). The narrative approach, with it's more explicit emphasis on power issues, is helpful here in that it insists on the worker taking responsibility for the scope of their work:

> Every viewpoint taken by an observer has moral and ethical implications for those over whom the observer has power and influence [it is] very important to underscore the notion that our point of view should be thoughtfully chosen and that ethical obligations, responsibilities, and values arise from that choice. (Freeman *et al.*, 1997, p. 298)

## Narrative approaches to antioppressive work

### *Externalising the internalised discourse*

Reflecting on my first attempts at combining the two approaches, there emerged obvious gender differences. I found that I tended to adopt a mainly solution-focused approach with girls and young women, whereas with boys and young men, I would quickly move to externalising the problem in narrative style. For example, Thomas was referred for help in coming to terms with his emotional responses to his parents' separation some six years previously; these 'responses' including long-lasting depression, persistent soiling, and uncontrolled anger. He could hardly speak at all, not surprising, really, as soiling is an embarrassing problem for a twelve-year-old, but he whispered that 'rows' and 'misery'were his biggest problems. I set about separating the person from the problem through an externalising conversation:

*Me*: How long have you been feeling like this?
*Thomas*: About three, four years.
*Me*: That's rotten. Misery has quite a hold on you. What does it look like?
*Thomas*: Don't really know [prompt] it's grayish black … like a cloudish … a damp cloud … makes me feel angry and sad [prompt] … about fifty fifty. When I'm angry, I swear back and when I'm sad, I run upstairs.
*Me*: Which bothers you most, angry or sad?
*Thomas*: Angry really bothers me.
*Me*: How does the cloud get to you?
*Thomas*: When someone says something, I just react.
*Me*: How many times a day does the cloud get to you?
*Thomas*: About twice.
*Me*: Are any times worse than others?
*Thomas*: When we have a big argument.
*Me*: Any times of the day worse than others?
*Thomas*: Probably in the evening … as soon as I get in the house … I put my bag and coat in the hall … go upstairs and play on the play station, then it crashes and I get angry and Mum comes up and shouts … [prompt] … it lasts about half an hour.
*Me*: How do you get over it?
*Thomas*: She says, 'stay in the bedroom till you calm down' … it works sometimes.
*Me*: Does the cloud laugh at you?
*Thomas*: Yes. In my head. It says, 'keep going, keep going'.
*Me*: Has the cloud got any friends to help it?
*Thomas*: Not really.
*Me*: This cloud has been around for quite a while, has it got crafty?
*Thomas*: Yes. At school I was [he continues with the example in such a low voice that I am unable to hear him].

*Me*: Perhaps we need to be a bit crafty back, fool it ...
*Thomas*: [first smile of the session] Yes!
*Me*: Okay, possible solutions, what would the cloud dislike?
*Thomas*: Me being nice to my mum.
*Me*: Do we need some sunshine to make the cloud go away?
*Thomas*: My friend, he has one. He ticks it off.
*Me*: That's great. Can you join forces to come up with ways to get rid of your cloud?
*Thomas*: Yes. [And he's off on his own solutions.]

We had a further session two weeks later where he reported that he had successfully fought off the cloud. Apart from thickening the counter-plot, no further sessions were needed. His parents were puzzled but delighted at the change in his behaviour.

This difference in approach partly reflected the nature of the referrals for males; many of whom responded to violent experiences with violence of their own and, partly, it was a way of getting the less articulate boys to talk at all. Also, externalising the problem lends itself to 'fighting' metaphors which have considerable appeal to males brought up in a home with violence. This is, however, to neglect the discourse in which male violence is storied and to which they, too, subscribe; ignoring the fact that they (and their mothers) are telling me *someone else's* story about themselves. Simply taking someone's story at face value does not allow a full examination of the possibly oppressive nature of that story: 'We enter into stories; *we are entered into stories by others*; and we live our lives through these stories' (Epston, 1998, p. 11, my emphasis).

For women, the powerlessness which violent experiences engenders often leads to lethargy, despair and hopelessness while, for males, it often manifests itself in aggression. Removing the aggressive behaviour without putting anything worthwhile in it's place often reveals an underlying despair as they, too, have internalised, and are dispossessed by, feelings of alienation and worthlessness (for a fuller discussion, see Milner & O'Byrne, 1998, Chapter 5). The narrative approach, being underpinned by Foucauldian ideas on the self-regulating nature of power, and it's capacity to be productive as well as oppressive, emphasises the need to externalise the internalised discourse which defines the problem. It is not enough to simply externalise the problem as this neglects the context in which it is storied (White & Epston, 1990; Roth & Epston, 1996).

This externalising takes the form of developing alternative stories and providing challenges to the original story – or plot. For example,

Freeman *et al.* (1997) examine with parents the sociocultural backing for certain parental practices and expectations; particularly the social expectations which lead to self-blame: 'Instead of lecturing about right and wrong, we can externalise the effects and operation of "isms" so that the personal misery and social alienation they promote can be seen more clearly' (p. 56). White also suggests that each interview is evaluated by the service user as part of this process; to enable the worker to be honest about their own values and allow the service user to speculate on these to open up 'possibilities for dialogue and for the consideration of alternative views and opinions' (White, 1995, p. 69).

### Evaluating the interview

My experience of working with young women who have experienced sexual violence has influenced my opinion that giving evidence in court against the abuser is largely a damaging and humiliating experience to be avoided; plus the reality that the low odds of it leading to a conviction also makes it unproductive (see, for example, Lees, 1997). I explain not only my views but how I have arrived at them so that young women can make their own evaluation and not be 'nudged' by me towards my preferred outcome for them; there being a fine line between responsible therapy and therapeutic abuse (Jenkins, 1996, p. 129). Indeed, by successfully challenging my opinion on this matter, fourteen-year-old Soraya – a particularly timid girl – was not only able to take a first step towards asserting herself but also to pursue her wish to give evidence in court with more confidence; a course of action I was able to support because we both put my views to one side.

Similarly, the service user evaluation of a session permits a fuller appreciation of class and power differences. For example, I had puzzled over sixteen-year-old Kylie's recurrent use of a particular word: she tended to refer to anyone she didn't like – foster parents, social worker, etc. – as 'snobby':

*Me*: But I'm snobby. I don't understand what you mean. How can I be being helpful if I'm being snobby?
*Kylie*: You're snobby in a nice way [laughs embarrassedly].
*Me*: I'm still not sure what you mean ...
*Kylie*: Well, you're not dead serious all the time ...
*Me*: Is that helpful?
*Kylie*: Yes ... a bit ... but you're dead bossy [she smiles at me and turns my pad round. Taking my pen, she draws a line for a scaled 'bossy' question and asks me where I would put myself].

*Me*: About 95 ... ?

*Kylie*: NO. ONE HUNDRED. [She falls about laughing.]

*Me*: What would I be doing differently if I was at 99?

*Kylie*: You wouldn't be paying me those compliments.

*Me*: But you have been doing so well, which compliments do you want me to stop?

*Kylie*: Yeah, I'm pretty pleased with myself ... but I think I'll still need to come and see you ... probably next week. ...

*Me*: What will I be doing next week that will be helpful to you?

We continue slowly and carefully; what Weingarten (1998) refers to as attending to the small and the ordinary, enabling Kylie to express her discomfort with some aspects of middle-class life in her foster home – what she had lumped together as 'snobby' earlier; address the power imbalance in our relationship (although I am not sure how 'bossy' I am if she dare tell me), and discover that I have been guilty of 'cheering on change' prematurely: Kylie eventually tells me that she is worried about her drinking – something she had been keeping secret and which she wants to stop.

Another part of the evaluation consists of asking the service user what has not been relevant or useful to them. Most service users are incredibly polite, so when they answer 'it was a bit helpful', I follow up with something on the lines of 'Well, that's OK, but what would have been *more* helpful?'

### *Communities of concern*

Although asking the service user what advice they can offer to others with the same problem is intended primarily to thicken the counterplot (and increase the worker's stock of ideas), when this advice is added to a newsletter, it has the advantage of circulating ideas to a community of people struggling with the same problem; what Madigan and Epston (1995) refer to as communities of concern. For example, Freeman *et al.* (1997) describe one in which league members share their struggles and ideas for revising relationships with anorexia and bulimia and some members take an active part in revising the definition of the problem through education programmes in high schools:

> Facilitating such movements from the personal to the political is a powerful avenue for individuals as well as social change and consequently a value-laden pursuit that demands high ethical standards. This requires a constant process of informed consent from clients and takes place in a context which is highly collaborative. (Freeman *et al.*, 1997, p. 127)

The importance of attending to the social, gender and cultural aspects of the problem as well as the psychological aspects is highlighted in a Young Carers' group which is facilitated by Northorpe Hall Trust. Initially the social workers involved organised this group around their own agenda; one grounded in *their* existing knowledge of the likely effects of being a young carer but, as the members became involved in their evaluation of the group, they not only changed the focus of activities but also made their own educational video which broadcasts *their* realities of being young carers and the services *they* would find helpful. This has the effect of not replacing one ideology with another, rather, 'sites of resistance' are increased (Law & Madigan, 1994, p. 5).

The notion of 'communities of concern' as a means of holding one's work accountable to oppressed people is extended to the organisational arena by Tamasese and Waldegrave (1996), who devised 'just therapy' to address both institutional and individual modes of cultural and gender discrimination responsibly. Not only is their work with families directly accountable to therapists of the same culture but they also established caucuses of women's and cultural groups to which policy-making groups are accountable. These caucuses have the right at any time to call the agency, or parts of it, to address equity issues. The groups are self-determining, enabling the voices of subjugated groups to be heard and white, male groups to check out key aspects of their orientation and projects with caucus groups. There remains progress to be made as the white, male policy-making groups usually respond to requests for meetings rather than initiate them but it is a positive step in changing the organisational culture. The gender dimensions in narrative work are addressed more fully in the following two chapters.

## The ethics of influence

There remains the issue of how much influence the worker has over the solutions arrived at and how this influence can be made visible. Jenkins, (1996) describes how a sense of outrage and grief on hearing abusive stories tends to arouse his 'inner tyrant'; one which operates from a sense of frustration and self-righteous superiority. He views these experiences and feelings as an inevitable part of working with abusive men, recommending that they be named and discussed with colleagues; although he does not go so far as to recommend that he consults a caucus group of abusers. It is not just in work with abusive men that one's inner tyrant emerges; I am only too aware that I have a feminist inner tyrant in me which continues to classify and categorise people. This too needs to be named and questioned; a process which I attempt to do honestly in the case examples in this book. Respect, say Essex and Gumbleton (1996), comes from openness about one's values and an explicit recognition of the position of the service user; including their values, beliefs and meanings; especially where these differ from one's own. The impact of the gender of the social worker and service user is examined in Chapters 3 and 4.

## SUMMARY

- The anti-oppressive basis to solution-focused approaches enables social workers to actualise their value systems in terms of measurable outcomes. Service users' cultural ideas and 'theories' are respected and viewed as valuable as professional knowledge.
- Service users are encouraged to gain control over their lives through the identification of existing competencies and the exercise of choice in the co-construction of solutions. The emphasis on discovering service users' unique ways of cooperating with the social work endeavour creates genuine partnership. The process is speedy, simple, and value for money in that it seeks always to be least invasive through minimum intervention.
- In rejecting the notion of fixed truths, the reality that some social truths have more power than others may be disregarded in solution-focused approaches. Narrative approaches adopt a more overt stance against structural inequalities and their impact on solution finding.
- Narrative approaches extend the notion of identifying exceptions; actively deconstructing problem-saturated stories by externalising both the problem and the internalised discourses which support the problems. This enables social workers to examine with service users the possibilities that their reality may be a story into which they have been entered by others.
- Narrative approaches to evaluating the social work interview permit a fuller appreciation of power differences than solution-focused approaches. The development of communities of concern enables service users to develop competencies at group as well as individual levels.
- Both solution-focused and narrative approaches encourage respect for service users through openness about professional values; especially where these differ from service user values.

# 3

# Women talking with women: serious gossip

Despite a growing confidence in the effectiveness of a combined solution-focused/narrative approach in helping service users identify and meet their goals, I became aware of a growing unease about the development of my personal style. There were two issues which needed untangling. First, although I was engaged in regular, reflexive discussion with a supervisor (with whom I shared an enthusiasm for the approach to such an extent that we co-authored a book on social work assessment without a single disagreement), it was becoming increasingly obvious that my work was different from his in a gender-specific way. Apart from noticing that I 'got up close' with women, he could not identify how I 'feminised' his suggestions.

Secondly, Dermer *et al.* (1998) present a feminist critique of solution-focused therapy in which they argue that the emphasis on competence and strengths tends to overlook gender and power differences; being, at best, subject to a *beta-prejudice*: neglecting difference. They also point out that solution-focused approaches ignore feminist-informed therapy groups where women are encouraged to connect with each other and deal only with productive blame at the expense of other-directed anger. If this is so, why did I find myself adopting a predominantly solution-focused approach with females and a more narrative approach with males? Surely the more explicit acknowledgment of power issues in the latter would have made a narrative approach more appropriate for women; especially externalising internalised discourses? My initial evaluation did reveal a neglect of how women are positioned socially, economically and politically. There was an urgent need, therefore, to address the questions of how a woman does solution-focused and narrative work; whether this is different from how a man would do it; and whether she does it differently with male service users.

As I take verbatim notes in each session and then type them up for supervision, I had ample data to study. Themes emerged in the initial analysis, revealing differences in my work which could be labelled womanly. First is the way in which I actualise empathy. de Shazer's focus on behaviour rather than emotion, and the present and future rather than the past, leads him to listen to – but show little interest in – florid expressions of distress, pain and failure. He remains interested in the exceptions to these expressions. This neglects an important dimension for women, it being well established that a major source of resilience for women is the sympathetic receiving of a disclosure (Madge, 1997), and my personal style is softly to interject comments about the abuser during the telling of an abusive story (my internalised discourse?). I am not neutral and service users respond to this with initial surprise and then delight. We sometimes have very strong conversations about what we would like to do to abusers and this is helpful for them in expressing anger about what has been done to them – dealing with *both* productive blame and other-directed anger; one of the criticisms of solution-focused approaches levelled by Dermer *et al.* (1998).

Sometimes we share tears. For example, I invite the reader to listen to nine-year-old Jenny, who has been sexually abused over a period of years by a pensioner in his home. She tells me that the other girls he abused blame her for involving them with the man; that she has had to change school, her family are about to move to another area (in the meantime, she cannot go out of the house), and her sister is highly critical of her for bringing 'trouble' on the family. She deals with her multiple losses by going to her bedroom to read and be sad. With silent tears pouring down her face, she whispers that she wakes each morning wondering what can possibly happen next:

*Me*: What is this sadness like?
*Jenny*: Don't know.
*Me*: If you drew a picture of it, what would it look like?
*Jenny*: A big heart, broken into pieces.
*Me*: Can broken hearts be mended?
*Jenny*: Sometimes.
*Me*: What would mend your heart?
*Jenny*: Nothing. [said despairingly]
*Me*: Is it broken for ever?
*Jenny*: [nods, and the tears flow faster]
*Me*: What have you done with the pieces?
*Jenny*: Chucked them in the bin. [she is racked with harsh sobs]

Could you remain disinterested? Could you, indeed, should you, remain cool, calm and 'professional'? But it is not all tears; I also discovered that what my supervisor had referred to as my 'creative craziness' arose from 'having a laugh' with people about their (sometimes) dire situations. Women laughing at themselves is, I think, a particularly womanly thing. I also found that sharing tears and laughter was the way I got into an externalisation of the internalised discourse; albeit one I hadn't been operating consciously in my efforts to pursue the discipline of a solution-focused approach. I had also been influenced by women writer/practitioners. Dermer *et al.*'s criticisms are based on an examination of solution-focused texts largely written by men and these do not particularly address gender issues. Women writers, while acknowledging their debt to the pioneering work of de Shazer, do address women's issues. For example, Berg and Reuss's substance abuse manual (1998) challenges the male professional domination of alcohol abuse therapies: 'many clinical indicators show that women are not comfortable with the confrontational treatment approaches and prefer programs that appeal to women's approaches to problem solving' (p. 151).

Berg (1991; Berg & Miller, 1992; Berg & Reuss, 1998) finds that women tend to hide their misuse of substances; internalise their problems; are devastated by the destruction of relationships and self-esteem, which explains why some women are described as pathologically codependent; have a stronger sense of lack of control over their lives; tend to self-blame; take responsibility for problems beyond what is realistic and reasonable; and feel vulnerable in decision making. From this, she develops a unique approach to solution finding with women which involves consensus-building approaches; negotiation through give and take; conciliatory rather than confrontational approaches; paying attention to personal issues and their personal meaning to women; and the use of tentative language which women can more easily challenge, for example, prefacing statements with 'perhaps', 'could it be' and 'I wonder'. I would add to this by saying something like 'some women tell me that they feel like … is this how it is for you, *or is it different?*' In this way, women workers are accepting and reinforcing the idea that a woman is unique and that her feelings are valid. I am also influenced here by Carol Gilligan's (1982) work on moral development. She proposes that because women are concerned with the activity of care, they define morality as the understanding of responsibility and relationships, whereas men claim that morality is defined by fairness, leading them to think of rights and rules.

Similarly, Lethem (1994) stresses the importance of recognising the accomplishments of women which may seem modest unless account is taken of the adverse circumstances in which they have occurred; the need to clarify what is and what is not within and without her control; and the advisability of using 'just therapy' (Waldegrave, 1985;

Tamasese & Waldegrave, 1996). A helpful way of making visible the modest achievements of women is to use the recovery charts devised by Yvonne Dolan (1991) for work with sexually abused women. These reflect the essential components of resilience: disclosures being positively received, thinking positively, having a good friend or supportive family, and achievement and success (Madge, 1997); and the importance of supporting mothers so that they can become 'strong mothers' (Peake and Fletcher, 1997). Within this womanly framework, I find that I can help women reauthor their lives in a way that enables them to cope with certain repetitive themes of oppression which stultify women's creativity in solution finding. Some of the ways in which this is achieved are briefly illustrated below.

## Safety and control

George *et al.* (1990) find that when working with domestic violence they cannot let women lead in terms of the goals for therapy: 'in cases where it is clear or we suspect a woman to be at risk we unilaterally put the woman's safety at the top of the agenda' (p. 91). Similarly, Berg (1991) places the safety of children at the top of her agenda in her work on family preservation. Both she and Dolan (1991) use scaling questions for assessing child safety and Dolan also recommends externalising it, i.e. 'What could you truthfully tell social services which would convince them that safety is present in your home?'

When the experience of violence shatters a woman's illusion of safety, she often loses further control over her life; for example, she does not venture out without an escort, takes to wearing 'big clothes', suffers panic attacks and flashbacks, and increases her attempts at appeasement. The reality of life for a woman is that it is not very safe; she may have been abused by one man but there is the potential for abuse by many others so it is never a simple case of helping her to come to terms with one bad experience; she needs to develop a range of effective safety strategies. Even where young women are currently in warm, supportive relationships with men, they not infrequently find the relative calm more unsettling than the previous turmoil where they could more easily recognise their resistance and coping skills. Here the starting point for me is to explore what control and responsibility taking is reasonable and what is unreasonable and the easiest place to begin is by helping the person gain control over their thoughts and feelings.

Cassie had experienced sexual and physical violence almost all her life; having been abused first by her father and then by a series of partners.

Although she was now in a stable relationship with a gentle man, the violent men she had known were still in her life. Her father lived locally and hoped to 'give her away' when she married her current partner; and she was due to give evidence in court soon against an ex-partner who responded to her ending the relationship by breaking into her house and raping and attempting to strangle her as she sat on the sofa watching television with her daughter. She has had counselling previously but did not find it helpful: 'she just sat there. Then she said my mum hadn't kept me safe, how did I feel about that? I was right upset. I thought my mum didn't love me. I was dizzy and panicky having to talk about it.'

Her main problems were dizziness and intrusive thoughts which came more frequently now she had no worries about being being hit by her partner; when she was in violent relationships she knew where she was. She cleaned the house to make the thoughts go away:

> I would clean with a toothbrush to avoid the kind of life I was leading, blanking stuff out, being beaten. My doctor says stop cleaning ... give up my job, sit on the sofa and relax. I can't sit on that sofa! I only relax at work. I don't feel safe at home during the day. I'm a real worrier. I get tense and then I overbreathe.

She became increasingly tense as she told me this, walking round the room until she suddenly sat down and burst into tears. When the tears stopped, we looked at exceptions to her dizziness and intrusive thoughts.

As well as cleaning, these involve telling the thoughts to 'fuck off', putting music on full-blast, singing at work, decorating and baking. We then explored life in the future without the problem and baking was central to how she envisaged this; a warm kitchen with pine furniture and the smell of fairy cakes baking while she mixed the butter cream. She was unable to envisage other parts of her life in so much detail so I suggested that she carried a paper bun-case in her pocket as a comfort cue for the times when the intrusive thoughts returned and she couldn't dash into the kitchen to bake; and to remind her to think about what life will be like when the problems have gone.

This may seem like a trivialisation of a huge reaction to multiple trauma but Cassie was sufficiently in control of her thoughts by the second session to begin disentangling the various threads of her misery. She was much clearer about what she needed to do more of to achieve her desired future and achieved her goals in four sessions.

Also useful in helping women gain positive control over their lives is a coin-toss experiment (Berg & Reuss, 1998). Berg and Reuss use the coin-toss experiment in work with women who appear to be 'codependent' on men who abuse alcohol but actually are struggling with making a decision whether or not to sever a relationship. Before going to bed, the woman is to toss the coin. If it comes up heads, she is to pretend for the whole of the next day that she has decided to stay with the problem drinker, no matter what he does. If it comes up tails, she has to pretend for the whole of the next day that she has decided to leave the problem drinker, no matter what he does. She is not to tell her partner about the experiment. This task allows her the experience of detachment one day at a time. The fact that is a pretend task, an experiment, allows her to discover how she feels about herself; solutions are not being forced upon her. I find that this works very well in cases where women are unable to decide whether or not to stay with a violent partner but modify it slightly. I keep a selection of foreign coins from my holidays and allow the service user to choose which currency she wants for the coin toss. I will say what happy experiences each coin reminds me of and ask when she last had a holiday. This allows her to entertain the possibility of a carefree holiday for herself at some time in the future as women usually choose a coin from the country they would most like to visit (I have been known to declare a penny to be a Scottish one). Then I use whatever comments they make about the coin part of the experiment. For example, Janet chose a 200-lire coin because she liked Italy and 200 was her lucky number. Tails therefore became the logical side of the coin to indicate that she would pretend that she was safe and her problems were resolved that day. As the heads side depicted a *man's* head, she chose this side for pretending to have a nightmare day where all her worst fears came true. I continue to express innocent surprise when women report back that the coin came up tails most days. Strength to resist quickly grows from such small beginnings. It is a fruitful way of creating space for any woman with a difficult relationship decision to make.

## Women reclaiming their bodies

Young women who have been sexually abused often disassociate from their bodies in a variety of ways; possibly the least understandable to their families being that of seemingly reckless sexual activity, and the most destructive being severe self-harm in the form of cutting and suicide attempts. Dolan (1991) considers it important to help such women regain a sense of control over their own bodies but acknowledges that 'Empowering a formerly sexually abused client to reclaim her sexuality may be a delicate step for the therapist. It is imperative that the client not feel intruded on, lest the invasive aspects of the original trauma be symbolically re-enacted' (p. 165). She recommends following the woman's easiest path by asking her to identify any times when she does experience feelings in her body. Additionally, she recommends dance as a means of re-establishing awareness in her body and providing a vehicle for self-expression but this latter is not always appropriate in that it often has overt sexual connotations. I find that there are simpler and more fun ways for women to reclaim their bodies.

Shannon was an intelligent seventeen-year-old woman who was raped by a stranger at the age of eleven, sexually assaulted on a school holiday, and, more recently, sexually abused in an appallingly degrading way by a known man over a period of time. After three sessions, she had made good progress in a number of areas; she was back in school, had stopped drinking, drug use and cutting; rebuilt relationships with her mother, and her flashbacks had reduced in intensity. However, she continued to engage in casual sex with complete strangers several times each week – what she described as 'having a slaggified week', requiring yet another visit to the clinic for sexually transmitted diseases. Previous attempts at exploring her 'easiest path' to recognising body sensations having failed completely, I decided to do 'something different', suggesting that it was about time that she reclaimed her virginity. She looked at me in astonishment and told me not to be so ridiculous, she could never get it back, 'it's gone for good, Judith'. 'Not so', I countered, 'I'm reading *Captain Corelli's Mandolin* at the moment and apparently in some parts of Greece, a woman is considered to have lost her virginity the moment she fancies a man sexually, sort of mentally lost it.' Shannon did not consider this fair but I said that if it were true, then when had she fancied a man sexually? Of course, she never had and this gave me the opportunity to build up a case for her never having lost her virginity in the first place as it could only be voluntarily relinquished in 'Greek' terms. Shannon was intrigued with this idea even though not entirely convinced of my logic; her comment being, 'you are daft at times, Judith'.

Nonetheless the seeds of an alternative story were sown and she ceased casual sex shortly after this discussion, reporting proudly that she was in a celibate stage. Her health and school work improved as a result of her change of behaviour and she obtained a breathing space in which to discover her body. This took the form of discussing what sort of clothes celibate women wore – she wore all black clothes for a while as she toyed with the idea of becoming a nun, later exploring what she termed 'being girlified', adopting pale pink cardigans. Some months later, she wrote to me about beginning to go out with boys (the first time she had ever been out with anyone younger than herself); always emphasising that she didn't let them 'go as far as they want', until one letter arrived in which she informed me that she had met 'a smashing lad and, guess what, Judith? I've just lost my virginity!'

## Self-blame

Taking an unreasonable amount of responsibility for what has happened to them is a common theme in my conversations with girls and women. The violence they have experienced is internalised as a relationship failure on their part, even when they have been badly abused as small children. This is not just a simple matter of women feeling responsible for relationship maintenance but also includes the influence of dominant discourses around mothering. Mothers are expected to love, nurture and protect their children, even in conditions of extreme adversity. The unanswerable question for many girls and women, whether they are attending as a result of recent child abuse, a long history of parental rejection, or domestic violence, is 'why me?' The solution-focused worker's response to this question is 'Which would be better for you, to find out why or get better?' Invariably the service user response to this is 'to get better' but it is possible to address both parts. An integral part of this is to attempt to restory the culturally dominant discourse of natural maternal love by saying that we have no choice about what sort of family we are born into, followed by a comment to the effect that 'it doesn't seem that you were at the front when parents were given out', before completing an adaptation of Dolan's (1991) sexual abuse recovery chart for use as 'recovery from poor parenting' (see Appendix 1). This is a way of changing the story the service user has struggled with for many years and which has what Freeman *et al.* (1997) call a 'thick plot'. This 'plot' is thickened not only by the mothering discourse which refuses to allow a person to admit to not liking their mother but also by the circumstances of the abuse; frequently only one child is abused and therefore that child thinks that there must have been something wrong with them. Where the abuser is a father, the self-blame is compounded by the failure of the mother to protect or to choose the father over the child. Where the abuser is a violent partner, he has usually told the woman that her behaviour has driven him to abuse.

Monica was a twenty-three-year-old woman who was rejected by her mother at fourteen years of age and spent the rest of her childhood in care. This was punctuated by periodic returns to her family, all of which quickly broke down on the (supposed) grounds of her unreasonable behaviour. She had made a life for herself since leaving care and was about to get married but was plagued with doubts that she deserved this relationship and her ability to make it work. She wished to read her child care records and had been advised to seek counselling as preparation for this. In our first session, she related her story: one in which she could not understand why her sister was retained in the family and she was rejected. She thought that there must be something wrong with her, the common theme of being a 'failed child', but this was overlaid with resentment at her mother. She was convinced that her father loved her and 'went along with Mum to keep the peace'. Although much of the period in care was nothing more than a hazy recollection of chaos, she had early memories of her mother beating her.

Monica resisted any attempt on my part to introduce possible alternative stories of her life so I decided to explore her story in more depth, using a modified version of a life story book (Ryan & Walker, 1985). I asked her to write down her memories for us to sort out at the next session. To make more real her 'lost period' in care, I also asked her to undertake a newspaper search to find out what major events happened during that part of her life. She arrived at the next session with a sheaf of papers, apologising for the lack of structure of her memories and the complete absence of dates. We read through these together and she began to piece together her life. Her talk was still full of happy times with her father and beatings from her mother but there was only one happy memory of dad in her writings and this was slight as it referred to a happy holiday during which she saw little of her father. As our discussion continued, it emerged that Dad had been involved in the beatings also. She added that she had only looked at local newspapers so far and had been amazed to find references to various family members quite regularly. She commented that she had never known that she came from such a violent family. I asked her how she had survived in such a family and we began a new story in which she had moved from failed child to victim-turned-survivor. The old plot still retained its density so I asked her to continue with her research as a way of thickening the developing counterplot.

The third session was our last one. She arrived merely to report that she had read her file and that it had made complete sense in terms of what she had read about her family in the newspapers. She had also rung her father and told him what she thought about him for the first time in her life – thoughts she hadn't realised she entertained before. She explained to me that she considered herself lucky to have been in care, away from such a family, and she intended to 'get on with life.

I feel I can get married and be happy now.' I asked her what advice she would give me to pass on to other people in similar situations and she said the local newspaper search and reading her records had been most useful. Although asking this question was mainly to 'thicken the counterplot', I asked for her permission to use this information and it has proved useful on many occasions, one of which is detailed below.

Pam, a forty-year-old woman with a 'care history', was depressed, failing in her relationship with her partner, on poor terms with her sons, and suicidal. As she put it: 'I don't know who I am or where I'm going. I'm lost.' As she lacked both the motivation and the energy to visualise any sort of future for herself, I told her Monica's story. Although dubious about the advisability of researching her past – she too suffered from the 'why me' question as her mother had remarried and subsequently successfully cared for a second family – she agreed to 'give it a go'.

For Pam, the key documents were her case records, of which she was allowed to make selected copies. She brought an account written by an NSPCC officer of the circumstances surrounding her admission to care. 'It's like something out of Dickens', she commented in amazement. The bald facts of her appallingly deprived childhood and her parents' replies to the NSPCC officer's questions helped her to make sense of her parents' behaviour to her when she was in care – mostly brief and disappointing contacts when they wanted money. With a new story of her childhood, one which freed her from self-blame, she rapidly began to make a new life to fit the new story. She enrolled at college, began babysitting for her sons, renegotiated the terms of her relationship with her partner – recognising his behaviour as loving despite a reluctance on his part to say the words, and bought herself some new clothes.

The new story was a weak one, though, so I attempted to strengthen it by listing the successes which we identified at each session and asked her to print them on a postcard, headed 'well done, Pam', and stick it on the fridge door. Although seemingly small, her successes were enormous considering her adverse circumstances but she continued to discount them, her sense of control over her life being still tenuous. At our fifth session, she returned to dwelling on her relationship failures and she expressed doubts that she would ever find happiness. Somewhat exasperated, I said, 'Well, you won't, at this rate, because you will keep looking in the misery cupboard.' I mimed her rooting in an imaginary cupboard, pulling out one failure after another and saying 'Oh look, here's another failure, I can't find happiness anywhere.' She began to laugh and said that maybe she had better look in the happiness cupboard. 'Huh,' I responded, 'and just where is it? I bet you don't even know.' A story soon developed in which she locked the door of the misery cupboard and began to build a bigger happiness cupboard. She decided that the misery cupboard made her dwell too much on herself and her failures and that she would find more happiness if she focused on helping other people. She concluded counselling at the next session.

## Undermining psychiatric stories

Often young women tell me that their problem is 'depression'. I have a problem with this as it is enters them into a story which will require an expert to diagnose and then treat the 'patient'. The treatment may work for a while but the woman is cast in a dependent role and is unable to exert control over her life; for example, although Ruth's psychotropic drugs muffled the voices which told her to cut herself they put her so out of touch with her body sensations that she became bulimic. Furman and Ahola (1992) suggest that psychiatric diagnoses become self-verifying and that 'watchful wording' can be helpful in developing an alternative story to help women gain control over their lives. For example, they coined the term 'latent joy' as an alternative to 'depression' and suggested that 'borderline personality disorder' was better described as 'a search for a new life direction'. Similarly Smith *et al.* (1998) say that labelling people is an unhelpful and mistaken attitude which invalidates the means by which a person has found to communicate something extremely painful about which they cannot speak openly. It may be a harmful way, such as cutting, but it is a form of resistance.

When I first saw Ruth, as well as receiving conventional psychiatric treatment, she had been in counselling elsewhere for over a year for assistance in coming to terms with sexual and emotional abuse by her father. She had become extremely distressed by her experiences of being encouraged to retell her abuse in counselling, had dropped out of college, and her self-harming behaviour had escalated alarmingly. She was extremely intelligent, had clear aims for her future, and knew what solutions she hoped to put into operation. Although, as mentioned above, the medication had obscured her 'voices', this did nothing to reduce the extent of her self-loathing. Smith *et al.* (1998) suggest that women with auditory hallucinations should be asked to talk more about these voices to find out where they come from and to develop challenges to them on the grounds that if 'hearing voices in your head is part of your experience, trying to develop a stronger more protective voice is really important' (p. 32). When encouraged to talk about her 'voices', it emerged that Ruth was hearing all the obscenely derogatory things her father had said over many years. We explored how he had got into her head and what it felt like. Ruth described it as 'a sort of octopus; it's inside my head and it's wrapped round my neck'. We then explored which tentacle would be easiest to chop off first; her self-harming being so entwined by the 'octopus' that, if she managed to stop cutting herself, she would revert to some other method of self-harm (indeed, Ruth had the largest self-harming repertoire I have ever met; I had no idea that is was possible to inflict damage on one's body in quite so many ways). We began small, with the most damaging message the voice delivered, being told she was 'a fucking fat elephant'. Although working on eating management is probably the most difficult place to start for a woman with such enormous difficulties, it was important to accept that this was where Ruth wanted to make her first effort so I suggested an experiment. She was to study her eating behaviour and watch for the 'full sign'. She wasn't to attempt to stop gorging at this point, just see if a 'full feeling' ever happened. Ruth was sure that she never had such a feeling but agreed to try the experiment, which we supported by a self-pampering programme. To her surprise, she did identify several occasions when she 'felt full' and, as she was under no pressure not to eat, managed not to overeat at some of these points. This was only a tiny success in the overall scheme of her desired weight loss of many stones but it provided a lift-off point. She attended six sessions in all and then stopped her medication and returned to college.

Her confidence in being able to continue to cut off the 'tentacles' was fragile so she asked if she could write to me. She wrote to me several times in her first term, always at times of acute stress but, interestingly, she chose to communicate her distress via a novel she was writing about her father. She sent me the first chapter in which we both appeared as vengeful characters, torturing her father; pouring out her anger in elegant prose. I wrote back, admiring her literary talent and added a second chapter in which she was slim and successful, my character asking her 'How did you do it'? The book continued to develop in a sporadic fashion; the literary style changed and a positive plot developed. Recently there have been no chapters coming my way although I had a letter telling me that her overall year one results were at B + grade. Now that she can appreciate that her successes are attributable to herself she has been able to think of the 'voices' as inconvenient, annoying background noise. She has also achieved her goal of beginning to lose weight. She ascribes this to a realisation that negative thoughts weigh heavier than positive ones. This is an intriguing notion which I have since discovered interests many young women who have difficulties managing their eating habits, as it changes what they see in the mirror.

## Valuing oneself

The referrers of the young women I see almost always identify poor self-esteem as a problem. This is actually a complex (and white, male, middle-class) psychological concept, including self-concept, self-image and self-achievement. I find 'selflessness' a more useful way of looking at this issue as it includes both the broader effects of female socialisation *and* the internalised self-blame resulting from the specific abuse which women have experienced. Dolan (1998a) offers a range of helpful exercises aimed at helping women to value themselves which I have adapted to the individual preferences of the young women I see. All involve a task which necessitates the women spending some time on themselves. I discovered the value of this quite accidentally. Women would commonly report that they had left the first session feeling much relieved but then experienced a let-down feeling later in the evening. To counter this, I included an explanation of the effects of counselling at the end of the first session, emphasising that they had worked hard, so not to be surprised if they felt tired afterwards. I would then ask them to tell me how they would treat themselves when this happened. At Sally's last session, I asked her what had been most helpful and she said 'the treats'. She added, 'I didn't take it all that seriously at first; I thought you were just being nice. But it built up. It made me realise that I am *worth* a treat. I felt really good doing the treats' (my emphasis). Treats, pampering, 'bedroom therapy' and 'comfort contingencies' for panic attacks and dark days are now an essential part of my work with women.

Women report that intrusive thoughts, flashbacks, nightmares and feelings of worthlessness are most commonly experienced in the period after going to bed and before falling asleep, therefore I explore how changes can be made to bedtime routines which will counter these. Jane was a twenty-year-old woman with severe learning difficulties who had been receiving psychiatric treatment for suicidal behaviour for many years. She had been sexually abused by her uncle over a long period of time and continued to be emotionally abused by her parents, who never called her by her name, 'useless cow' being much more usual. She had nightmares every night. During the day, she had better thoughts about herself when she was either with her dog or babysitting her only friend's little girl but she had a very foreshortened view of her future. Jane identified bedtime as her biggest problem so I suggested that she make a special dream-catcher.

A dream-catcher is a Native American artefact, a network of feathers and beads, which is hung where it will catch the morning light so that bad dreams caught in its web are dissipated. I provided Jane with a hoop and a selection of ribbons, thread and beads and explained how to make a web to catch the dreams. Jane was excited about this and recognised a hidden achievement – she was good at making things. She proudly brought her partly completed dream-catcher to the next session and explained that she had covered the hoop with blue ribbon because that was her favourite colour. She had rejected the thread for the web, preferring instead to cover the centre with pretty lace. Her nightmares had diminished in intensity but were still a problem so I added a combination of Dolan's self-care techniques (1998a, Chapter 9). We explored at length her hopes and dreams, what made her feel most comfortable and safe, and her proudest achievement. This conversation strengthened her sense of self-value but I recognised that her emerging sense of self-worth was fragile so I asked her to identify symbols for each element which she could then suspend from the dream-catcher. It was not easy explaining to Jane what a symbol meant (I ended up using an essential oils simile) but she eventually decided that a keyring would symbolise her hopes for the future (to learn to drive); a pink bootee for her greatest achievement (she was proud of her babysitting); and a tape of her friend's little girl laughing for her comfort cue. Jane's dream-catcher turned out to be a most elaborate affair, which not only stopped the bad dreams but also gave her confidence in her achievements. With more experience, I have found that dream-catchers are most effective with children or women with few sources of support (and time to make one), while a similar exercise involving the construction of a comfort drawer is more suitable for others. In all instances, the contents are decided upon after a long conversation, which in itself helps the woman to begin valuing herself.

I also explored ways of challenging selflessness with young mothers by introducing 'doormat' therapy. If they were unable to put themselves 'first', then how could they begin to put themselves a strong 'second' or 'third'? It doesn't seem to matter which level one chooses; the important thing is to get into a discussion about how it feels to be always at 'the bottom' and how to move up. For example, Trish reported at her second session that she had moved up from doormat to kitchen-sink level. After meeting Catherine, I began to extend this idea to young women.

Catherine had been sexually abused by an uncle four years previously and, again, recently. She was living with her father and brothers, all who admired her uncle so she was unable to tell them what had happened to her. Neither did she feel able to tell her mother, who had remarried and was pregnant with a much wanted child. It quickly became clear that working on exceptions to the effects of the immediate trauma would be insufficient as Catherine not only lacked support but her father and brothers depended on her for emotional and practical back-up. Matters were further complicated by her uncle moving to a house opposite where she lived.

As Catherine's story unfolded, the unconscious, continuing emotional abuse on the part of her father and brothers emerged as more damaging than the sexual abuse. We devised a comfort drawer which she kept in her bedroom and she retreated there whenever she experienced a flashback as a result of her brothers beginning to talk admiringly about her uncle. She also worked out how to claim part of the house as her own – she put up her paintings in the sitting room; the only room, other than her bedroom, which she felt was in any way her territory as the kitchen was 'a mess' and the dining room used a games room. She also identified two female friends who could be depended upon to be supportive and stayed away from friends who she tended to 'run after and try to please all the time'. All these things helped in the short term and an alternative story developed; one in which she viewed herself as warden of a men's hostel. This reauthoring of her life enabled her to accept only reasonable responsibilities and she was able to begin put herself 'a good second'. At our fifth session, she gave me a copy of a poem she wrote at the time of worst hurt to share with other women I see and a thank-you letter in which she spelled out her solutions and how she would take the 'next step'. She also informed me that she had moved out of her home and gone to stay temporarily with a nearby female cousin so that she could concentrate on exam revision and enjoy being pampered.

There exists, then, an identifiable womanly way of doing solution-focused work even though it has not been articulated within an explicitly feminist framework. As it seems that women do *do* it differently, questions remain about the extent to which both de Shazer's dismissal of power as a *metanarrative* and White's poststructural underpinnings can be assumed to include women's issues. On one level there is an obvious fit; feminist analyses have highlighted how dominant discourses, or practices, misshape women's identities and become 'truths' and postmodernism is known most of all for it's hostility to totalising discourses. If the most significant form of power held by the weak (largely women and children), is the refusal to accept the definitions of oneself that are put forward by the powerful, then the underpinning theory is sufficient; whether it be social constructionism, poststructuralism or postmodernism.

However, it is worrying that the male writers of the theories which have influenced the pioneers of solution-focused and narrative therapies have not bothered to mention women: 'mainstream postmodern theory (Derrida, Lyotard, Rorty, Foucault) has been remarkably blind and insensitive to questions of gender in their own purportedly politicized readings of history, politics and culture' (Di Stephano, 1990, p. 76); ignoring, for example, black concerns (hooks, 1990). Di Stephano raises the possibility that since men have had their Enlightenment, they can afford a humbleness regarding 'truth' but for women to take on such a position is to weaken what is not yet strong and, like Dermer *et al.* (1999), she sees a need for a strong feminist politics. There are problems in putting this into practice as it imposes a world view on women service users; particularly what sort of consciousness is desirable. Encouraging women to 'connect with each other' through feminist-informed group therapy assumes that they will naturally achieve some consensus. As Orme (1998) comments: 'To tell a woman user she is oppressed, is no more liberating than labelling her as depressed, unless there are ways of changing the situation' (p. 225).

I find women's preferred solutions complex. For example, Sally requested help in coming to terms with her father's sexual abuse of her as a young child. A story unfolded in which it was obvious that he had abused all his daughters in turn. When the sisters linked together and attempted to share experiences, they each expressed different solutions. These ranged from wanting their father to be prosecuted or, at least, the police informed so that other children were protected, to feeling sorry for him and hoping that he could be understood and treatment obtained for him. These competing senses of personal responsibility were intertwined with worries about the possibility of harm to his current and previous wives. Similarly, Cassie talked of a chance meeting with the members of a battered women's group: 'It's been four years since I went [to the group]. They're still the same old lot, talking about the same old things. I can't be arsed with it. I want to get on with my life.'

## Is a feminist politics necessary?

The difficulty lies between accommodating women's differences while still recognising their need to be repositioned more favourably through recognition of their shared oppressions (Dominelli & McLeod, 1989; Hanmer & Statham, 1998). For example, a university lecturer colleague was offered a sabbatical on the condition that *she* found someone to take on her administrative duties (duties which were unusual for someone of her grade), while her male colleague was offered a sabbatical unconditionally. This is clearly a gender inequality issue but was complicated by the fact that she found it difficult to give up her responsibilities because of her concern about her students with whom she had an excellent relationship and a reluctance to put her male colleague's sabbatical in jeopardy by querying the allocation process. He was free of any of these considerations.

However, several women writers warn against the pitfalls of developing an oppositional politics. Rowbotham, for example, says that feminist politics needs a proviso that it does not let 'the desire for self-preservation turn into the oppression of others' (Rowbotham, 1983, p. 143). Similarly, Chanter suggests that oppositional politics run the risk of not challenging the rules of engagement, merely applying the rules of the game more rigorously (Chanter, 1997, p. 90). Or, to put it more simply, most women service users would probably agree with Hudson (1996), who finds feminist politics problematic because she plans on continuing living with a man. As Rowbotham points out, this relationship 'is like no other relationship of oppressor to oppressed. It is far more delicate, far more complex' (1973, p. 34).

While solution-focused women writer-practitioners have hijacked the new approaches in an implicitly womanly way, narrative women writer-practitioners have addressed the possible problems of oppositional politics more explicitly; highlighting the complexities of women's relationships with men and children's relationships with their fathers. Stacey (1997) reflects on the protest metaphor in narrative work (in itself a 'masculine' notion), and suggests how the concept of resistance can be broadened. She comments that patriarchal versions of resistance typically take the form of large-scale, visible and verbal protests in which a 'cause' takes precedence over individuals and communities of concern. She recognises that women service users often conceptualise protest and resistance in more subtle ways and that the woman worker needs to recognise these; some of which include:

- refusing to submit to other's perjorative definitions of oneself
- subversion of the problem
- holding on to connections and relationships which the problem threatens
- enduring hardship while refusing to give up one's beliefs or life
- raising one's children to recognise both dominant and marginalised cultures
- supporting the dailiness of people's lives.

It is within these forms of resistance that Freer (1997) suggests that we can stand alongside service users rather than in opposition and create 'loud' spaces where women's voices can be heard. Elliot (1997) cautions against assuming that a woman worker's experience of being a woman is the same as the service user's and suggests that the worker create space for evaluation of the session; have people who are experienced in the problem available as consultants; and refer the service user back to others in her community for comments on the work. For example, Cassie was worried that her current, gentle partner did not love her as he did not want sexual intercourse every day as had her previous violent partners. We exchanged views on what constituted loving sex but it was a discussion of our talk with a friend, who also had experience of violent partners, that enabled her to make sense of her sex life: 'we think we've been being used all these years,' she commented.

As a woman reader, you can probably recall many and varied ways in which you have resisted oppression in your life. Even when oppression is experienced acutely, there is always some space in which to manoeuvre. For example, Gilbert and Gubar's analysis of nineteenth-century literature (1979) suggests that although 'the woman writer acknowledges pain, confusion and anger that what she sees in the mirror is usually a male construct' (p. 17), the fact that this construct places her in a mythological/domestic space in order to ensure the well-being of others means 'she *can* manipulate; she can scheme; she can plot – stories as well as strategies' (p. 26).

Broadening the concept of resistance reveals not only the ways in which women practise resistance but also how these resistances are processed. The key notion for me is subversion; probably because I like to laugh with women. And women laughing together about problems constitutes a counter-discourse which has a long history across cultural boundaries: gossip. Spacks (1986) suggests that 'serious gossip' frequently has a subversive effect because it does not conform to the official values of society: 'Gossip as a phenomenon raises questions about boundaries, authority, distance, the nature of knowledge; it demands answers quite at odds with what we assume as our culture's dominant values' (p. 12) and 'Gossip creates its own territory ... using materials from the world to create a new oral artifact. Its special value as a resource for the oppressed or dispossessed derives partly from this fact' (p. 15).

Because it belongs to the realm of the private (although it incorporates the possibility that people utterly lacking in public power may affect the views of people with power), it is the 'natural' discourse of women in which participants use talk about others to reflect about themselves, to examine certainties and uncertainties – and this talk travels. This 'natural' discourse will necessarily influence how women *do* social work. This discourse may be what poststructuralism and postmodernism have only just discovered; inspired not by the fact that men can afford complexity because they have had their Enlightenment, but because the complex nature of fratriarchal power structures has forced them into it. Perhaps the narrative approaches to social work theorised by early male writers are no more than men learning to talk like women? If White and Epston's narrative explanation helps male workers and their service users to learn how to talk like women, negotiate, value relationships and embrace complexity; and de Shazer's prescriptions keep the worker within women's discourses, then a combined solution-focused/narrative approach to social work has the capacity to be antioppressive – but not as gender neutral as de Shazer professes it to be in that its discourses actually reflect *women's* complex views of their worlds and their solutions. Perhaps this should be more clearly acknowledged?

## SUMMARY

- A womanly way of practising solution-focused and narrative approaches to social work is based on clarifying for a woman service user what levels of personal responsibility are reasonable and achievable. This involves consensus building, negotiation through give and take, conciliation rather than confrontation, paying attention to personal issues, and the use of tentative language.
- Maintaining personal relationships is important to women service users but not at the cost of personal safety. Paying attention to personal issues and helping women clarify what is, and what is not, within their control involves helping them reclaim their bodies, resist self-blame, and learn to value themselves by deconstructing dominant cultural stories about wives' and mother's responsibilities.
- Narrative approaches caution against assuming that women workers' experiences of being a woman are the same as service users and recommend evaluating each session, using women experienced in the problem as consultants, and referring the woman service user back to others in her community for comments on the work.
- Women's preferred solutions are often complex. An important way in which women can increase their resistance to oppression but remain in relationships with men is through subversion of the problem through the use of 'serious gossip'. Serious gossip is a natural discourse of women in which participants use talk to reflect about themselves, examine uncertainties, and provide a source of influence.
- Serious gossip raises questions about boundaries, authority and distance, having capacity to subvert dominant discourses, strengthen resistance and increase the range of possible solutions.

# 4

# Women talking with men: attending to masculinist discourses

If 'serious gossip' is a central feature of a combined approach to working with women, how does this transfer to women working with men? And, if 'serious gossip' raises questions about boundaries, authority, distance, and attempts to subvert dominant discourses, will men want to do this? Although men can be 'unmanned' at various points in their lives (Mckinnon, cited in Evans, 1995, p. 150), particularly when they are small boys, disabled, old or homosexual, their power means that 'there is more that joins men across class and disability, and even race and sexual orientation, than divides them' (Cordery & Whitehead, 1992, p. 29).

That some men engage in 'serious gossip' is evidenced by the emergence of men's studies but for it to mirror the 'serious gossip' of women it would need to subvert existing power relationships between men as well as between men and women. 'Serious gossip' is probably a more attractive means of resistance to women who are largely attempting to reposition themselves in their relationships with men. And it is possible that women social workers' facility in the 'double' languages of home and work means that their strategies accommodate and support traditional masculinities to a certain extent. This is particularly evident in the gendered social work context in which they operate, which emphasises differences between men and women. The majority of voluntary service users are women and children; the interpersonal problem presented most frequently concerns their relations with men; and their social workers are most likely to be women (see, for example, Hanmer & Statham, 1998). The majority of mandated service users are men; their interpersonal problems are mostly defined by others; and their social workers are most likely to be men (see, for example, Newburn & Mair, 1996). In both instances the most likely commonality is that the basic-grade social worker will be managed by men in a male dominated system (see, for example, Hudson, 1992; Hearn, 1999).

This segregation of men and women service users in welfare services is supported by dominant cultural discourses which emphasise the capacity of women as carers and guardians of the emotional tone of families (Rich, 1977); spotlighting women as the targets of social work interventions and enabling men to disappear from much of the dailiness of social work. Men further disappear through the recycling of stories to fit dominant cultural discourses: the principle of 'individualisation' which, like the criminal justice system, promotes the minimisation of the impact on women and children of men's interpersonal problems through stories of denial and mitigation, and expressions of remorse; and the knowledge base of social work (for an overview, see Milner, 1993a; 1993b; 1996). Additionally, concern with understanding 'victims' has meant that women and children have been much more extensively studied than men. Even where initial research attempts intended to explore men's experiences, men have resisted being studied; for example, Brown and Harris's (1978) study of the social origins of depression hoped to include men but found them unwilling to be interviewed (Harris, 1993). Despite a more recent focusing on men as offenders (see, for example, Morrison *et al.*, 1994) and as victims of their inarticulateness (see, for example, Smith, 1996; Digby, 1998), it has been difficult for social workers to incorporate a nuanced view of masculinity which appreciates their ability to be both threatened and threatening. Not only are women and children no safer in their relationships with men but the differentiated postmodern man remains ever elusive in the social work task.

These processes influence how social work systems categorise, analyse and decide who becomes what sort of service user and what sorts of services are provided. While this has the effect of reducing the numbers of men defined as deficient in their interpersonal relationships with women, it also casts them as not needy in the same way as women. The result is that services have been devised which men perceive as irrelevant to their needs (Marsh, 1991). The main growth in social work interventions for men has been in the area of confrontational work, based on lessons learned from feminist research about the troublesome effects of masculinity for women and children. Despite most women service users being concerned about their relations with men, this sort of work is applied to only a small number of men who are unable to resist being entered into this story. Dobash *et al.* (1996) found that programmes for violent men were only really effective when the men were mandated to attend yet voluntary programmes proliferate, with male social workers recognising the power of feminist analyses to explain their service users' behaviour but not integrating this into their own lives so that it becomes a way of men oppressing men in the name of protecting women. For example, a probation officer resists what he perceives as an attempt to retreat from the tenets of radical feminism on the grounds that it is 'necessary to challenge early on the first avoidance tactic of denying ... remaining silent and allowing him to continue could be seen as collusive in allowing him to control the discussion agenda as he controls his partner' (Teft, 1999) but he fails to see that this is a means of *him* controlling the agenda.

Men social workers undertaking confrontational work with men then become the legitimate controllers of those men deemed to be overcontrolling; even though the overt aim is to help men develop the performance of masculinities less related to violence and control by assisting them 'to locate those different forms of masculinity in themselves and then extending their performance of them. For I am suggesting that we men all perform numerous masculinities at different times in each day' (Pringle, 1995, p. 142). What these 'numerous masculinities' are is not spelled out and Pringle is equally unsure about who is best placed to provide these challenges and in what contexts. For example, he recommends engaging men by using venues, settings and techniques that are 'regarded as more typically masculine' (Pringle, 1995, p. 153) but does not say what these might be. He also has doubts about men's abilities to work with men on the grounds that they may collude with each other; doubts about women working with men because it is potentially dangerous for women; and doubts about men and women co-working with men because the man worker may devalue the woman worker's authority! As Dominelli (1991) pointed out, confrontational work encourages male stereotyping of women needing men to protect them, men's contempt for women, the rights of stronger men to dominate weaker men; and maintains the status quo.

Jenkins (1996) considers that the sort of social work intervention which wants to break down a man's denial – 'to knock some sense into him' – constitutes a therapeutic tyranny. He suggests that the professional detachment of a male social worker also involves processes of minimisation and denial, with an inner tyrant operating from a sense of self-righteous superiority; giving a sense of entitlement, blame and vengeance. This 'management' of a subordinated masculinity (Harding, 1998, p. 190) creates particular problems for women working with men, as the following example illustrates.

Roy was a young black man who was referred by the probation officer responsible for preparing his social inquiry report (he was about to lose his licence, and probably his liberty, as a result of yet another drink-driving offence), for assistance in coming to terms with his early experiences of child abuse at the hands of his mother. His alcohol dependence was being dealt with at a specialist addiction unit. Had the referral form stated that Roy was black, he would automatically have been allocated a black worker but, in the absence of this information, he was allocated to me because of the nature of his 'problem'. On arrival, he sank into a deep armchair, closed his eyes and launched into a lengthy description of his problems before I had even finished introductory explanations about the service offered. This description centred around him burying memories of his child-abuse experiences and his partners' complaints about him in drink. He continued:

*Roy*: I've lost my licence three times and now I'm going to lose it again. So I cried for help. I tried on my own but it didn't last long. These problems and arguments crop up again and again. I tell the women I'm living with but ... I wouldn't say they don't care but it don't seem a problem to them. Life goes on. I say I've had a bad day and they say 'What about my bad days you give me?' Same old problems. I do what I have to do in the day and then sit down in an evening and the thoughts come so I have a drink. Bury it in drink. [his eyes are open by this point but he is lost in thought and barely seems aware of my presence]
*Me*: It seems that the women in your life don't listen to you, so how do you feel about being seen by me? And I am white and older than you. Do you think I will be able to understand you? [short silence] Would you prefer to be seen by one of my younger, black, male colleagues?
*Roy*: Colour, it don't matter to me. And I prefers women. I get on better with them. There's nobody to talk to. I'm just on my own. I've got girlfriends but they give you what you've done to them. You tell them about a crap day and they say , 'what about me?' and you go to the shop and get two cans. Then it don't seem so ear-biting. Drink's got me disqualified three times and I'm going to court in three months to get disqualified again. [he looks round the room – which is not particularly masculine] I really like this room. I'm doing a bit of decorating on my house to get it like this, sort of comfortable like.

He then describes a life which is centred on being able to drive. He has an unusually large number of partners and children in different towns, whom he visits when in the district doing casual car and house maintenance jobs. He does not declare the income from these jobs as he also draws welfare benefits and is resentful that this allows his employers to exploit him. He dissuades his partners from reporting him to the Child Support Agency by offering them occasional small sums of money on top of their welfare benefits. On a scaled question he rates himself as an 'OK, happy person' who has got to breaking point because of the threat of losing his licence; if he gets his licence back, all will be well. This story awakens my feminist inner tyrant, which is appalled at the way he regards the women in his life and the view he seems to have of me as a woman who will bail him out of his current difficulties.

Roy expresses satisfaction at the end of the session in being listened to but I have serious doubts about how I have handled my part of the session and consult with two younger male colleagues, in line with the accountability ideas behind 'just therapy' (Tamasese & Waldegrave, 1996). I explain that I would have liked to initiate a dialogue about Roy's perceptions of reasonable responsibility taking but was inhibited by my inner tyrant labelling him as sexist, and my fears of him perceiving any comments from me as racist criticism of his seemingly feckless fathering (Phoenix, 1991; Mirza, 1992).

My white male colleague was strongly in favour of direct challenging, while my black male colleague was of the opinion that the focus of the work should be limited to Roy's experiences of abuse at the hands of his mother. This colleague practised person-centred counselling and had a hypothesis that Roy had an underlying hostility to women. He also considered that the work would be better undertaken by himself on the grounds of his age, gender and ethnic compatibility. I was not happy with either proposal, especially as Roy was already being challenged to little effect by his probation officer and addiction counsellor, but acceded to my black colleague's view on the grounds that he was better placed than me to understand Roy's experiences and his very real inner pain.

The problem for me here was that Roy was, again, being entered into a story; one which did not acknowledge the complex construction of his masculinity. On one level, masculinity seems to women to be something fixed and inaccessible: 'masculinity is hardly ever defined as such – it simply exists and accretes around itself sets of behaviors and assumptions that are plugged right into the power grids of everyday life. This is the silent running of what I call *indefinite* masculinity' (Smith, 1996, p. 2). On another level, there is the difficulty for women in understanding the individual meanings of masculinity: 'Yet men suffer. Their suffering is most easily accounted for when they are furthest removed from the status and authority which "masculinity" presumptively confers' (Segal, 1997, p. xi). The individual meanings of masculinity for Roy were complicated by issues to do with race and class and I was in danger of entering him into a story which cast him as a passive victim of historical and cultural processes.

May (1998) suggests that one way forward is to learn from feminist standpoints and develop a progressive male standpoint as an egalitarian and practical position from which men can critically assess male experience and traditional male roles (p. 337); a viewpoint which is also suggested for women working with men: 'Feminist social work ... can only be achieved by critically engaging with men and developing a range of strategies which incorporate direct work with men' (Cavanagh & Cree, 1996). But what is this direct work to look like if it is to avoid the problems of either confrontational social work or women reconsigning themselves to the domestic sphere where they ensure the emotional well-being of men? In solution-focused terms, this should be possible through careful listening at the level of the word and identifying exceptions – the latter, particularly, has the potential to reveal those 'numerous masculinities' to which Pringle so vaguely alludes (Pringle, 1995, p. 142). However, this ignores the fact that the language of social work may well reproduce practices of domination (Stacey, 1997).

### Exception finding and 'masculinity'

Although experience of male violence is a common component of the task between women social workers and women service users, men do not usually present themselves voluntarily for change; avoiding this tier of social work until they become the mandated service users of (mostly male) social workers. Their sons do, however, have their violence defined as problematic by their women carers and are presented, in various degrees of willingness, for change. The gender dynamics of these social work encounters are largely ignored in both the narrative and solution-focused literature with the effect that the 'numerous', or alternate, masculine behaviours are prevented from emerging because the exceptions, like the problems, are described in traditionally masculine terms:

> Narrative therapy is, like language generally, filled with warring metaphors. For example, take phrases such as: "taking a stand against", "standing up to", "conquering", "battling with". Although we reason that we are turning the language of oppression around to work against the problem, we still perpetuate a patriarchal language of domination. (Elliott, 1997, p. 66)

Fourteen-year-old Barry, for example, was referred by his single-parent mother and female social worker for 'anger management' to reduce his aggression in the home. When I asked him what he thought the session was for, he replied that he 'loses it sometimes'. This was a huge minimisation of a loss of temper during which he would kick doors in at home, throw furniture around, and physically assault his mother and younger sister. This must have been extremely frightening for them as he was large and well built for his age, while they were both small and slender, but his mother accepted his story which minimised the violence and maximised his emotional pain. As he was only ever violent in the home, he obviously had a high degree of control over his temper but preferred to talk about his personal pain which triggered each episode.

He described these episodes as 'raging confusion'. 'Rage' is a term I find used mostly by males (women more commonly describe temper as 'upset'), and one which is not helpful to work outwards from to identify alternate masculine behaviours. In Barry's case, his proffered solutions were all embedded in a fighting discourse: he was the general in his battle to destroy 'raging confusion'; his mother was the infantry; and his weapon was a bazooka. My attempt to introduce other metaphors led only to a 'boxing' story in which his mother and I were recast as his personal trainers. Barry was able to reduce the frequency and severity of his violent behaviour but only by remaining firmly in control of the situation. Discussing the consequences of his continued violence – calling the police – only heightened the powerlessness of his mother in the situation. And the consequences of police action are not dire; the conviction rate and penalties handed out are kept low by the minimisation processes of the legal system.

Superficially, the situation with Jarvis looked more promising. He, too, was unusually large for his fourteen years which made his unpredictable rages, in which he broke up the children's home where he was living and terrorised both staff and residents, more frightening. The rest of the time, he was a helpful and polite young man who was eager to please. He was anxious to develop this side of his personality, being particularly keen to cease his violence towards a much younger and troublesome resident. Jarvis complained that staff 'used' him to control this resident. I was confident that he could develop an alternate future through exception finding and invitations to take personal responsibility for his behaviour.

Jarvis's initial progress was encouraging: he successfully resisted the younger resident's attempts to wind him up by walking away or ignoring him and he identified football and music as activities through which he could develop powerful but calm strategies. Over a four-week period he remained violence-free, learnt how to dance, and began voluntary work. The latter two activities did not last long as Jarvis's ideas about being a responsible male were grounded in his aspiration to become a policeman. There was no realistic hope of this as he already had a substantial criminal record but he had been told so often that this career was logical in view of his height that he saw himself as uniformed and attempted to take control of every activity in which he became involved. He had no idea at all of how to join a group as a junior member.

Although the number of violent episodes reduced dramatically for both Barry and Jarvis, they both became increasingly unhappy. Their exceptions to violence were framed in the same masculine discourses of male superiority and control so when they yielded this, they were no longer 'somebody'. As McLean says:

> Once men become aware of the realities of male violence, abuse and oppression, it is often difficult to know where to move next. If my sense of identity is deeply tied up with being a man, and men are oppressors, where does that leave me? In seeking change, am I in effect wishing myself out of existence? (McLean, 1996a, p. 15)

### Being a man, being 'somebody'

Listening at the level of the word in seeking exceptions is, therefore, only to track men along the well-worn lines of a dominant masculine discourse in which 'the need to be "somebody" is exaggerated and extreme. Competition and the struggle for power are central' (McLean, 1996b, p. 76) and where the metaphors of masculinity are about individual control – men 'standing alone'. Denborough (1996) argues that the central importance of dominating and controlling others underpins a theme of masculinity which makes it harder to develop an alternate way of 'being a man'. This theme includes the justification to use coercion; abdication of responsibility for the use of coercion; and rejecting and denigrating the feminine (and homosexual expression). 'Being a man' is thus supported by insult vocabularies which are influenced by sexism, racism and heterosexual dominance and these insult vocabularies limit the usefulness of exception finding through listening at the level of the word. Twelve-year-old Andrew, for example, was referred for help with his attitude towards women, undesirable behaviour in the home – setting fire to doors, taking money, drinking, fighting and arguments with his stepfather; all of which were ascribed by his mother to Andrew's previous experiences of domestic violence when she was living with his natural father. After considerable success in finding exceptions to his behaviour which Andrew could build upon (he couldn't resist a challenge), he arrived at the third session with his mother looking tired and stressed. She complained that he had insulted women in the bus station on the way to the appointment:

*Mum*: It were right embarrassing. He's got a bad attitude to women.
*Andrew*: It were the bus driver's fault. He were late.

*Me*: What were you saying that makes your mum say you have a bad attitude to women?

*Andrew*: It's me Dad [stepfather] who got me into it. He says "there's a woman in a right nice bikini". [his mum challenges this and they bicker about where the blame lies]

*Me*: What sort of names do you shout at women?

*Andrew*: Bird … chick … when we watch *Baywatch*, I say, "have you seen those big ones?"

*Mum*: When we're out in the car, he points and shouts "big bazookas".

*Andrew*: And I call you fatty … and me nanna butter buttocks, lard arse. But me mum and dad does it an' all. [Mum explains shamefacedly that it is a family joke]

*Me*: Do you know there's a word for what you are doing?

*Andrew*: Yes. Sexism.

*Me*: What can you do about it?

*Andrew*: Just don't do it.

*Me*: Is that hard or easy?

*Andrew*: Easy. Do you want to bet on it? [back to competition, being tough, being a man!]

Andrew was cheerful and buoyant throughout this particular exchange but he was also deeply unhappy about his conflictual family relationships. He wished to change his behaviour and displayed a concentration and willingness to work hard in the sessions which contradicted his poor school reports. The difficulty was that he was defiantly unhappy and found it impossible to stop 'being a man'. This was supported by his stepfather's behaviour – they argued constantly and childishly to achieve dominance over Andrew's mum – and Andrew has no idea how to be different from his stepfather. It was also supported by his mother's acceptance of being called 'fatty', even though she did not like this, and her collusion with the insult vocabulary which described Andrew's grandmother as 'lard arse'. Another way in which an insult vocabulary supported Andrew's masculinity was the denigration of girls by boys at school, where the vocabulary of the playground defines and controls girls through the use of such terms as 'slag', 'slapper' and 'lessie' (for a fuller discussion, see Lees, 1986). Andrew was popular with the girls at school where his macho behaviour appealed to them. Mac an Ghaill (1994) found that while girls do not value hypermasculinity in itself, they do perceive it as a legitimate defence against authoritarian male teachers.

Messerschmidt (2000) argues that boys construct masculinities in particular social settings and that different types of masculinity can exist simultaneously: 'differing types of violence by men and boys, depending upon the social setting, can be a form of social practice invoked for accomplishing masculinity under threatening social conditions' (p. 14). Thus Andrew could be said to be exhibiting hegemonic masculinity in his domination and control of women and girls at home and school, oppositional masculinity in his rebellion against his teachers and stepfather, and subordinated masculinity in his acceptance of a psychological story about his need for counselling.

Although Andrew's mother wanted him to become less violent, she also wanted him to fit into a family whose discourse was embedded in a traditional masculinity. Other than accept a demotion to being a junior male member, a subordinated masculine identity that Andrew did not want, having been the sole man in the house for several years prior to the arrival of his stepfather, there was no place for him to go; no place for him to be 'somebody'. The 'problem' for those for whom 'being someone' is based on dominance is that it is such a short, fragile career, with a long apprenticeship and one to which it is virtually impossible to aspire if the young man is positioned well down the socio-economic hierarchy. It is an identity which denies men emotional expression and keeps them in continuous, unsatisfactory struggle with other men. For example, although a hypermasculine workplace culture provides a precarious form of masculine unity, it is ultimately counterproductive as a form of resistance against men in management (for an overview, see Collinson & Collinson, 1989). It also has little potential for a life of hope and joy: 'it is men themselves, and their attachment to traditional ideas of manhood, which are very much part of the problem' (Segal, 1997, p. xix). As victims of their corporate identity, they can hardly be expected to identify alternate ways of being unless the internalised masculinity discourse, and its meanings for individual men and boys, is openly acknowledged. Whereas for women resistance can be located within their relationships with men and solidarity sought within women's friendships; for men supportive male friendships are more elusive because men position themselves vis-à-vis each other as much as they do against women. This makes the listening process for women working with men more complicated than when they are listening to women.

## Attending to internalised male discourses

The notion that solution-focused approaches are implicitly antioppressive simply because the service user's meaning system is elevated beyond that of the social worker's theoretical orientation and personal beliefs is at odds with its emphasis on the importance of language. Language may be culturally determined and infinitely fluid but it does have a constant theme in that it is basically man-made (Spender, 1985; Graddol & Swann, 1989). As O'Hanlon says: 'language and interaction are part and parcel of the therapy and problem, and problem definition, and also part of the solution, potentially' (Bertolino & O'Hanlon, 1998, p. 25). As can be seen from the case examples earlier, there is no 'potential' about it. Attending to, and tracking, male talk is to remain within a masculinist discourse which will dictate, and limit the scope of, the solution.

Although there has been some identification of the different nature of the therapeutic task with women in the solution-focused literature (see, for example, Berg & Reuss, 1998), there has been no attempt to identify how men might be different from women, how they may differ from each other, or how they may be with men and women social workers. In this sense the co-construction of solutions remains grounded in a masculinist discourse which renders men invisible by virtue of their position as the 'norm' (for a fuller discussion, see Brod, 1987). This limits the sorts of questions the worker is likely to ask and hinders the detailed listening process developed by women workers attempting to understand women service users' individual meaning-making. The 'gap' in attending to *beta-differences* became more apparent when I compared how I listen to young men and women talking about fighting. In the cases of Jarvis and Andrew, I asked no questions about their individual meanings of fighting as I *assumed* that these were grounded in traditional notions of competing to demonstrate 'being a man'. Where young women were involved in fighting in the company of young men, I made similar assumptions. For example, fourteen-year-old Charlene told me of her revenge on a young man who had stolen from her and other residents in a children's home:

We let him come with us [to a flat where the group regularly smoked heroin]. He had to sit in the corner and watch us smoke. We made him eat *all* the chocolate [the chocolate was only required for the silver paper wrapping]. Then we did him. We kicked his face in, in turns [she looks down at her heavy, stack-soled shoes with some satisfaction]. He were whimpering and there was blood everywhere but we still made him eat the chocolate. Served him right. He'll not nick from us again in a hurry. He looked a right mess.

I knew that the young man's injuries had required hospital treatment (he was insistent in ascribing them to a fall from some scaffolding when stoned) and that Charlene was usually even-tempered to the point of inertia but I showed no curiosity about the *meaning* of this episode to her. I was much more interested in her 'women's issues', particularly the risk of her being drawn into prostitution as a result of her heroin use. I assumed, probably erroneously, that she 'merely' followed suit as part of the pressure to conform to a violent and delinquent peer group. This view is bolstered by Segal's (1997) review of the research, which concludes that fighting girls had been encouraged to fight by their families and saw it as a good way of releasing anger, i.e. externally directed 'rage'.

However, when I was told stories of girls fighting girls, it seemed strange to me that the controls of traditional feminities had been breached to such an extent and I listened more carefully. The fighting they described was not only extreme – for example, sixteen-year-old Karen had been in intensive care for a week after one fight, a fate which she had delivered to another girl some weeks earlier – but the fighting was sec-ond-hand. Karen had beaten up her victim 'for a friend' and had been beaten up in turn by two 'hard cases' employed by her victim. Similarly, fifteen-year-old Samantha had received a police caution for fighting girls but she, too, lived in fear of retaliation by unknown, hired protagonists.

For both these young women the meanings they attributed to fight-ing were complex. They both enjoyed the reputation of being viewed as 'hard cases' yet constantly feared retaliation and were ashamed of police involvement – being a 'hard case' with peers was one thing; hav-ing a criminal record was not a desired identity as both had ambitions for careers which needed a clean record. Interestingly neither young woman sought a career which involved 'caring'. They were ambivalent about the shock their fighting had on other people, being very pleasant people outside the fighting. They were both concerned about the effect of their fighting on their ability to get, and keep, 'nice' boyfriends and they both said that the companions of fighting and temper were misery, despair and tears; although the actual fights were exciting. For exam-ple, Samantha said:

> I go for weak people 'cos I know it hurts them more ... like I was hurt ... it's a bit scary at the start. I get butterflies in my stomach and start shaking. Then I get this ... this sort of adrenalin rush. I like to see blood. When the blood runs, that's the best bit. I feel satisfied then.

This story is so similar to the stories of young women who cut them-selves; other than the fact that the blood is not Samantha's, that it became easy to locate her motivation for change in terms of learning to value herself as being worthy of having sustained relationships with both young men and women and how to become a 'tough softie'. Why did I not also attend to the relationship needs of men and the potential damage to their interpersonal relationships through fighting? Gardiner (1998) suggests that even where men are attached, they 'retain many features of traditional masculinity ... inexpressivity to adults and an unwillingness to seek help or admit weakness or failure' (p. 269) but could that inexpressivity be an unwillingness on our part to ask them questions about the effects dominant discourses have on their relationships or listen carefully to their stories about how they have adopted dominant disourses into their philosphies of living? Are we, as social workers, as trapped by notions around traditional masculinities as male service users?

## Externalising the internalised discourse

Jack had a temper problem of even greater magnitude than Barry and Jarvis but both he and his mother explained this as him being 'volatile' as a result of unresolved feelings about his violent father, resulting in him having difficulties in maintaining relationships with girlfriends. Externalising his 'volatility' revealed a long-standing anger which sometimes rumbled and simmered in a grumpy way for an hour or two but, at other times, erupted in a volcano, leaving him thinking, 'what have I done?' Jack found these violent episodes short but scary and they left him feeling restless for a long time afterwards. Talking about the effects of these episodes and exploring his internalised masculinity discourse showed how Jack was struggling with 'being a man' in many social settings. His anger rumbled at work, where he saw himself as subordinated, and erupted in his social life which focused around a group of hard-drinking mates. He knew clearly how 'being himself' would differ from 'being a man', identifying his well-developed sense of responsibility and his pleasure and pride in himself when he was involved in non-drinking leisure events, choosing to develop this side of himself. He took time to study the effects of his anger and made more space for himself by self-talking. For example, when the 'rumbles' began, he asked himself if he was interested in taking his anger further and found that it did not fit with who he wanted to be. He reported that he felt he was completely in control of his anger when asked by a slight acquaintance if he 'knew that dozy twat who beat up Michelle's new fella after she dumped him' and was able to reply, with wry amusement, 'Yes. I am that dozy twat.' When I asked him how he did it, he replied that he hadn't got rid of his temper; he had decided to keep it in case he needed it but it was no longer using him. He was confident that knowing it was 'there' would mean that he wouldn't need to use it and his confidence was obvious by his relaxed, carefree manner. There was no sense of the sullen, emotionally charged, young man of the first session.

Listening to men in an effort to identify their inner pain is simpler when they appear more threatened than threatening. For example, physically, Douglas was a large man employed in a traditional man's job but he began his story as a very young and vulnerable boy in care:

> I was one of the younger boys in the home. I remember the first time it happened, I remember crying. I was six at the time. I couldn't believe it. You sort of get used to it. The crying outside stops, you cry inside, sort of numbing it.... It happened, not isolated incidents. It was his specialty. I saw it happen with one lad. He could pick someone up by the ears. He did that to me. And threw you. And smack round the head, the face, the ears, the stomach ... just the way he was. He'd go red in the face when he got mad ... mental side of it was worst. I remember one incident when I did something wrong. I got a beating and had to stand in a corner, one to two hours, staring at a wall. I remember the plan of the house [he describes it in great detail], this cupboard by the locker room, full of cleaning stuff. I got thrown in there and locked in. At times I felt safe in there. I remember curling up, felt safe. Sometimes it would be an hour, come out, have my tea, sent to bed, didn't mind this at all. It carried on from me being six up to about I was fifteen. I left school at sixteen, came home from me first job, came home. He tried it on then and I retaliated.

This part of Douglas's story ends with him 'being a man' but the way he has told it prevents my inner tyrant from telling me that I need to confront his current worries about being aggressive towards his daughter when she becomes six. We are able to talk about how his experiences have affected his masculinity – he has problems with flashbacks at night, which make him feel small compared with his partner, and he is not coping with the male banter at work, particularly when he has to sit at a crowded table. He is also able to tell me how he resisted the early influences and give examples of when he is tender with his daughter. His solutions include taking her with him to view the children's home so that she will be with him as he lays the ghosts of his past; and he asks his employers to put on a stress-management course for manual workers as well as senior staff. This is his way of recognising that not only are his ideas about 'being a man' preventing him from getting the help and support he needs but also an understanding that other men may be like this too. Had Douglas been referred for inappropriate fathering rather than as a man with an abusive history, there would have been the possible consequence of me siding with the problem against the person, thus making it much more difficult to listen to him in a way that enabled us both to talk about what 'being a man' meant to him.

The context and meaning of traditional masculinity was similarly important in Alan's successful recovery from heroin addiction; a process made hazardous by members of his previous drug gang's continuing violence towards him. Some of his talk was located in white, male metaphors of competition and struggle but, as he was more threatened than threatening, I was able to talk with him about the internalised discourse – although as can be seen from the following extract, respectfulness verges on collusion with a masculinist discourse at one point when I offered to change the subject:

*Alan*: I'm still here. I'm going to be twice the person I used to be ... I'm building myself up. I'm doing it for me. I prefer to diffuse a situation rather than use my fists ... lots of people I used to know go there [the pub]. People are still saying, 'you look better. Where have you been?' I'm handling that. That part's getting easier. [long pause] I went shopping with my Mum and sister. There were gangs of Asian lads. I tried to avoid them. I don't know if its racist but I have a serious distrust of them. [we talk about what is and what is not racist and I share my experiences of fearfulness of any gang of youths] It made me feel helpless being with my mum and sister. They were all right about it but I felt I wouldn't have been able to protect them.

*Me*: So there's a masculine thing in it?

*Alan*: Yes. It makes me feel less of a man. I feel I couldn't protect my girlfriend if anything happens on a Saturday night. My main problem is Asian taxi drivers. They comment on drunk white trash. I don't want to start a race war. I know a lot of Asians. Can't tar everyone with the same brush. Its specifically Asian taxi drivers ... people involved in drugs. I feel I would want to run and she couldn't keep up.

*Me*: It's hard. But think, even Clint Eastwood's got so old that his girlfriends have had to get younger. And Arnie Schwarzenegger got beaten up. Masculine confidence can be a short-lived thing, and maybe most men have these fears? [he looks very embarrassed] I'm sorry, I'm embarrassing you. Remember, all you need to say is 'pass' and I will stop the questions. [a convention agreed at the first session]

*Alan*: No. It's important. Carry on. [We did, but I stopped taking notes so that I could be more conscious of when he had had enough. He used this conversation to develop a safety strategy for getting home on Saturday nights which was not dissimilar to those commonly devised by women service users.]

Although I also stop taking notes when women are telling me horrific details of sexual abuse this is largely so that I do not appear to be repeating their experiences of making formal statements. Alan's case was rather different; I was providing him with the opportunity to avoid masculinity issues and risked denying the importance to him of developing a satisfactory alternate male identity.


**Developing alternate male identities**

There is another danger for the woman social worker here; is she helping a man to work out what his preferred way of being will be like or is she treating him as an object to be brainwashed to her way of thinking? Jenkins (1996) asks: 'could therapy be a skilful con-job designed to trick the client into thinking that he has orchestrated and enacted his own ideas in changing his behaviour?' (p. 129). And is this any more satisfactory than previous practice which held victims responsible for their abuse?

Denborough's (1996) group work with schoolboys is useful here. These boys identified 'being yourself' as a preferred alternate way of being and were able to enlarge on what this meant to them when they were invited to consider when they felt compassion, consideration and caring for others; i.e. talking with them as we do with girls. This is work undertaken by men with young males but Elliott (1997) offers advice to women working with men. For example, she criticises focusing on developing talking skills for women service users on the grounds that this merely confirms a male way of being in the world; suggesting that it is more fruitful to *increase* men's listening skills. Additionally, she points out that men should be asked to take responsibility for their own behaviour; not depend on women to police their behaviour, and raises the issue of gender as a possible context for behaviour by asking such questions as, 'how as a father, a man, do you handle these issues?'

This can be a slow process, as I discovered when I attempted to find out what 'being yourself' would be like for Ricky, who was referred for an opportunity to explore his emotional problems, an area of work his social worker felt had been neglected due to his numerous moves within the care system. The 'complained about' behaviour which led to these many moves included: alleged buggery of a younger child, offending and threatening behaviour, drug use, and involvement in prostitution.

I asked Ricky a series of scaled questions and found out that his 'threatening behaviour' consisted of threats to kill care staff; actual assaults on them, teachers and peers; and verbal abuse, mainly swearing. His 'offending behaviour' included: stealing cars; smoking cannabis; 'accepting' money from a female resident involved in prostitution; frequent absconding; and 'pass' on sexual offending. It was relatively simple to discover exceptions to these behaviours: he did not steal cars with baby seats in them; frequently returned stolen cars undamaged; and did not abscond when he was involved in cooking or attending a boxing gym, so we were able to talk early on about responsibility taking. Unfortunately, although only twelve and small for his age, Ricky saw himself as a really hard man and demonstrated this throughout our sessions by challenging me to a series of bets (how much would I give him if he stopped swearing at staff, for instance); boasted about his high tolerance of cannabis; showed off his physical fitness (balancing and catching coins on his upturned elbow); and demonstrated his toughness (he stapled his finger while we talked). He hoped to 'turn his life around' but thought this would only happen after he had been to prison.

Ricky was so immersed in 'being a man' that he could only talk about responsible behaviour in the context of being a boxer; rather more masculine a topic than I would have liked. I asked him if he knew of a boxer who had 'turned his life around' and he chose Mike Tyson. Stifling a groan of despair, I used the opportunity to question whether a prison sentence for rape, subsequent assaults, and allegedly neglecting his ferrets, quite amounted to turning around a life. Ricky entered into a debate on this, but with a determination to 'win' the argument so I used written feedback to provide him with an opportunity to reflect on his life without him needing to compete at the same time; see the notes from the third session, which use his own words and expressions, below:

### *Problem*

1  Keeping out of Trouble – rather than not getting caught – so that Ricky can turn his life round.
2  Cutting down on spliffs and cigarettes so that Ricky can keep on with his boxing.
3  Finding something else to do that is more fun than Trouble.

### *Progress/exceptions*

1  Ricky has not done any swearing, fighting, or absconding this week. Pretty good, what?

2    He has been to school every day, apart from court days as he is not
     going to mess up his education. [The court appearance was for a
     previous assault on a female member of staff.]

### *Thoughts on solutions*

1    Ricky would advise other kids to handle Trouble like he does – by
     counting up to ten, saying 'yeah, yeah' when people try to wind him
     up, and going to his room. Stamping up stairs is not to be recom-
     mended as Ricky finds it makes things worse.
2    He can do responsibility taking even though he is not always quite
     sure how he does it.
3    Ricky cut down on spliffs and cigarettes one week so he can prob-
     ably do it again.
4    He can talk about the trouble that Trouble gets him into. This says
     a lot about Ricky as a person and his determination to turn his life
     around.
5    Ricky would prefer to go back to the past to change the time when
     Trouble first began making his life difficult. The past can't be
     changed but he has thought a lot about this and knows what his life
     will be like when it is turned round. He will be living in a flat with
     his girlfriend and keeping on with his education.

### *Homework*

1    More counting up to ten and going up to his room when people try
     to wind him up.
2    Judith and Ricky will do some hard thinking about what Ricky can
     do instead of letting Trouble run things. This could be quite hard as
     Trouble can be fun too.

### *Afterthoughts*

1    If Mike Tyson is a knobhead for hitting women, does this mean that
     Ricky used to be a knobhead when he hit [name of assaulted female
     care staff]? What does it say about him as a person now that he
     doesn't hit women any more?
2    People keep bringing up Ricky's past behaviour in [name of place
     where the alleged buggery took place]. This makes Ricky flip and
     gives Trouble the chance to get back into his life. Judith would be
     interested in how Ricky can handle this and what he can say to
     prove that there is no possibility of such allegations being made

again. Like how can he convince people that he is safe around young kids when he has turned his life around?

3   Has Trouble been sneaky and crept back into Ricky's life by telling him that it is all right to do Trouble as long as he doesn't get caught? Maybe Ricky needs a counter-punch for this?

Along with these notes, I included a paperback biography of Frank Bruno which detailed how he had gone from being a bully at school to a respectful boxer. At his next session six weeks later, Ricky reported that he had been to school every day, his behaviour in the home had improved radically (this was confirmed by staff), he had stolen his last car, smoked his last spliff, and was mixing with kids his own age. He had done this by comparing Frank Bruno's life with Mike Tyson's (the latter, fortu-itously, was in England for a fight and the subject of much debate in the national newspapers). Ricky worried that Mike Tyson would never turn his life around because of his alleged links with New York rappers. He had worked out that there was only one certain way out of a New York rapper 'project' – death – and that he did not want to get stuck in such a lifestyle, however 'cool' it had seemed to him earlier.

I asked him what he would like people to see if they were to meet him for the first time and not know anything about his past. He replied that he would like them to see a good boy who did not get into trouble. This was the first time Ricky had ever described himself as a boy and not a hard man. We spent some time working out how he would do 'being good' as this was new to him, although he was an expert in 'being bad'. This will take time as his social worker and staff at the children's home are still telling him not to be 'bad' (he did steal another car), and failing to notice his efforts at being good (stopping swearing at staff, going to school regularly) but at least he stands some chance of growing up and growing the problem down; and, hopefully, avoiding prison.

Developing alternate 'ways of being' is possible even when a man is in a violent environment such as a category B prison. The experience of spending long hours locked up in a cell with nothing to do lends itself to self-reflection and I have found that setting homework on mapping the effects of violence on men's lives is a fruitful way of encouraging change between sessions (see Appendix 2 for examples of worksheets).

Jenkins (1996) says that to allow an alternate way of 'being' to develop without coercion to change involves males in learning respect for others and self-respect – and the worker being respectful too. The research evidence shows that violence-reduction programmes are most effective when they run alongside women's and girls' programmes (Dobash *et al.*, 1996; Denborough, 1996), as this ensures that women's voices are heard. I am not at all sure how I feel about this. Yes, I do want men to listen to women but is it women's responsibility to help them do this? Can they really not think of this for themselves? And when will they start listening anyway? Although I enjoy working with men and boys, I do get exasperated at their, and male social workers', dependence on women to help them solve their problems.

### SUMMARY

- There are complex differences between working with men and working with women. The gendered context of social work which emphasises the capacity of women as carers and guardians of the emotional tone of family life means that services are not designed for men's needs and that women social workers are cast in traditional mothering roles.
- Some men service users minimise their abusive behaviour and are stuck in discourses of domination. While it is important that social workers avoid colluding with this, confrontational work holds the danger of encouraging male stereotyping of women needing men to protect them and the development of a therapeutic tyranny which can result in social workers operating from a position of self-righteous superiority.
- Exception finding and narrative metaphors are embedded in male language which describes solutions in masculine terms, such as 'taking a stand against' and 'battling with', perpetuating a patriarchal language of domination.
- The central themes of 'being a man' involve dominating and controlling others, which makes it difficult for male service users to develop alternate ways of being.
- Attending to the meanings of 'being a man' when talking with male service users enables social workers to understand how these service users can be simultaneously threatening and threatened. Externalising internalised masculinity discourses provides a useful way in which men can develop ways of 'being themselves'.
- Violence-reduction programmes are most effective when they run alongside women's programmes so that women's voices can be heard. If women are encouraged to limit their responsibility taking for the emotional tone of the family to what is reasonable and attainable, then both men social workers and service users will need to take more responsibility for their emotional needs and behaviour.

# 5

# Writing: developing the dialogue

The introduction of service user access to their case files reflects a growing awareness of their needs as well as their rights. Prince's study (1996), for example, found that service users expressed 'a sense of longing (almost hunger) to possess, know and get hold of the information and opinion which they felt the social worker committed to paper' (p. 88). Just how far access meets that need is questionable. Service users do not have unrestricted access to their files; often being requested to undergo counselling before they are permitted a single viewing of an edited edition of which they may, or may not, be permitted to make copies. If this were done in the name of protecting the person from possible trauma then surely counselling should be made available before the subject of any unauthorised biography was permitted to read that account of their life? Like that reader, service users have no means of challenging the assumptions made about them. Indeed, 'open access' has probably made social workers more reluctant to record assumptions so service users have even less information on how decisions have been made about them.

'Open' or otherwise, the case record remains closed to its subject because it is in no way co-authored. It is a means of distancing the social worker from the service user in which the former becomes the expert author of the subject's life. White and Epston (1990) argue that such an author has 'a library of terms of description that have been invented by and considered the property of this particular domain of knowledge' (p. 188.) This 'expert' knowledge, combined with the invisibility of the author, creates the impression of the possession of an objective and detached view that does not actually exist. One that bolsters a view of the social worker as benevolent expert, with the moral assumptions implicit in their specialised discourse hidden by *their construction* of the subject.

Narrative approaches challenge this view of recording by providing service users with continuous written feedback. Epston (1998), for example, considers his principal role as a sort of 'scribe who faithfully notes down the proceedings for posterity and makes available a client's history, capturing on paper the particular thoughts and understandings with which they make sense of their lives' (p. 96). 'Capturing on paper' expands, and makes real, the conversations we have with service users; provides a check on the accuracy of one's perceptions; reduces the power imbalance between worker and service user; and encourages co-authorship. For example, James said about his notes: 'It helped 'cos I knew what I'd said and then I could think and it solved the problems. I just started doing them [the solutions].'

Epston writes long letters after each session which include the metaphors people use to tell their stories, any unique outcomes he has identified or moments when the problem is subverted, but there is no need to follow this approach slavishly. There are as many different ways of providing written feedback as there are styles of working and abilities of service users. With experience I have found that my written feedback turns out rather differently depending on the age, abilities and preferences of the service user. Initially I began making written records for service users from what I perceived as my existing area of competence: the provision of 'minutes' of meetings. This expertise had its roots in my earlier experiences of providing accurate feedback for social work students on their practice performance identified at three-way meetings between student, practice teacher and tutor and the care I took in the preparation of child-protection comprehensive assessments which I co-authored with all the family members. In both instances, accuracy was vital because of the implications of my ultimate 'judgement'.

The first 'case' in which I conscientiously applied a solution-focused approach consisted of two sisters and a cousin who had been sexually abused by a family friend. I took notes in each session and then edited these to provide each girl with 'minutes'. At this stage I was concerned primarily with providing them with an accurate summary of our conversations but rapidly realised that there were additional benefits to this practice. With the girls' permission, I took almost verbatim notes which meant that I was so busy writing that I talked much less than usual and listened more carefully. This slowed down the session and provided the girls with space to add to their first thoughts on my questions; what would have been a gap filled with another question now became an opportunity where the girls engaged in eye contact with each other instead of me and pondered out loud more. This had the effect of 'taking me out' of the conversation to a certain extent, foregrounding the girls and enriching the conversation. Going slowly actually speeded up solution finding.

It also provided a running accuracy check in that I would read parts of the record back to them, particularly when their talk overlapped, making my note taking difficult. I would say things like: 'Lindsey, you said that Susan can't influence her parents' decision to separate; its not her business but Susan, you said that you still worry about this. Is that right?' The note taking and summarising also enabled me to emphasise the discovery of strengths and expectations, which I listed in capital letters. Service users enjoy this emphasis and often make statements such as, 'did you get that, have you written that down?', then giving me time to do so. Sometimes they take my pen and add their own comments. Comprehensive note taking shows respect for what the service user is saying, signifying that this is important and establishing them as experts in their own lives as well as making the therapeutic process open to scrutiny.

The 'minutes' also had the effect of externalising the problem for other family members; freeing them up from their own feelings so that they could join forces against the 'problem' rather than persons. Susan's parents' relationship breakdown was accompanied by recriminations about which of them had been responsible for welcoming the abuser into their home. Susan was extremely distressed by this but could not tell them, indeed, she was taking on unreasonable responsibility for trying to keep their relationship intact. She opted to communicate this to her parents by showing them her copy of the 'minutes'. Her parents were then able to help her sort out what was *her* worry and what was *their* worry and became much more supportive of her. From this point, her recovery was rapid. From this small beginning, my written feedback to service users has developed considerably and I find that even the briefest feedback speeds up the therapeutic process. White and Epston (1990) researched the effects of their letters; the recipients reporting that they valued them as equivalent to 4.5 sessions of talk. Some of the different ways in which written feedback can be delivered are detailed below.

**Verbatim copies of notes**

When asking permission to take notes, I also explain what will happen to them; not only the 'official' version on file, to which they have access as well as their own copies, but also the typed-up version I prepare for my supervisor, and our promise to destroy the latter after sessions are concluded. No one has, as yet, asked me to destroy their notes but some have shown great curiosity about the supervision process.

They are particularly curious about how their story is received by a third person. In these instances, I offer them a copy of these notes too; complete with my thoughts, doubts, questions for supervision, and afterthoughts. At no extra work for me other than running off another copy, this practice expands the conversation in that it allows the recipient to reflect on their story at one stage removed from the emotional content of the actual session. This enables the person to do their own editing and focus in the subsequent session on the elements which are most pertinent to them. It also makes the supervision process more transparent, adding to accountability. That there is also an additional therapeutic advantage became clear by happy chance. Shannon started one session by reporting that she had mislaid her copy so I gave her mine, which contained handwritten supervisory comments responding to my request for advice. Shannon was deeply appreciative of the time and effort that had gone into studying her story and wrote a thank-you letter to my supervisor in which she expressed a curiosity about what he looked like. He then sent her a small photograph of himself and a poem which he hoped might be comforting on 'dark days'. This added to Shannon's feelings of being valued and contributed markedly to her early recovery from feelings of worthlessness.

People tell me that they keep these notes for constant rereading; gaining strength from visible evidence of their progress. At the end of the work they have a complete record of their story of hope and resistance and I usually round this off by sending a thank-you letter such as the one quoted below.


Dear Sally

I sat down today to write up your notes and decided to write a letter of thanks instead. I saw my 'new' person today and it was so much easier knowing all the things which you found helpful. Most people I see add to my store of 'accumulated wisdom' to some extent but your contribution has been substantial. The 'new' person liked the idea of the letters and got straight into the 'future thing'. We made such progress, I could hardly believe it.

It sounds a cliché to say that it has been a privilege to know you but it is true all the same. Your courage in tackling a really difficult problem has been amazing and the poems were such a creative way of doing the letters. I feel sure that your 'thoughts' book will soon be complete and you will be able to put it safely away somewhere.

Thank you so much for helping me. All best wishes for a happy and successful future.

## Edited notes

Epston's long letters (1998) are more than simply a summary of what takes place in a session. He edits out his questions and the answers which did not produce any useful narrative line, 'always tuning in to what opens up new possibilities, any glimpse of an alternative to the client's problem-saturated story' (p. 98). This (mutually negotiated) editing is necessary for most written feedback, both for the recipient and the case file; few people on either side of the therapeutic encounter want to read through pages and pages of a verbatim transcript. The problem for social workers is that an Epston-type letter does not fit easily with the agency case-file requirements, particularly where there are specific demands such as the Looked After Children forms for children in residential care or set assessment formats for access to adult resources. Neither does the busy worker want to have the bother of completing two sets of records. After experimenting with several different forms of written feedback, the 'session notes' used with mandated alcohol abusers (Berg & Reuss, 1998, p. 167) seem to provide the most useful all-purpose format; an example of how this was adapted for James is given below.

### Session notes

**Name**: James

**Age**: 14 years          **Date of session**: 15th July

*Problem*

1  James's granddad got really ill with a heart condition after his grandma died. James is concerned about a combination of death and illness worries. He wishes his grandma was still alive and that his granddad was in better health. This happening would be James's miracle – it would make life better but it wouldn't solve anything between him and Daniel. James doesn't need a miracle for Daniel as he can handle this.

2  He would like to be able to go to school and just behave. A combination of Daniel and granddad's problems are stopping James doing school at the moment.

Stabbing himself with a compass is not much of a problem to James as he thinks it will stop when he is working at school. Also, his lack of eye contact is more of a problem for his teachers. As James says, it doesn't mean that he isn't listening.

## *Progress/exceptions*

1   James rates his control over his behaviour as about 75 per cent and he is pretty satisfied with this.
2   He rates himself even higher on the happiness scale – 80 – and is satisfied with this.
3   Coping with school rates 50 but James is satisfied with this under the circumstances. If he was at 70, he would be doing his lessons, being reasonably behaved, coming in full school uniform, treating the teachers with respect, concentrating more. He is already going to school in full uniform about one day in five – especially those days when his trainers are in the wash. Full uniform would be the easiest place for James to start on his school problems.

## *Thoughts on solutions*

1   James is intelligent (he is expected to get 8/9 GCSEs) which means that he brilliant at analysing problems. He is also 75 per cent in control of his behaviour and this means that his solutions are likely to work. As he says – 'I will wake up in the morning and think I might as well wear my school uniform and just put it on.' He is also independent for his age and doesn't think he will need any help with going to school in full uniform.
2   James has a pleasant personality and is easy to talk to. He has a good friend he can talk things over with – it might be useful to ask this friend for ideas on solutions.
3   Judith thinks that avoiding eye contact and walking near the corridor walls at school is probably a good way of keeping out of trouble – another of James's good solutions.
4   James copes with a difficult home situation very well in the circumstances.

## *Homework*

1   James will go to school in full uniform for the last three days of school. If he does this, Judith will pay a penalty to him of a big bag of prawn-flavoured crisps. If he doesn't, James will give Judith a small bag of plain crisps. The summer break will be a difficulty in James trying out his solutions. Judith will be interested to hear what ideas he has on how we should tackle this.
2   James will list his good qualities in time for the next session so that we can look at the strengths he has to use for solutions to his

problems. Judith expects this to be a long list as he impresses her as an interesting person, so maybe James will need to ask his grand-dad, mum and teachers to add to his list.

**Name of counsellor**: Judith Milner

**Date and time of next session**: James to ring for an appointment when he is ready.

**Session notes**

**Name**: James

**Date**: 17th August

---

### *Problem*

None. Next year, James is going to school all the time. His brother is going away for a bit and hopefully he will be better when he comes home. Granddad is better, Mum's coping. Life is satisfactory. He's happy with it.

### *Exceptions/progress*

James went to school in full uniform the last days of school – apart from the last day which is not usually a full uniform day. His friends were very pleased to see him. Mrs [name of referring teacher] noticed that he looked smart, was standing up straight, not hugging the walls. She was pleased too.

James has started to get over his grandma's death. He is also getting on better with his brother – keeps out of his way to avoid arguments. His mum has noticed this.

### *Thoughts on solutions*

James has many good qualities which he brings to solutions. His intelligence means that he can quickly work things out – he has solved his problems in record time, Judith is most impressed. Also he is popular and this means that he has friends he can rely on for support. He knows how to treat his friends right and can keep them as friends. Judging by Mrs [name of referring teacher]'s comments, he is obviously a well-liked pupil, too.

His solutions will be useful to Judith when she sees other lads with problems. James considers that school problems are helped by the encouragement of friends and teachers and not allowing himself to be put down. Home problems, he says, are best handled by talking.

### *Homework*

Do more of the same when school starts next term. James is confident he can do this – he rates his chances as 9 out of 10. He also knows he can come back to Northorpe Hall to talk about things should anything unexpected throw him off track.

Judith is confident that James will be in school, in uniform, doing well in his subjects next term and she expects that he will get his O levels. He is an exceptional person. Well done.

**Name of counsellor**: Judith Milner.

**Date and time of next appointment**: James will ring if he needs one.

### Letters

Narrative letters (see, particularly, White, 1995, Chapter 8; Epston, 1998, Chapter 9) are a more personal version of the edited notes described above:

> What distinguishes a narrative letter is that it is literary rather than diagnostic; it tells a story rather than being expository or explicatory. The letter engages the reader not so much by developing an argument to a logical conclusion as by inquiring what might happen next. Structured to tell the alternative story that is emerging along with the therapy, it documents history, current development, and future prospects. (Freeman *et al.*, 1997, p. 112)

I find such letters useful in the externalising of problems for young people and in identifying weird and special abilities. This latter comes from an idea developed by Epston (1998) after a ten-year-old girl told him that she had resisted a long-standing thumb-sucking habit by enlisting the assistance of an imaginary friend, available only to weirdly able kids. Weirdly able kids turned out to be those who see things in a different way from others who then tease or push them around. These ideas proved useful in the case of ten-year-old Christopher who arrived with a problem-saturated story. He was accompanied by his parents who pressed lengthy reports written by themselves and Christopher's teacher on me. The reports told of his depression, suicidal thoughts, sadness and weeping, body piercing, wetting and soiling, inability to cope with boys in the playground, concentrate on school work, or play out at home. He had been seeing psychiatrists and psychologists since he was four years old without any improvement.

Christopher whispered to me that he wanted to work on the 'toilet thing'. Mum interrupted to say that they were more worried about his suicide threats but Dad gave me permission to listen to Christopher. Slowly we externalised the 'toilet thing'. It had been making his life a misery since he was four years old. The most sneaky thing it did is when he went to the toilet – an extremely frequent occurrence in each day and always at mealtimes. Christopher sat for ages on the toilet and when he managed to pass a motion, he flushed it away but it was very sneaky and 'comes back up and goes up my bum again'. Christopher decided to call the problem WM (for wee machine) and PP (for poo pants). He had managed to outwit WM and PP on a few occasions; he thought they wouldn't like it when he wore his glow pyjamas. He also thought that they liked white toilet paper but might dislike green or peach-coloured paper. And a badge inside his T-shirt might help. Mum and Dad offered to help with the provision of materials for his solutions. Interspersed with all this discussion, he spent time drawing happy and sad faces of his family. I admired his drawing ability but did not comment on any possible meaning of his artwork. Using an Epston letter as a guide, I sent him the following letter;

27th November

Dear Christopher

Thank you for coming to see me this week; I always enjoy meeting young people with special abilities like you have. I was very impressed with how you were able to talk about the things bothering you – and do those super drawings to help me understand your difficulties. If everyone I saw was like you, my job would be a piece of cake! When I think how long WM and PP have been making your life miserable, I am amazed at how well you have stuck it all. What I would like to know, is how you managed to beat them on Mondays and Wednesdays? Perhaps, if it is not a secret, you might tell me next time we meet.

I think it is most unfair of WM and PP to sneak up on you when you are not looking. It is a rotten trick to make you look younger than you want to be. Still, you have some terrific ideas for getting your own back on them. I wonder which will work best – the green toilet paper or the peach-coloured paper? And I bet you have made a really good badge.

WM and PP are so sneaky that they will probably be thinking up new ways to trick you. I wonder if you will be able to spot them coming? Mum and Dad might be able to help if this happens; especially if you can tell them what sort of help will work best. I must say that I agree with all the things they say about you that makes them proud of you.

I can hardly wait to hear how you get on with the battle.

At the next session, Mum reported that there had been no wetting or soiling at all. Christopher said that the green paper worked. He had made a badge and was wearing it inside his T-shirt. He asked to begin work on his sadness and we used scaled questions. He talked and drew at the same time – mostly elaborate genograms. Again, I commented only on his drawing ability and did not make interpretations even though I was beginning to wonder if this was a habit he had picked up in his previous family therapy sessions. We began working on what he will be like at eleven: see the follow-up letter below:

11th December

Dear Christopher

As I promised when I saw you last week, I have been doing some hard thinking. You are such an interesting person that you certainly gave me plenty to think about! I was so impressed with the way you were successful with the green paper thing and the badge you made is brilliant. I expect that you have got WM and PP completely confused by now. I wouldn't be surprised if they have given up trying to make your life miserable and moved off to pester some other boy.

I know that much of what you have been doing to fight your problems is a secret – and secrets are so important – but I was very touched that you were able to share your secret with me about being sad inside and happy outside or sad outside and happy inside. This must be very useful at school with the bullies. They won't be able to suss you out at all. It is a terrific weapon. I wonder if they are a bit jealous of your popularity with the girls? You might be able to tell by their expressions on their faces at playtime. Perhaps you can tell me about this when we met next time?

And on top of this, you have a truly amazing ability to be 50–50 which is really well balanced. But you don't have to be 50–50 if you don't want to. Not many people know how to be sad and happy at the same time so they sometimes get too miserable or too silly. I wonder if anyone else in your family looks different on the outside from how they feel on the inside? You could ask them how they do it but, of course, you don't have to do it their way as you have such good ideas of your own. Like the trampolining idea and getting to be ten at school without anyone spotting how you did it. My idea is a bit ordinary in comparison. I thought you could go in for your Certificate of Achievement in Taking Eleven-year-old Responsibility. What do you think? You could start with the bronze certificate and work your way up, or go straight for gold. It all depends on how much responsibility you want to take on. Anyway, you can let me know next time. I expect you are pretty busy with Christmas at the moment.

Please give your family all my best wishes for a good Christmas. I really look forward to seeing you in the New Year.

At the third session, there was still no wetting or soiling, his teacher reported that he was coping well with school and Christopher asked to work on his relationship problems with his brother. By the fourth session, he was handling his brother's attempts to wind him up well. No sad thoughts. Most of the session was spent on deciding what sort of certificate he should aim for. Six weeks later, he returned for an awards ceremony for his silver certificate. Mum was awarded her trainer's certificate at the same time.

## Certificates

The silver certificate referred to above is a development of yet another idea from narrative work; what Freeman *et al.* (1997) refer to as 'growing up and growing the problem down' (p. 42). As they find many children are keenly interested in 'growing up', they ask about developmental shifts, growth and readiness for change, as well as abilities, interests and qualities. I devise a certificate to meet the needs of any particular situation; the categories of bronze, silver and gold have no particular significance other than they allow the young person to opt for what they think they can reasonably achieve. I tend to discourage 'going for gold' by insisting on one criterion of my own: advanced bedroom tidying, as I have found that a neater bedroom adds dramatically to a mother's good moods and capacity to be supportive to her child, and so many boys share a bedroom with an untidy brother. After the criteria for each award has been agreed between all interested parties (more 'slip-backs' are allowed for in the bronze category), no further sessions are held until the awards day, although any member of the team (the young person is assigned trainers as a means of enlisting everyone's help in solving the problem rather than criticising the child) is given permission to book an emergency appointment. There have been no emergency appointments to date. The awards ceremony is held in the hall of the building in full view of passersby who usually stop to ask what is happening – and then add praise. The certificate is handed over and photographs taken. While the photographs are being printed out on the computer, the young person gives everyone present a slice of chocolate cake – the cake is decorated quite simply with the words 'well done [name]' and I use this time to thicken the counterplot by asking the young person how they did it.

My early experiments with certificates tended to be of the temper-taming, good behaviour type but I now find that Taking [age appropriate] Responsibility is a more useful category; especially in some child protection situations (see Chapter 6 for a further discussion of certificates and safety training) but, below, I give the example of my letters to twelve-year-old Joshua. Joshua was referred in a last bid to avert his exclusion from school. After only three sessions (including the awards ceremony, at which he was the first person to achieve a gold certificate), Joshua was in complete control of his temper and doing well at school. The letters are included here as an example of how letters were used to influence the other people in Joshua's world to side with him against the problem instead of complaining about him. Raymond, the education social worker, and the teachers were enthusiastic about the certificate but tended to phrase the criteria in negative terms. The cigarette referred to in the first letter is an 'in-joke' from the initial session.

21st April

Dear Joshua

I had a cigarette break and read through my notes when I got home, so I thought I would write and let you know my second thoughts on your difficulties. First of all, I can't remember ever seeing a kid who is as well motivated as you are. I am really impressed by your determination to solve your problems. And you have lots of skills that you can use to come up with good solutions to the problem of the teachers picking on you for small things. Both your mum and Raymond had a lot of good things to say about you. In fact it's quite a long list: Raymond finds you polite, articulate, pleasant and witty. Mum says you are good at singing, acting (I'll say!), drawing, building, computers, reading, keeping your bedroom tidy, shopping, keeping clean. Also you are good-looking and popular with girls, and good with your brother. There must be something in all this we can use? Perhaps some of the girls might help? Or could you use your acting skills to pretend to be a model pupil for a while and fool all the teachers? I expect you will have lots of ideas of your own.

My only worry is that the teachers might not be ready for you going for gold. You will need lots of help and support from them – just like athletes in training need to have coaches urging them on. Perhaps you could ask Raymond to have a word with the teachers who are most critical of you and ask them to see if they can spot all the times you are helpful? Or is there anything else they could do to make sure you get your gold? I am very excited at the thought of you getting it as it will be a first for me and Molly (our cook) will have to make a big chocolate cake.

Whatever you decide, make sure that lots of people are helping. I look forward to hearing how you get on.

14th May

Dear Joshua

I have been reading through my notes and I just have to write to say how impressed I am with your successes. Three merits in one week! Pretty good going – although I expect you will have got a lot more by now. And all those positive comments in your planner. I have booked Molly for the chocolate cake already.

I saw a new lad this week and I passed on your solutions for handling the temper. He thinks he will try the counting thing and walking round the block to cool off. So thank you very much for the helpful advice.

Just one thing. Could you make sure that Raymond, or someone, lets me know what your teachers will count as polite behaviour. I can't put 'has stopped being rude' on your certificate. In the first place, it's a bit vague and, in the second, how can I work out if you get a distinction if I don't know exactly what they expect of you? After all, you might turn out to be super-polite.

I look forward to hearing how you are getting on. Please give my best wishes to your mum.

1st July

Dear Joshua

I was reading through my notes last night and I thought I would write down all the things you told me helped you get your gold certificate – just in case you ever decide to go in for training other lads with difficulties at school.

For coping with frustration, Joshua:

1    takes a walk round the block to cool off
2    asks his teacher for permission to leave the classroom

3   keeps his anger in until later and then lets it out safely – hitting the
    couch and things like that
4   counts to ten – in French!

To help him, Joshua enlisted the help of these people:

1   Judith (counsellor)
2   teachers (especially the ones who had been most difficult)
3   Raymond and Mum.

For coping with slip-backs, Joshua:

1   asks his mates to help him keep calm
2   makes any slip-backs up the next day.

As I said on Monday, this is such a brilliant plan that it will come in
useful when I meet other lads. I did worry when you opted to go
straight for gold that you had bitten off more than you could chew. It
looked like a tall order but how wrong I was! Well done, Joshua, and
thank you for being my first successful gold award holder.


**Women writing to themselves as well as me**

Writing has tremendous therapeutic potential; a written story can tell of
endurance and resistance against all odds; why else should Jane Eyre be
mentioned most regularly when I am suggesting a woman borrows from
a life she admires? A poem allows painful emotions to be expressed in
dramatic form. A diary allows crushing injustices to be protested. A
story not directly about oneself provides a distraction from other concerns; why else should I be writing this book? Most of all it is a means
by which women can reconstruct themselves: 'The woman writer ...
searches for a female model not because she wants dutifully to comply
with male definitions of "femininity" but because she must legitimize
her own rebellious endeavors' (Gilbert & Gubar, 1979, p. 50).
    Women writing to themselves, for themselves, to me, to their oppres-
sors is, therefore, a valuable part of their resistance to problems which
is well defined in women's solution-focused literature. For example,
Dolan (1998a) describes writing a letter from the future for discovering
hopes and dreams (p. 75); rewriting negative messages for flashbacks
(p. 141); letters to abusers for releasing internalised negative messages
(p. 146); and rainy-day letters for dark days (p. 167); none of which
are posted. I have found all of these ideas useful but prefer to link
them to a more flowing, written dialogue in which we continue our

conversations through a variety of written media. This is especially productive when both I and the service user are 'stuck'. This sometimes happens when the problems are so numerous and intertwined that goals cannot be easily formulated and I prefer it to the standard solution-focused task of requesting the service user to make a list of what they do not want to change. This latter has occasionally elicited the response, 'but I want to change everything'. Fifteen-year-old Chandra was a case in point.

Chandra was referred by her mum. From being a home-loving, affectionate and academically successful daughter, her behaviour had changed dramatically. Her schooling had gone downhill to the point where she was about to be permanently excluded; she had constant, violent rows with her mum and friends; and she had become involved in gang fights with girls from another school. Mum ascribed this change in behaviour to the breakdown of her marriage after a period of domestic violence. Discussing the referral details at the first session, Chandra told me that she was never happy before; her behaviour had changed but her thoughts had not. She felt that she was in conflict with everyone to an equal degree – her temper being a response to 'whoever happens to be there'. She identified 'upset' as her major problem, with 'sadness' being more prominent than 'anger', but could not work out what she felt sad about or identify a single exception.

I admitted to being completely baffled at the end of the first session but promised to think about it and write to her with any thoughts I might have. My thinking yielded no bright ideas so I wrote a narrative letter listing the ways in which 'upset' affected her and ended by asking Chandra to make a list of the 'sad' and 'less sad' things that happened in the coming week. This was the beginning of a written dialogue which soon clarified 'upset'. Chandra appeared at the second session with a short list of 'sad' and 'happy' events – progress! We discussed these and a story emerged of difficulty in maintaining peer friendships; she was never a 'home-loving child', but she stayed in because of her peer conflicts. These conflicts had exacerbated recently because of rivalries over a boy's affections. Chandra was deeply in love with Darryl who had rejected her in favour of a meddling friend. Chandra was suffering the pangs of unrequited love and these were added to by her friends 'not being there for me'; both through her mismanagement of relationships and losing acquaintances through her mother's house move and the death and illness of an unusual number of peers and relatives. She has no energy or ideas about a first, small step so I sent her the following letter expressing my puzzlement.

2nd July

Dear Chandra

I have been reading through my notes and doing some thinking about your problems. The notes you made on 'happy things' gave me an idea. You say that being far from everyone helps as well as Rebecca's support to watch your back – and the pair of you managed to have a laugh and forget your problems when you had a drink. And, of course, the chance that you might get things back together with Darryl brightens up your life. This made me think that you may be trying to create a space in which you can be happy. Could it be that there is lots of happiness hidden inside you that can't get out because of all the misery which is around you?

I wonder if 'upset' is not really inside you at all but presses on you because of all the upset which other people are landing on you? I am not sure what this is like exactly but I am getting a picture of you having to handle other people's misery as well as your own – your parents' separation, for example. And those deaths and suicide attempts around you can't be helping. Plus all the miserable students at school who don't feel good about themselves so they pick on you. Sometimes I find this happens a lot in schools. It is almost as though they see someone vulnerable and have a go because that person looks like an easy target. Even some of your teachers seem to be putting their unhappiness about their jobs on to you.

If this is the case, then it must be hard for you to make sense of *your* upset, which bits are due to your own feelings and which you have been landed with. The good thing is that even though 'upset' is trying very hard to ruin your life, you can still get the happiness to creep through in the little bits of space you make. Writing the 'upset' and 'happy' things on separate sides of the paper is a good idea as it helps to untangle things. Would it be an even better idea for us to spend more time working on what helps the happiness rather than concentrating on the upsets? I suspect you have more control over the happiness bits as these are more you – the upsets seem to belong to other people and we perhaps need to work out how you can shove them back where they belong. I don't see why you should have to take responsibility for misery which doesn't belong to you.

You probably know this already as you are protesting as best you can about the teachers making you feel like a shit for forgetting your folder. You know that you are not a shit and their comments are unfair; it doesn't help anyone to be only told negative things about themselves. I reckon it could help for you to remind yourself of all the good things about your happy self so I will make a start for you. From our two meetings, I see you as an intelligent, good-looking, sensitive, funny, kind and imaginative person (with a lovely smile). Plus, you have the capacity for really hard work – you are a great person to counsel as you concentrate well, don't duck any difficult issues, and come up with good solutions. Can you add to this list? And can your mum? I expect she knows more good points about you than you do – even if they do get a bit lost when you are having rows.

I may be completely wrong but would be interested to hear more about how we can get the happy person to show more. Anyway, you can let me know when we next meet.

Best wishes (and good luck with the teachers).

Chandra came early to our third session proudly bearing a huge folder which she invited me to read. It consisted of an elaborate life story book with photographs of friends and relatives at happy events. She had included comments about which people could still be counted friends and why. In the middle was a long story about her relationship break-up with Darryl, his insensitive response to an assault she experienced, her attempts to get him back, and her hopes that this would happen despite his firm rejection of her. We discussed what a really good friend did, how to maintain friendships (having 'a laugh' as well as 'being there' in times of trouble), and the sorts of expectations she could have of less supportive friends. She identified giving people 'evil eyes' as a precursor of rows. She had also found two imaginary friends under a bush to help her with this problem. There was no time for me to read the Darryl story carefully so she allowed me to take her life story book home.

18th July

Dear Chandra

Thank you for letting me read your story about Darryl. I must confess to having a bit of weep over it. It is bad enough to be assaulted as you were without then having absolutely no support for all you have gone through. I can understand that Darryl couldn't cope with the situation but to abuse you verbally and then hit you is completely unacceptable. No wonder you are confused about your feelings for him. Graham comes across in your story as a much nicer person but I expect nothing can measure up to that first kiss with Darryl! It is going to be hard to get him out of your head. Perhaps you could make a list of the good and bad bits for your Valentine box; a sort of 'the price of love' list?

I also counted up your friends. You have more good friends than most people: [listed]. Friends do move away and it is important to work out how to keep in touch. You are good at writing, you know, so maybe a letter or two would be a welcome change from the mobile? Even your unreliable friends aren't all that bad [listed]. And to think that you told me the first time we met that you weren't very good at keeping friends! There are only four 'fun' friends in your book [listed] but I am willing to put money on there being more.

I realised after you left last week that we had completely ignored [names of imaginary friends] on the sofa. What a lost opportunity! We could have asked them for their advice. It makes me smile to think of the effect of them on Mr [teacher] and Miss [teacher]. Have they gone to camp with you? I do hope you are having a good time and that there is a great-looking bloke to take your mind off Darryl.

Your life story book is brilliant. I appreciated you letting me borrow it for a little longer as it gave me time to enjoy all you had written. Would you mind if I used the basic idea with other people? I wouldn't use your name or give them any details. If the answer is 'yes', could you also give me some advice on how best to get them started on it?

I look forward to our next meeting.

At the fourth session, Chandra was much brighter – her clothes were colourful and cheerful and she was smiling. She was in less trouble at school (no 'evil eyes') and had had fewer rows with her peers. Mum also reported that she was a different person at home. There was much work still to do but it was made easier by our written, as well as spoken, dialogue.

## Essential components of narrative writings

If service users are to recognise their own stories in your letters and notes, then these need to use the same words that were used in the spoken conversation. You do not need to reauthor them in official jargon as this creates a distance between you that didn't exist when you were talking honestly. Equally it is vital to avoid interpreting events as this, too, is you authoring a subject. This doesn't mean that you can't ask further questions by way of clarification – as long as these are phrased tentatively and the recipient of your letter is given permission to disregard or dismiss your thoughts.

Dolan (1998b) suggests that 'instead' is probably the most important word used in solution-focused work, therefore you can ask people what they do 'instead' of misery, temper, confusion, etc. Where problems appear overwhelming, the externalising process can be assisted by changing nouns for emotional states to verbs; i.e. 'how do you do misery?' And to strengthen emerging resistances, you can use verbs ending in -ing as nouns, i.e. 'when you go to your bedroom, how do you do self-calming?' Also useful are phrases which open up possibilities; i.e. 'do you think you might be developing a knack for knowing when other kids are winding you up in class?'

Also, it is necessary to give some thought to the age and ability of the recipient of your writings. I find that I can be as discursive as I like with teenagers and upwards but young children prefer something simpler, such as cartooning. All of them appreciate the words *PRIVATE AND CONFIDENTIAL* on the envelope, especially young children. A card which depicts something talked about (often a pet figures in a child's happy memories), with a brief message, is usually welcomed; as are short, congratulatory letters. Young people frequently bring me stories, poems, and life stories but children are more likely to bring me pictures and models. As I enjoy stitching, I sometimes respond by making them a hand-stitched card which symbolises their hopes – a singer, a footballer, a dancer, etc. These very rarely have the same impact as jointly-authored writing (they are too much my authoring of their stories) but are appreciated for the effort put into them. It is worth remembering that most people in trouble receive either no letters at all or the 'brown envelope' variety, so even the shortest note from you will be valued. Jenny, mentioned earlier, got a short letter from me about 'broken hearts' and a Beanie Baby with a pink heart to 'put her on'. Eighty-six-year-old Mrs Brown, discussed later, received a short account of a day visit to a residential home to remind her where she had been.

## Ethics of written feedback

Not only is written feedback an effective way of speeding the therapeutic process, it is necessary in ethical terms: 'Records actually occupy a "hot seat" in the power relations between social workers, their managers and consultants, and functioned not only as an index of power but also as a bearer of meanings, codes, resources and emotions' (Prince, 1996, p. 180). Written feedback increases the worker's accountability, makes visible the evidence on which they base their decision making, and demonstrates the effectiveness, or otherwise, of the worker's ability to be helpful. As service users may hesitate to correct any inaccuracies in your written feedback, it is important to include a phrase to the effect of, 'as promised, here is copy of your notes. I hope I have got

/erything right but, if not, you can let me know next time we meet so 
⌐hat I can make any necessary alterations.'

Once something is written down, it gains authority and, if only one person holds the pen, then the service user is captured and fixed in the writing which is subject to distortions. These distortions include those arising from post hoc selection and analysis in editing (Kagle, 1991); inaccurate information and the 'shaping' of that information to fit the writer's theories (Sheldon, 1995); the racist nature of language itself (Denney, 1992); and the 'silences' about women's experiences (Maynard & Purvis, 1995). Where a report is written for a decision-making forum, these distortions are likely to increase as the 'evidence' is recycled in an attempt to make either a 'pitch' or a 'denunciation' (Dingwall *et al.*, 1983; Aronsson, 1991). This latter will be discussed further in Chapter 6, which addresses child protection issues but, mean-time, I invite you to begin a process of co-authoring records with your service users. It takes a little time to get used to but this is time well spent as it provides you with space to think about the service user's life; speeds up desired change; and makes recording less of a chore.

## SUMMARY

- Genuine partnership is more likely to be developed when the subject of a case file has contributed to what is written and their own words and definitions of the problem used.
- Narrative therapists use long letters containing the metaphors people use to tell their stories and any unique outcomes to help service users reflect on their competencies and resistances to the problem.
- Accurate feedback on the social work process can also be achieved by sending service users copies of verbatim notes taken in sessions or edited notes. Edited notes can be used for agency recording.
- Edited notes can be adapted for the development of certificates in age-appropriate responsibility-taking for young people.
- Shared recording not only provides service users with space for self-reflection, encouraging change between sessions, but also helps to reduce the power imbalance between social workers and service users.
- Further benefits of shared recording include accuracy, clarity, accountability, and respect for service users.

# 6

# Child protection: developing safe solutions for women and children

Many child protection social workers I meet seem to be perpetually angry and dissatisfied with the families they see, their managers, and the general public; all of whom expect them to intervene in only a selected few, 'high-risk' cases (never themselves), and 'get it right' on every single occasion. To meet these expectations, they would need unqualified public support for the endeavour, based on a body of knowledge about what constitutes parental competence and child well-being and a consensus about the skills required of social workers in a well-functioning child protection system. Unfortunately, as Turnell and Edwards (1999) point out, this is not the case.

The Children Act 1989 does not provide a clear framework for action, reflecting instead public and professional ambivalence about every aspect of child protection work. Although the Act established the welfare of the child as its primary principle, it neglected to say anything about what significant well-being would be like. The Act is clear enough on what constitutes significant harm (a risk focus), but the comparison with a 'similar child' has limited potential for a safety focus as well as encouraging class divisions about what is considered a 'good enough' environment for a child.

The Act further compromises notions about the best interests of the child by qualifying the context in which social workers may intervene. The maxim of minimum intervention in family life (the 'no order principle') and the emphasis on working in partnership with parents, but rarely consulting children (see for example, Mullender, 1999a) means that social workers cannot remove children from their families of origin as easily as public criticism suggests. Should they obtain care orders, they find that satisfactory substitute care is not freely available – it is one thing to close down children's homes on the grounds that they provide unsatisfactory alternatives for children but there hardly exists a large number of concerned adults willing to offer themselves as foster parents. And, should social workers attempt to work with families, community support is equally scarce; there being little public support for the resourcing of family centres and respite care similar to that available for families with disabled children.

For example, Stephanie, mentioned earlier, originally requested support for her efforts in caring for four young children, one of whom was sickly, at a time when she was working nights to support her family and attempting to separate from her unemployed, drug-dealing, and emotionally abusive partner. Social services could only offer a distant nursery placement and Stephanie found the task of delivering the two youngest children to this nursery and getting the other two to school a further pressure which resulted in her physical and mental health breaking down completely. As there were then no foster placements which could accommodate all four children, the two eldest were placed with her parents – with whom she was on poor terms and who had failed to support her earlier. On her complaining about this, these children were found a short-term placement seventy miles away.

On her discharge from hospital, the two eldest children were returned to Stephanie. Concerns about the neglected state of the two youngest when they arrived at their foster home (concerns which Stephanie had raised as the reason why she sought help in the first place) led the social worker to decide to leave the younger children in foster care while she undertook a risk assessment. Stephanie's parenting competence was assessed according to government guidelines (DHSS, 1988), which depend largely upon psychological theorising about the nature of a 'healthy' mother–child relationship; particularly the importance of secure attachments. This knowledge base is underpinned by psychodynamic thinking (see, for example, Fahlberg, 1988; 1991) which, in turn, dictates the skills base required for both assessment and intervention. Here importance is accorded to mothers' abilities to reflect critically on past traumatic experiences which may be hindering the expression of appropriately sensitive mothering behaviours.

This knowledge base may well accord with public beliefs about natural mother love and the sanctity of the mother–child relationship as the source of emotional growth but it is by no means uncontested. For example, Jack (1997) argues that the parenting concept is not especially helpful unless seen as a way of describing behaviour and competence within a broader ecology, which would include the influences of the extended family, friendship networks, and neighbours. These influences were significant in Stephanie's position as a young, unwell and unsupported mother but the assessment ignored these factors. Given the remit of a psychodynamic knowledge and skills base, it consisted of ten interviews at social services' offices, during which Stephanie's own past care experiences were rigorously analysed. Her (now homeless) ex-partner had offered to care for the younger two children if social services could find, and furnish, him with a home so he was included in later sessions. Not surprisingly, Stephanie protested vigorously at the process of the assessment – she particularly did not want to talk about her past experiences of sexual abuse in front of an ex-partner she had found emotionally abusive and who had previously beeen unaware of their existence. Her protests were viewed as resistance and denial resulting from a presumed lack of insight into her behaviour and a pathological need to control events. The decision was to recommend a Residence Order to her ex-partner in respect of the younger children and support him in the care of them; for Stephanie to continue to care for the two older children under a Supervision Order; and for both adults to have two days' contact with all four children. At no point was Stephanie observed caring for any of the children, nor were the children consulted about their wishes.

Berg (1991) argues that this form of child protection work is paternalistic and that taking the side of the child against the parent and telling the parent what to do naturally engenders an adversarial and hostile relationship. Faced with following a plan devised by professionals in a formal arena is also a process which parents find stressful and alienating (Mylam and Lethem, 1999). Building on the work of Thomas (1995), Turnell and Edwards view such stressed and alienated parents as at the bottom of a trench with academics on one side and professionals on the other. Certainly this is how Stephanie felt; not only did she disagree with the decision but she saw it as insulting to the older children that she was deemed 'good enough' to care for them but not the younger two. During the assessment phase, her protests were interpreted as resistance and manipulative attempts to control the 'expert' professionals. When she tried to vary the terms of the contact so that her ex-partner could attend football matches at weekends and she could take the younger children to nursery, this was recast as obstructing the 'agreed' plan – the senior social worker informing me that this was a further attempt on Stephanie's part to manipulate events. The 'experts' determined to stick rigidly to the original plan, confirming findings that once judgements have been made, little further information is collected or is processed in the light of that judgement (for a fuller discussion, see Milner & O'Byrne, 1998). Once parents have been identified as lacking competence, it is difficult for them to change this view (Turnell & Edwards, 1999).

However, it is not only service users such as Stephanie who are at the bottom of the trench. Social workers are there too; stuck in the same process of denial they ascribe to 'uncooperative' parents, making 'pitches' or 'denunciations' (Dingwall *et al.*, 1983), clinging to their initial judgements, holding unrealistic expectations, worn out with unsatisfactory, conflictual relationships, and lacking sufficient substitute or domiciliary care resources to offer useful choices. I realised how true this was for Stephanie's social worker the first time I saw them together. Four weeks into the plan, Stephanie told me that her ex-partner was using the contact arrangements to move back into her home and life. She admitted that she was blocking out the emotional distress his presence caused her by taking drugs. After answering a series of scaled safety questions, she acknowledged that her children were not safe and her preferred solution was to return the children to foster care if the same placement was available while she sorted out her relationship with her ex-partner and they obtained separate housing some distance apart. She thought it would be difficult to explain this to her social worker because of their poor relationship, saying:

> I have a problem with people who piss me off. It's my problem. But when I'm ... I can't explain ... makes me feel inferior. Makes me feel I'm doing something wrong ... then I get mad ... it's mad-embarrassed. It reminds me of when I was younger and I don't like it. With social workers ... then they ... they just throw me straight on the defensive. I don't know why ... not the others ... because it don't feel good. Me kids don't make me feel like that ... I'm getting paranoid ... they keep saying I'm manipulative.

We talked about how she could handle this and she set off to see her social worker; only to ring me shortly afterwards asking if I would help her explain things to the social worker. They arrived looking tense and miserable. Bristling with annoyance, the social worker informed me that she would take notes. I looked questioningly at Stephanie, who nodded her agreement. I began the explanation, checking with Stephanie for confirmation that I was telling it correctly. She soon took up the conversation, honestly detailing her difficulties. The social worker responded with a list of objections: the children must be consulted (we readily agreed this), the foster carers might not be available, it would disrupt the children's lives, she would never get another house, she was strong enough to tell her partner to leave, he was a very nice man anyway, she was putting her needs before those of the children. Stephanie said, 'you're not listening to me' and began to cry. The social worker's face became pinched in an effort not to burst into tears of anger herself; it was impossible to tell which of them was feeling the frustration and pain most deeply. I really should have 'taken a break'; instead I summarised what they were saying and they did begin to listen to each other. The social worker conceded that Stephanie's plan had some merit but came up with more objections: she would never get it past the 'challenge to care' panel, three men who never gave her any placements anyway, and she would have to talk it over with her senior.

The placements were arranged and I was hopeful that Stephanie and her social worker could make a fresh start. It was not to be; the senior social worker felt manipulated and decided to institute care proceedings in respect of all four children. Eighteen months on, Stephanie had been assessed by a bewildering array of 'experts': a Guardian ad Litem, two psychologists and two psychiatrists, as well as having her contact with the children supervised. During this process, she still managed to work successfully with me on her past experiences of sexual abuse and refrained from drug use. Her relationship with social services was such that she was at stage three of the local authority complaints' procedure and, as she said, it would have been cheaper and easier if they had given her the help she requested in the first place. None of us were any clearer about her mothering ability, as she had not been stress-free at any time during this process.

Stephanie was not the only victim of this process; the children had become increasingly disturbed and the social worker had a horrible time too. It would be easy to criticise her but I have no doubt that she was basically a caring and conscientious person who would have preferred a better solution and more effective child protection system. Inquiry report criticisms have not improved the process; their most common recommendations being more interagency meetings and further training. Both of these activities must seem more appealing to child protection social workers than continued conflictual direct contact with parents and the experience of children being harmed by the 'care' arrangements. Fortunately there has been a fundamental policy shift which will better support the system and a combined solution-focused/narrative approach to social work practice provides a skills base for interventions which have the potential to increase engagement and reduce hostilities.

**A way out of the trench**

The principles underpinning the revised government guidelines include:
- assessment should centre on the needs of the children, with direct work with children to ascertain their wishes and feelings;
- assessments should be rooted in a thorough understanding of child development and the significance of timing in a child's life;

- an ecological approach that takes into account poverty, unemployment, racism, poor housing, etc., needs to underpin assessments of parental capacity;
- the parents' capacity to meet those needs should be considered, *building on strengths* as well as identifying difficulties; and,
- professionals should work in partnership with families *and* children. (DoH, 1999, pp. 10–13, my emphasis. See also, DoH, 2000, p. 10)

While the key parenting tasks used in the recruitment and selection of foster and adoptive parents are to be applied more widely in work with children and families in the community (basic care, ensuring safety, emotional warmth, stimulation, guidance and boundaries, stability), there is an acknowledgement that this does not take place in a vacuum. People with cumulative risks can still show resilience if they have resources within themselves, their families and other social groups (Gilgun, 1999). The emphasis on the need to build up a strong, supportive community in which parents can develop competencies means that the social work task will both widen and contract. For example, should Stephanie have referred herself when the new guidelines are operating, her social worker would be expected to undertake a needs assessment which was carried out in parallel with other action and providing services (DoH, 2000, p. 10). There would have been less time spent exploring Stephanie's psyche because the assessment would be focussing on her parenting strengths as well as her weaknesses.

The key features of assessments equally signify a shift in focus from risk to safety needs; from deficits to strengths; from expert knowledge which categorises to individual assessment, including:

- clarity of purpose about questions asked;
- evidence, not opinion, of what is seen, heard, and read to be carefully collected and recorded;
- the meaning of the information to family, children and social worker to be distinguished;
- clarity about sources of knowledge which inform judgements;
- severity, immediacy and complexity of the child's situation will be important influences;
- assessments to be followed by clear decisions and coordinated planning and intervention; and,
- clarity about what needs to change, how it will be achieved and how it will be measured. (DoH, 1999, pp. 14–17)

Child protection social workers are likely to say that they 'do this already'; to which the reply is 'do more'. The evidence shows that case conferences are so preoccupied with risk that they only spend an average of nine minutes discussing the care plan (Farmer and Owen, 1995), and professional responses discourage interest on the part of natural network members who are left feeling irrelevant, marginalised and deskilled (Gilligan, 1997). In the absence of consensus over what constitutes child well-being, the knowledge base developed around resilience factors is also welcome; as is the evidence that small change often has a ripple effect (Berg, 1991; Katz, 1997; Turnell & Edwards, 1999; Gilgun, 1999; Gilligan, 2000).

Child protection social workers cannot be expected to embrace a broad ecological perspective without, first, management support and appropriate resource provision; and second, an effective skills base from which to engage with families. Pilot studies show that a great deal of preparatory work is required; for example, North Lincolnshire Social Services began a population needs analysis to predict the extent of need among children and families in the authority and this was followed by detailed planning of service requirements, dependent upon child and family need. Only when these fundamental building blocks were in place were staff provided with the opportunity to develop a skills base which utilised an 'exchange model' of interviewing (for a fuller discussion, see Milner & O'Byrne, 1998), within which service users were viewed as experts in their own lives; the social worker helping them to identify appropriate resources to reach their own goals. Professional concerns about the safety of children were managed by the adoption of the 'signs of safety' approach – a solution-focused approach to child protection initiated by Berg (1991) for work in a US family-based service, and further developed in the UK by Essex *et al.*, (1996) and Turnell and Edwards (1999) in Australia.

## The signs of safety approach

Turnell and Edwards argue that all families have signs of safety but that talking about the '5 per cent' of problematic behaviour which has brought the family to the attention of the child protection system ignores '95 per cent' of ordinary family competence. This reduces whole people into problems and undermines hope, respect and cooperation:

> there are many times when the family does provide a safe and 'good enough' environment for the child. To work effectively with a family, it is invaluable for workers to be able to elicit these aspects of family experience and functioning. These signs of safety provide a

balance to the problems and dangers and provide many clues for developing a cooperative relationship with the family and for the development of appropriate, case-specific plans and interventions. (Turnell & Edwards, 1999, p. 37)

They have developed six practice principles which promote engagement with families without collusion; are respectful of people; and promote change while still maintaining a focus on safety. Their work not only results in positive change in families but social workers rated themselves as significantly more skilled after using the approach. So, if you feel chronically dissatisfied with your child protection work, you might like to consider adopting these principles – doing something different.

### *Understanding the position of each family member*

Jenkins (1996) comments that we treat those who abuse with considerable disrespect at the same time as we expect them to learn to show respect to others. Therefore the first step to building a partnership approach is to quell one's 'inner tyrant' by treating alleged abusers as people worth doing business with; seeking to identify and understand the values, beliefs and meanings of family members. This does not involve colluding with the alleged abuse, say Turnell and Edwards, it is more about being open and honest about any disagreements. For example, Stephanie found the Guardian ad Litem and one of the psychologists helpful because they gave her specific details about aspects of her interpersonal behaviour they considered were contributing to her difficulties. Similarly, Tina found that the Guardian ad Litem's calm, supportive manner meant that she could accept her comments about her shortcomings as a mother whereas the psychologist's criticisms were experienced as destructive because they were delivered in an abrasive and confrontational manner: 'I felt totally destroyed. She made me feel like a criminal. And what she said about my relationship with my mother; she hadn't even met my mother. I was in floods of tears. She just sat there. Said, "it's no good crying. That won't get you anywhere." I hated that woman.'

Turnell and Edwards also recommend social workers accept that a focus on the alleged abuser's denial of responsibility is an unhelpful way of organising their work, as this leads to a sullen stand off between worker and parent: 'Acknowledgment [of responsibility for the abuse], while preferable, is neither a sufficient nor a necessary condition of safety' (1999, p. 140).

## Finding exceptions to the mistreatment of the children

Rather than analysing the '5 per cent' of parental behaviour that is considered risky, seek to identify exceptions to the problem; that is, times when the child could have been harmed but was not. This creates hope for parents and social workers and may indicate possible solutions. While it is useful to know when an abuser could have mistreated a child but didn't, it is even more useful to know when, where and how this happened, what was different about this, and how the abuser understands what they did on these occasions so that they can be encouraged to repeat this behaviour.

For example, Charlotte, who had been referred following a recurrence of flashbacks of earlier sexual, physical and emotional abuse as a result of appearing as a witness in court, told me that she had ground a facecloth into her daughter's face when the child whined about shampoo going into her eyes. Charlotte was very worried that she was becoming an abuser herself and it would have been easy to concentrate on her early experiences and a possible tendency for these to establish a cyclical pattern of abuse. However, careful questioning elicited the fact that this child was invariably difficult at hair-washing time and that Charlotte usually managed these occasions well. Her usual coping strategies when tired and stressed by the whining included calling her husband or eldest child to take over or, when they were not available, pulling the plug out of the bath before walking away to count to ten and then returning to the child when she had calmed down. All she needed to do was reinstitute her existing coping competencies which had been threatened by her recent experiences. Where no exceptions exist, the worker is alerted to a more serious problem.

## Discover family strengths and resources

It is a sad reality that the less supported a mother is, the more her mothering behaviour is scrutinised and criticised; as one single mother said to Lethem, 'You're the only person who's ever said anything good about me as a mother' (1994, p. 36). Such a focus overwhelms and discourages everyone involved and, as Turnell and Edwards say, it is extremely difficult to get a parent to *stop* doing something; and much more productive to help them *start* something. It doesn't minimise the abuse so much as reinforce the idea that the family's life and experience form a foundation on which change can be built. For example, Della had been referred for counselling by psychologists who were failing to effect any improvement in the extremely disturbed behaviour of her two sons. She was inconsistent in her handling of them, being unable to cuddle them but displaying obsessiveness about their safety. She was prickly and difficult about the advice offered to her on how to handle the children and was unable to take up the psychologists' suggestions that she stop letting her previous violent partners return to the house as and when it suited them. She had been sexually abused in childhood and identified an inability to accept praise as well as criticism, or like herself, as her main problems although these were things she wanted to be able to do. I asked her to listen for compliments, an idea she found intriguing. At the next session she reported receiving compliments about her looks and built on this by eating better, growing her nails and dressing more carefully. Over the next six weeks she began to praise herself, became more relaxed, got rid of her ex-partners and settled into a warmer relationship with her boys – whose behaviour improved.

### Focusing on goals

A family's goals to improve the safety of the child is the first thing to establish; using the family's ideas wherever possible. These will not necessarily be the same as the agency's goals, but the two sets of ideas can be compared. For example, where it is apparent that some behaviour has to stop, the worker can explore how it will stop, what will happen *instead*, and how the agency and family will know that it has stopped. This process is particularly useful in identifying concrete, measurable outcomes which are agreed by both parties. Case conference minutes are full of references to failure to thrive and subsequent comments about the child 'blossoming' but there are rarely any details to supply evidence of what the 'blossoming' looks like (Kelly, 2000).

Where the family is unable to suggest any constructive goals, danger to the child is probably increased. For example, John's children requested admission to care after a period living alone with him during which he made strenuous, but terrifying, attempts to get his estranged wife to return to him; culminating in the children finding him hanging by the neck when they returned from school. The only goal he could identify was one of being reunited with his wife, which he saw as the complete answer to his problems. He could not provide any answers to questions aimed at broadening the detail of a family safety goal; such as, 'what can *you* do to improve matters in your family?', 'what do you think the children would say needs to happen before they are willing to return home?' and 'if I were to ask your wife to return, what messages could I give her that would convince her that she would be safe?'. Any family safety goal plan needs to include *each* family member's individual goals.

### Scaling safety and progress

Risk estimation is professional rather than family knowledge so it is extremely difficult to estimate the extent to which risk has been reduced. It is considerably easier to identify family members' sense of safety and compare these with professional judgements. For example, in the meeting with Stephanie which led to her decision to ask for the children to be accommodated temporarily while she 'sorted herself out', I had used the Children Act 1989 welfare checklist as a framework for scaled questions about her parenting capacity after she had admitted drug use. I also incorporated the professional concerns listed in the agency risk assessment – that she did not meet her children's emotional needs; was unwilling to tackle unresolved issues from her past; and had neglected her children.

These latter concerns were not very specific so we also looked at her ideas about 'good enough' mothering – 'I used to think like me mum, clean the house and that were it really. Now it's responsibility for paying bills and do the material things when they're in bed. I was like a sergeant major, I knew that.' She acknowledged that she had neglected her children and not met their emotional needs – 'I wasn't fit for nowt' – and that her eldest child had begun to show signs of role reversal – 'I'm trying to get her to behave like a nine-year-old. I let her make a sandwich but not use the cooker. She could play out with other kids more. I could get her in a club.'

She was also able to rate their development as satisfactory on a number of the checklist items: they were meeting their developmental milestones, attending school regularly, eating and sleeping well now that she had established a routine, they were up to date with clinic and hospital appointments, and her eldest son was OK socially. Having identified her areas of competence, she then felt able to acknowledge openly that her lack of support, the pressures from her ex-partner, and her resumption of drug taking threatened all this progress. Hence her decision to ask for the children to be accommodated temporarily in a familiar foster placement to minimise their stress – a not unreasonable safety goal.

I do not find it unusual for parents to be able to acknowledge what is going wrong when they are involved in scaling questions; the range of points on a scale means that they are rarely totally condemned and they do aspire to 'doing better'. They can also identify what is going well and work out their own solutions. What was unusual in Stephanie's case was that we were not able to get the senior social worker to spell out what she would view as safety signs, therefore Stephanie had no hope of ever meeting the senior social worker's expectations.

## *Assessing willingness, confidence and capacity*

In order to maintain a safety focus it is important to determine the family's willingness and ability to carry out plans before trying to implement them. However, Turnell and Edwards also make the point that motivation should be shared between the worker and service user; that the social worker has a responsibility to create a context that maximises the likelihood of family members displaying motivation. When relationships become characterised by hostility, a context can be created which reduces motivation. For example, Stephanie found social services' delays in paying her travel expenses to the distant foster parents' home made contact with her children almost impossible but the social worker interpreted this as Stephanie not 'being bothered' to maintain contact and evidence that she put her own needs before her children's. Walsh (1997) also finds it important to provide practical support for parents who are themselves often neglected and impoverished.

Above all, Turnell and Edwards recommend that the worker assumes nothing; and doesn't make hasty judgements or expect everything to work in order to remain flexible and creative to opportunities for change, even in the most difficult cases where abuse is strongly suspected but vigorously denied.

## Working with families where the abuse is denied

Understanding the position of each family member in a non-confrontational way enables an abusive parent to collaborate in devising safety plans even where the abuse is strongly denied. Essex *et al.* (1996) maintain that denial does not necessarily equate with untreatability as the denial may well be rooted in an understandable reluctance to admit responsibility for fear of the consequences – prosecution, family break-up, job loss, social stigma, etc. In Trudy's case, her motivation turned out to be a long-term fear of what her daughter would think of her.

Some months after seeking assistance in coming to terms with her early sexual abuse experiences, she made an appointment to discuss how she could get her baby daughter returned to her care. The child was the subject of a full Care Order following investigations into two unexplained injuries and general failure to thrive. Social services were seeking a Freeing Order for adoption. Trudy was not able to give detailed answers to scaled questions about the child's safety, being much keener to 'explain' the injuries:

*Trudy*: That settee I had, I was sitting there and she was up on my shoulder. I had her like this [demonstrates]. She seemed safe to me. She fell. She was falling asleep in my arms. I was desperate to go to the toilet so I took her upstairs with me, laid her on the bed ... not put her in the cot. 'Cos I didn't want to wake her. I wrapped my duvet round her and shut the door while I went to the toilet. Next thing ... I heard this du ... ff sound. I ran out and there was red mark on her face. [Raising her voice] The doctor says my explanation isn't con ... cons ... you know. He says its a grabbing bruise. [She described a series of angry confrontations with doctors and social workers where they have obviously spent considerable time trying to get her to accept culpability. She could recite accurately the details of linear bruising and fingermarks but was not accepting these alternate explanations. Rather than pursue culpability, I expressed puzzlement.]

*Me*: It doesn't sound like you. I've seen you with Echo. You were always fussing over her. What were you doing holding her carelessly like that? [I mirror her demonstration.] It's just not you. What were you doing that was making you behave like that? [She admitted to smoking a spliff and we talked about mothering responsibilities generally.] What will be best for her if your mothering isn't quite what it used to be?

*Trudy*: She'd be best adopted, but honestly I don't think I can do it. I'd feel like I threw her away.

It was easy from here on – if emotional – as she became involved in devising a safety plan for her daughter which also saved her from future recriminations. She decided that accepting the recommendation of the Guardian ad Litem (which she knew would be freeing her daughter for adoption) would be the most responsible course of action. As she said: 'he's independent and he's fair. I wanted a second chance but Echo needs it more.' She gave me permission to inform her daughter's social worker (with whom she is not on speaking terms) while she went to another telephone to ring the Guardian ad Litem and make arrangements to 'sign the papers'. Feeling pleased that a contested court case would not be necessary, I asked the social worker, whom I knew to be dedicated and careful, what she would consider to be the best outcome of mine and Trudy's discussion. Her answer dashed my elation: she hoped that Trudy would be prepared to sit down with her and talk it through, accept what she did and work through it so that she could go forward. And I thought that was what Trudy had just done as best she was able. (Fuller details of this intervention are analysed in Parton & O'Byrne, 2000.)

Where there is insufficient evidence to remove the child and difficulties in working with the family because of refusal to accept culpability, Essex *et al.* (1996) have devised a three-part 'Resolutions' programme which has been remarkably successful; largely because families have a sense of ownership of individual safety policies they have devised on the programme. Equally professional concerns are addressed fully.

### Part one

A non-confrontational approach is taken but collusion is carefully avoided by responding to questions such as, 'why are you here when I haven't done anything?' with answers on the lines of, 'my training says be worried but you say not, that's why we are working together today'; 'if it were that simple, it would have been sorted out by now' (Essex *et al.*, 1996). Then a family safety policy is drawn up without the alleged abuser present but including extended family to reduce the power and opportunity of the abuser. It is probably also sensible to include any family pets in the safety plan as research in America has found that not only are there links between child abuse and animal cruelty but also that a significant proportion of women in refuges report delaying leaving the abuser out of fear that a pet would be harmed if they were to do so (DeViney *et al.*, 1983; Ascione, 1993; AHA, 1995; Lockwood & Ascione, 1998). The agreed plan is then shared with the abuser, who is responsible for ensuring that the rules are adhered to and for monitoring their own behaviour. This is useful to them because it reduces both professional anxiety and the occasions when the alleged abuser's behaviour could be misinterpreted.

### Part two

All family members are asked to take part in a 'similar but different' exercise, looking at the issues from the respective points of view of various members of a hypothetical family. In role, the non-abusing parent can express their feelings openly and ask difficult questions of the alleged abuser. The abuser also has the opportunity to understand the impact of their behaviour on the family. After this exercise has been completed, the family is asked what issues arose that are relevant to their situation and how they might be used to ensure their children's safety.

*Part three*

The children are asked to identify a significant adult to whom they can turn if they are worried at any time in the future. Variations on this idea have also been developed by Dolan (1991), such as giving the children a prepaid card which, if posted, will ensure an immediate response or a 'secret sign' (an agreed ornament, for example) which can be moved to alert a significant adult that the child feels unsafe but dare not say so openly. Where children are old enough, Essex *et al.* (1996) also undertake education and safety work with children. This can also be adapted for work with children who have been sexually abused by non-family members.

## Safety work with sexually abused children

Kirstie, a twelve-year-old who is big for her age, was referred by her social worker for assistance in coming to terms with the negative effects of a sexually abusive experience by a distant family member outside the home. Kirstie identified her problems as not getting on with her dad's new partner, Mary; being on the child protection register; and the 'mess over what happened'. She ranked the first as her main problem, followed by 'being on the register'. The 'mess' she viewed as not much of a problem at all because she had reported the incident as soon as she got home and the abuser had been arrested. Despite the referral request, I began with Kirstie's definition of her problems and asked a series of scaled questions. She entered into this discussion freely but her dad said little other than, 'I'm keeping out of this' and 'stop turning your feet over, you'll break them shoes'. Kirstie identified the occasions when her relationship with Mary was argument-free and decided to improve the relationship by being more helpful in the house, telling jokes, and asking Mary if she would teach her how to cook. Dad then complained that Kirstie goes into his and Mary's bedroom, taking things, which meant Mary having to check through Kirstie's room in search of them. This led to arguments, after which Kirstie would stamp out of the house and wander the streets. I suggested that Kirstie might put anything she takes back and she liked this idea. We then moved on to the problem of being on the child protection register:

*Me*: What do you need to do to get off the register?
*Kirstie*: Don't know. Stay away from trouble and nowt happen to me.
*Me*: How will everyone know that you are safe?

*Kirstie*: By telling them where I'm going. By asking what time to be back in. If I sleep out, Mary and Dad can ring up.
*Me*: On a scale of 1 to 100, how much can you keep yourself safe?
*Kirstie*: 60, 65.
*Me*: If it was 70, what would you be doing differently?
*Kirstie*: Keeping myself safe even more. Like telling my dad where I'm going. I used to go to building sites. Sleep at my mum's, not somewhere else.
*Me*: How can you prove this score to everyone?
*Kirstie*: Mum doesn't really want me there. [she scores Mum zero without me introducing a scale] I only go to Mum's to see my sisters.

We then scaled her organisational and 'keeping to plans' ability and motivation. I suggested that she try out her ideas and perhaps we could consider her going in for a twelve-year-old responsibility-taking certificate at the next session. I was hopeful that if she could get on better with Mary she would stay home more and not roam the streets after arguments, putting herself into unsafe situations.

### Second session

*Me*: What's better?
*Kirstie*: Me and Mary. Started talking, just get on better. We haven't argued for three days. We used to do it every day.
*Me*: How did you do it?
*Kirstie*: Kept talking and kept out of each other's way for a bit.
*Me*: That's a new solution. When did you think it up?
*Kirstie*: Last week.
*Me*: How did you work that out?
*Kirstie*: It just came to me. Go next door to the neighbours.
*Me*: When do you do it?
*Kirstie*: When she's ratty. Like yesterday, she went to bed at half-past eight.
*Me*: How do you know when she's ratty?
*Kirstie*: Tell by her face.
*Me*: Pretty good. Are you pleased with yourself?
*Kirstie*: Yes.
*Me*: How often is she ratty?
*Kirstie*: Not a lot now, just now and then.
*Me*: How long do you need to stay round at the neighbours?
*Kirstie*: I go anyway 'cos I'm friends with them.
*Me*: Do you tell Mary where you are going?

*Kirstie*: Yes. Or I tell my dad.

*Me*: How do you do talking with Mary?

*Kirstie*: Just say hello every time she comes in from work, like 'did you have a good day, was it busy', whatever.

*Me*: And that works?

*Kirstie*: Yes.

*Me*: Mary sounds as though she gets tired...

*Kirstie*: Yes. Sometimes. She's a lot to do.

*Me*: Have you been helping?

*Kirstie*: Yes. We was about to have an argument yesterday but I dried up, put the stuff away and went out and we didn't argue.

*Me*: Would Mary say things are better?

*Kirstie*: Yes.

Me: How would you score getting on with Mary?

*Kirstie*: 80, 85 [anticipating my next question with a smile] and Mary would say 50, 60 and dad 90, 95. Dad said well done.

*Me*: What do you need to do to get Mary to 70?

*Kirstie*: Start talking more and helping. I can do it.

*Me*: Have you done any baking yet?

*Kirstie*: Yes, some buns. Just plain ones but I'm going to start making more. And they wasn't hollow inside neither.

*Me*: How did you do it?

*Kirstie*: Just asked and she said yes and got this book and we started doing them together.

*Me*: Did you pick a day when she wasn't ratty?

*Kirstie*: Yes.

*Me*: Crafty. How many points do you give yourself for being crafty? [she smiles modestly so I give her 95]

*Kirstie*: We might do chocolate cake next and cook a whole Sunday dinner: chicken, cabbage, potatoes, all that lot.

*Me*: Where are you on the happiness scale?

*Kirstie*: ONE HUNDRED.

*Me*: How did the experiment about putting things back go?

*Kirstie*: I did not take ANYTHING AT ALL, not even a paper hankie.

*Me*: How did you do that?

*Kirstie*: Don't know.

*Me*: Well, it must have taken a lot of self-control...

*Kirstie*: I did it by making up my mind and watching myself. Only time I go in their bedroom is when I'm told to get something by them two.

*Me*: Is Mary still checking your things for missing items?

*Kirstie*: She says well done. Dad says he would leave me in the house on my own a bit but [name of social worker] says no. I'd just have a friend from next door and if anyone came to the door I'd say Dad was in, up in the bathroom.

*Me*: I don't think your social worker can give a twelve-year-old permission to be in on her own, especially after the difficulty you had...

*Kirstie*: The mess, you mean. [matter-of-factly]

*Me*: Yes. What else have you been doing about being out but keeping safe?

*Kirstie*: Dad let me stay out till ten, next door, 'cos I'd been so good. Helping in the house.

This was not a particularly productive answer so we began to work out what she needed to do to convince everyone that she is safe and devised the following programme for her certificate. All the items were suggested by Kirstie:

### Kirstie: 12-year-old responsibility-taking certificate (silver) plan

Kirstie would like to get off the Child Protection Register and is planning to take her silver certificate so that she can convince the August case conference that she is able to take reasonable responsibility for her own safety and general behaviour. If she is successful, the certificate will be presented at 4.00 p.m. on 10 August – all the people who have helped are invited to come and have a piece of celebratory chocolate cake (and be in the photo). She has agreed to keep up the following efforts from now until August and identified who she will need to help her:

1  Tell Dad and Mary where she is going at all times.
2  Tell them what time she will be back (currently she is allowed out until 9.30 p.m.) and be back within five minutes of this at most.
3  Only go to someone else's house where there is a sensible woman.
4  Keep weekly appointments with her social worker, except when either of them changes the agreed date for good reason.
5  Always have 10p with her for making phone calls. Dad and Mary to make sure she has this money.
6  Inform her social worker if she has a planned overnight stay away from home. Dad to ring too.
7  Own up to her social worker if any of the above things go wrong and work out how to put them right.
8  Handle relationships with her mates so that she can keep friends and keep out of trouble. Her year head to help with this.

9   Keep her shirt tucked in at school.
10  Hand in her homework on time.
11  Begin to learn how to be quiet in class. Her German and English teachers to help with this.
12  Keep having conversations with Mary. Mary to help with this.
13  Finish all the jobs she starts in the house.
14  Cook a whole Sunday dinner with Mary's help.
15  Accept any punishments Dad or Mary give her without arguing (but she needn't look as if she doesn't mind!)

Kirstie will need lots of help from everyone to get her certificate, especially people telling her when she is doing things right as well as telling her off when things go wrong. This is a draft plan worked out by Kirstie and Judith so comments from Dad, Mary, [name of social worker] and teachers are welcome. They might have some better ideas. Also they will be important trainers to coach Kirstie through to silver, so please let Judith or [name of social worker] know what sort of help you can offer.

Both the social worker and myself thought it an ambitious plan for a twelve-year-old. The social worker was also concerned about lack of support and interest from Kirstie's dad as he had not been very cooperative with the social work effort to date. Despite these concerns, all looked promising until a week before the case conference. At the suggestion of her social worker, Kirstie went into town to attend a sporting event but found it cancelled. She then spent the day with her grandmother and forgot to phone her dad until 8.00 p.m. She was grounded for a week, a punishment she accepted with unusually good grace, and reported herself to her social worker so that she could 'get back on track'. Unfortunately the teacher representatives at the case conference considered this 'failure' sufficient grounds to contest deregistration.

At the following session, Kirstie and her dad expressed their disappointment. Apart from this one slip-back, Kirstie had worked on every item by reading the plan each night and 'just doing them one at a time'. Dad was a completely different person. He acknowledged how much better things were at home, he had changed his work shifts (at considerable financial cost) so that Kirstie was not spending long periods in the house alone, and he was willing for social services to continue visiting but could not see the need for continued registration. We decided that Kirstie should receive her bronze certificate and rewrote the plan so that she could go in for her silver certificate in three months' time. As she would be thirteen by this date, some of the items were altered to allow for this. The social worker made sure that the teachers were fully involved in this stage of the plan.

People freely give me permission to tell their stories to help other people with the same difficulties but Stephanie, Tina, and Kirstie's dad were particularly insistent that I tell people about their unsatisfactory experiences of the child protection system as well as their successes. 'Please tell people, no one should have to go through what I went through', was Stephanie's comment. 'They said I'd to take all the children's feelings into consideration but *they* didn't', Tina complained; while Kirstie's dad wanted people to know how embarrassed and hopeless he had felt when Kirstie's name was put on the register but he hadn't been offered 'usable' help. Kirstie simply wanted me to use her real name as she was proud of her achievements. I explained that this was not possible. I tell their stories here in the hope that the reader will be convinced that a safety approach has the potential to reduce social workers', as well as service users', frustration with the current system and enable them to identify existing competencies which will form the basis of an effective safety plan.

## SUMMARY

- An emphasis on risk assessment in the child protection system has a detrimental effect on both social workers and service users. A signs of safety approach addresses this difficulty and builds on a needs-led assessment model.
- Most families have signs of safety as well as risk. Building safety provides a balance to the problems and dangers for children, encouraging the development of a cooperative relationship with all members of families.
- There are six important principles to a safety approach: understanding the position of each family member in order to treat alleged abusers as people worth doing business with; finding exceptions to the mistreatment of children so that parents can repeat acceptable behaviours; discovering family strengths and resources; focusing on family and agency goals so as to be clear where these differ; scaling safety and progress; and assessing the willingness, confidence, and capacity of families to carry out safety plans.
- It is possible to work with families where abuse is suspected but denied by adopting a safety approach which uses a family safety policy, a 'similar but different' exercise, and builds in safety checks for children.
- Age-appropriate responsibility-taking certificates can be used in safety work with children vulnerable to sexual abuse outside the family.

# 7

# Child care planning: children's solutions

The Children Act 1989 gives a clear message about the desirability of involving children in the decisions which affect them; a message which few social workers would view as either contentious or problematic. Most social workers aspire to good professional practice identified by young service users: listening carefully, without trivialising; being available and accessible, with regular and predictable contact; accepting, explaining and suggesting options and choices; building rapport through the use of humour; being realistic, reliable and straight-talking; and being trustworthy in terms of both confidentiality and consulting with children before taking action (DoH, 1999, p. 45). However, the same government guidance on the assessment of children in need considered it necessary to spell out the need for direct work with children on the grounds that 'it is clear from research that this is often not done at all or not done well' (DoH, 1999, 3.38, p. 44). The main reason for this state of affairs seems not to be unwillingness to talk to children but rather the way it is done; there being a tendency to ask questions, listen to the answers and *interpret* what children are saying within an adult frame of reference (Dalrymple & Burke, 1995). Similarly, Braye and Preston-Shoot (1995) suggest that adultism remains a stumbling block as the concept of need is located within an *individual dependency-led model* which is also influenced by adult, white, Eurocentric norms and assumptions (p. 16).

In other words, although social workers listen to children, consult them and invite them to meetings, in the final analysis, as adults they consider that they know what is in children's best interests. This retention of expertise by adults in traditional social work interventions would not be a problem if children could be shown to benefit from this wisdom but, as White (1999) commented, the social construction of children as vulnerable dependants incapable of finding solutions to their problems has not served children particularly well. For example, comparable numbers of children die, or are seriously re-injured, at the hands of their care-takers each year (Herrenkohl *et al.*, 1979, 1995;

127

Cleaver & Freeman, 1995; Farmer & Owen, 1995); if admitted to care, are separated from their sibs against their wishes (Selwyn, 1999); and have low levels of satisfaction with family services (Sinclair *et al.*, 1995; Blyth *et al.*, 1995; Dearden & Becker, 1996).

Neither will DoH recommendations that assessments of children's needs be grounded in evidence-based knowledge (2000, p.10) necessarily improve matters particularly. Despite a plethora of available psychological research findings about children's developmental needs, this 'does not have the capacity to predict anything about any *individual* child' (Mullender, 1999a, p. 11, my emphasis). The use of the term 'the best interests' of the child is, says Mullender (1999b), a suspiciously catch-all phrase, implying an inability to spell out what children's needs actually are (p. 324). It best describes how a well-meaning adult views a child's relationship with that adult and, when that relationship is not going smoothly, the child is often 'totalised' within a pathologising discourse. It is not only social workers who do this; all parents understand and explain their children's behaviour within their existing adult ways of meaning making, influenced largely by their *own* experiences and traditional psychological explanations. These interpretations are rarely made explicit to children and are probably not shared – as the example of Maggie illustrates.

Maggie used compensation money awarded in respect of her early sexual abuse experiences to pay for a private investigator to track down the father of her middle child, Jon, in the hope that she could arrange for Jon to have regular weekend contact with his father, as did his older brother and younger sister with their fathers. Unfortunately the investigation revealed that Jon's father had served a prison sentence for sexually abusing his daughter by another partner. Maggie sought advice on how best to explain the situation to Jon, who regularly asked about the progress of the investigation. She was torn between telling him the truth or a lie. In the case of the former, she anticipated him being badly affected; she did not want him to be hurt by abuse as she had been and her nightmare was that 'He will be crying all day; really messed up; and there won't be a single thing I can do about it.' On the other hand, if she told a lie, this would be a blow to his hopes: 'I feel his pain at not knowing his dad, especially when the other two come back from seeing their dads with presents. It is particularly bad on Saturdays and at Christmas. I hoped for a reconciliation between Jon and his dad and I might have put this over to him too much. I wear myself to the fingers overcompensating for the kids not having dads around but they don't go without anything a family with a resident dad would have and do.'

As her description of all three children was of healthy, emotionally resilient young people, I suggested that she ask her children to travel to a happy future in a 'back to the future' car and say what this looks like in two years' time to enable her to listen to their wishes without having to put herself constantly second to their needs – or to second-guess what these needs and wishes might be. She was confident that she could predict with 75–85 per cent accuracy what they would say, but agreed to try it. To give her space to try out what it would feel like living with either decision without constantly weighing up the pros and cons, I also asked her to do the coin-toss experiment: pretend that she would tell Jon the truth about his father when the coin came up heads and a lie for tails.

Two weeks later she reported a comfortable conversation with Jon about his dad while the other children were out with their dads, where she had been able to listen to him:

*Maggie*: Then on Sunday ... I wrote all this down because I didn't want to forget it ... we played the game on Sunday. I'm shocked. I said I could get 75 per cent and I only got about 5 per cent. This I felt ... I want to stop, how do I cope with this? I asked them where they will be two years from now. Karen, she's content how she is ... stay in the house we're in and she wants me to get married! Jon, he wants to stay as we are. He's quite happy. That's his main thing. Maybe live a bit nearer school. Mum to have more money. Do rugby training and Mum to pass her driving test. Mum not to get married at all. They were all laughing and chipping in as it got going, agreeing with each other. Dougal, live nearer school ... it's an hour on the bus and he gets bus-sick. Me to get married ... to have lots of friends, pass my test and have a car. The last bit nearly knocked me off the bed – he wants Jon's dad to be in that car in two years! Jon didn't mention his father but Dougal did. I've never thought how Jon not being in contact with his dad affected my other two children.
*Me*: Do you reckon that Dougal has illusions or dreams about how Jon's dad might turn out?
*Maggie*: [thinking hard] No ... I think that when Dougal and Karen go [to see their dads] ... Dougal is really sensitive and I think he feels that Jon's at home and not going.
*Me*: What was the 5 per cent you got right?
*Maggie*: The money. They all wanted a lottery win and maybe a car would come into it. I never thought marriage would come into it ... or that they would want to move. What concerned me, from thinking this is a problem for me and Jon, it's also a problem for Dougal.
*Me*: And the coin toss?

*Maggie*: I only tossed it three times and I'll tell you why. I wasn't ready to put all of me in the first day. Second day, I thought I was strong enough to take it. Landed on a lie day. I was tempted to toss it again. But thought, no, see it through. I didn't feel like I could get into it full ... a part of me didn't want to. I felt really crappy. Day after, thought, don't know if I want to toss this. Landed on a truth day. Sat down and visualised it. Just felt that the day I had, you know, I could push myself to do that. I didn't feel crappy that day. Felt for two days overall, whose needs do I want to meet? If I lie, I meet my own needs, not Jon's. Third day, it landed on a lie day and I didn't even go into it. It told me what I'm going to do. There's about 600 people in [name of her town] tossing coins. And getting into that car. That's a really nice thing anyway, whether you have problems or not. I'd definitely do it again with them. I'm still analysing but not thinking about what they might be thinking. I really expected the conversation [with Jon] to go on a lot longer, in more depth. But he got what information he wanted. I left my feelings and concentrated on how Jon really felt. And then thought, well, we do seem to be having a few good days.

*Me*: What's your next step?

*Maggie*: Is to carry on, be able to carry on with these conversations. Be able to feel that I don't have to stop them. Stop thinking that I know what they're thinking because I obviously don't ... I don't feel like I did three weeks ago. At all. Don't feel so desperate. [I ask her a scaled question and she rates herself at 90 for how she is handling it.]

*Me*: What would make it 95?

*Maggie*: Answering in the best way I can to an eight-year-old. When I walked out of here two weeks ago, I thought, I'm my mum. All the things, I was doing the exact same things. Not much different. My mum brushed things under the carpet, like they did in those days. Hope it'll all go away. By shutting Jon up, I'm sweeping it under the carpet. But he'll carry it all on with him. If I'd talked openly with my mum, my life might have been better. I want to be that honest person for my kids. And life isn't always easy. I could have carried on talking, *had* Jon. At the moment, I feel ready to face what I've got to face.

## Children's concerns

Being less influenced by psychological explanations of behaviour than adults, children tend to describe their problems in terms of their present and future functioning. They describe being very much more affected by the misery which accompanies current unsatisfactory peer relationships and parental conflict than they are by past emotional traumas. This should not be surprising as, whatever emotionally damaging events occurred previously in their lives, they still have to cope with the dailiness of school life. Even where both teachers and parents are supportive of children, their influence can be minimal if the child lacks a supportive peer group, children's self-image and self-evaluation being strongly influenced by the informal culture of school. Unpopular, bullied or absent pupils are at increased physical and emotional danger (for an overview, see Blyth & Milner, 1997, chapter 2), so it is not surprising that they express concern about ongoing social and economic problems; the former, especially, have the capacity for sustained emotional misery. If they are not attended to, and the child fails to negotiate the informal, social culture of the school, they are unlikely to be any more successful in the formal, academic school culture or the adult world as measured by longer-term outcomes in education attainment, training, employment, housing and personal relationships (for an overview, see Milner & Blyth, 1999).

Children discuss these concerns initially in terms of falling out with friends, not having the right trainers, being picked on, and so on – all of which seem minor in comparison with the big emotional problem identified by adults, resulting in their significance to the child being trivialised. This leads to frustration on both sides, further misunderstandings and, often, a child resisting adult descriptions of their problems by increasing the 'complained about' behaviour. This, in turn, reduces the capacity of adults to help the child: 'when a therapist listens to, and accepts, and then furthers the investigation of a pathological description of a child, the child's identity suffers' (Freeman *et al.*, 1997, p. 9).

For example, Steven had a history of suicide attempts at the time of his parents' separation for which he received pyschiatric in-patient treatment. His school referred him for counselling three years later, saying that he had very low self-esteem and could not cope with school. After a playground falling-out with a friend, he had told a teacher that he wished he had never been born and his school was worried that he would attempt suicide again. Additionally, the school's fears were fuelled by an 'interpretation' of his black, spiky writing with many crossings-out as indicative of 'suicidal ideation' – a 'totalising' of him within a psychiatric discourse.

Listening to Steven revealed that he saw his problem as the reaction of other pupils to his psychiatric history: 'people making fun of me ... calling me hangman and stuff ... 'cos they know all about me ... seems like the whole school knows'. He was miserable with the name-calling, which isolated him from his previous friends (children tend to avoid a pupil targeted by others in the interests of self-preservation), and had responded by walking along the school corridors with his head down. He had begun to believe the pathological story into which he had been entered: 'I'm not good at socialising face-to-face', he told me seriously. 'Good gracious', I responded, 'Whatever does that mean?' 'I'm scared of girls. I back off', he replied.

Once we stepped outside the psychiatric story, it was possible for Steven to devise his own straightforward solutions to his problems. These consisted of putting his hand to his neck in a pretend pull whenever called 'hangman', walking with his head up in the corridors, and walking home with a girl he identified as both friendly and intelligent enough to help him with his maths homework. Three sessions later he rated himself at 70 on a 'happiness at school' scale and the improvement in his peer relationships was confirmed by his referring teacher. However, the teacher remained worried about the suicide risk he considered Steven to represent; the weight and mass of the old story. Steven and I discussed this problem and Steven came up with the idea of smiling brightly whenever he met teachers in the corridor and engaging them in cheerful conversation but this was only partially successful. His teacher remained worried about his black, spiky writing with crossings-out; he was sure that the psychiatric problem had merely gone underground and was being revealed symbolically. Steven explained to me that his handwriting had nothing to do with misery, just that he had never learned joined-up writing properly at junior school and made mistakes when he was rushed. I thought that I would have to spend time teaching him how to do 'proper' joined-up writing (an unusual use of counselling time, to say the least) but, once again, Steven came up with the answer. He bought a bottle of Tipp-Ex! Children are surprisingly capable of resolving their own problems: 'Instead of simply reflecting a child's language or listening and making theoretically-based interpretations, we seek to be a welcomed and active participant in the *child's world of meaning ...* the child often finds a 'solution' we could never have anticipated' (Freeman *et al.*, 1997, p. 7, my emphasis).

Even where a child has experienced an horrific assault, the reactions of peers often cause more distress than the original trauma. For example, Suzanne had been seriously sexually assaulted by a stranger who met her on the street whilst she was truanting from school and invited her into his flat. She was referred for counselling to help her come to terms with the (presumed) resulting trauma. I asked her what she hoped to get out of counselling and she replied that people who had a hard time came to talk about this. When asked what 'hard times' she had

had, there was no mention of the sexual assault. Her list included: missing her mum who died three years previously, being poorly and not being believed (being sent to school when she had a headache), being bullied at school and by her brother at home, not getting trips to the seaside, and the police taking her school blouse and jumper for forensic evidence (this meant that she 'stood out' at school in a different jumper, which increased the bullying and subsequent truanting, nor could she get into her locker to get her schoolbooks as her key was in a pocket of her blouse). She was 'not bothered' about the sexual assault because 'he's been arrested and he'll get sent to prison'.

She chose 'missing her mum' as her main problem and we worked on this over three sessions. Towards the end of the third session, Suzanne began playing with a toy troll; commenting that it couldn't breathe because it had a tube stuck in its mouth. Conscious that her assault had involved oral ejaculation, I leapt to a psychological interpretation – maybe she was trying to talk about the abuse through third-party play? Before I could frame an exploratory question, she held up the troll and asked, 'what shall we call him?' I suggested one of the names of the seven dwarfs, thinking this would give her a range of emotional states to consider. We took some time remembering all the names and, as I was writing them down, she asked me which one I was. I chose Sleepy, again to leave her a wide choice of emotional and behavioural states. We then filled in who she was and all the others. The troll was left without a name, her final list being:

*Grumpy*: Grandma ('cos old people are)
*Doc*: her brother's girlfriend ('cos she's sensible)
*Dopey*: Dad ('cos he drinks and plays Mum's old records)
*Bashful*: her brother (no explanation but a giggle)
*Sleepy*: me
*Sneezy*: her best friend
*Happy*: herself ('cos I am now I spoke to my mum and I know she's all right)

So much for my psychological insights! Suzanne attends a local club and I bump into her occasionally. She is happy and attending school regularly.

Adults often find it incomprehensible that children can be more concerned about everyday difficulties than previous trauma. They then try to make sense of this seeming incongruity through the use of psychological explanations; the child must be dissociating and denying the experience and, therefore, in need of lengthy therapy. However, since beginning to listen to children more carefully and accepting what they say as their reality, I have discovered that the effects of sexual abuse, in particular, are infinitely variable. Regardless of the 'severity' of the assault, recovery seems much more dependent on the supportiveness – or otherwise – of friends and how it is handled by adults.

For example, Amy was raped at a party by a boy from her school. Her family and teachers were supportive but concerned about what they viewed as her excessive tearfulness. She told me that she found school incredibly difficult because some of her girlfriends had taken the boy's side and he had boasted in the playground that he had 'had her all the way'. He was subsequently excluded from school but his comments became incorporated into the masculine insult vocabulary of the playground. Whenever any boy wished to insult Amy, instead of the more usual 'stuck-up snob', he would make remarks such as 'oh, go and get yourself raped again', to which taunt, the other boys would shout 'been there, done that'.

By carefully listening to Amy's descriptions of her life at school, it emerged that she had struggled with peer relationships ever since entering secondary school, where she stood out as different due to her musical ability – she was a talented cellist. After a period of intense loneliness, she was grateful when a group of low-achieving girls accepted her into their social circle. She had little in common with this group; certainly, she lacked their street wisdom, thereby making herself vulnerable to the assault by attending a party at which she not only felt socially insecure but lacked the necessary skills to rebuff the boys' crude sexual advances. Although she subsequently developed her own coping strategies for the playground taunts, this amounted to no more than survival and she decided that she needed to attend a school where her musical ability would be valued if she were to be really happy. Her parents were able to accept this when they realised that she was not running away from her problems, as demonstrated by her dogged attendance at school and reduced tearfulness. Even so, she had to use a counselling session to practise what she would say to her parents so that her solution could be viewed as a sensible one.

The adults in these three young people's lives acted out of concern; the difficulty was that they expressed this concern from a point of view that *they* knew what was in the best interests of vulnerable young people. This adult pathologising of children's problems invalidates children's expressed concerns about their struggles with the dailiness of life; their desire to be accepted by their peers, their need for respect from adults, and their anxieties about relationships with the opposite sex (unrequited love is a common theme of my talk with teenagers). It is not that they avoid discussing emotional trauma, simply that they often ascribe less importance to them than adults do. They do not necessarily need to address individual emotional events in order to move forwards, rather they need to gain control over their everyday lives so that they can address these events from a position of competence.

Casting children as inherently vulnerable is also to deny them competence in their devising their own solutions to their problems. When children are allowed to frame their problems from their own perspectives, they show not only the capacity to exercise considerable responsibility and make sensible choices but they are also much more creative in their solutions than adults. Given the scope, they frequently solve problems for the adults in their lives as well as themselves.

## Children's solutions for themselves and their families

Entering a child into a pathological story frequently makes the problem worse as the child resists being defined in a way that 'fixes' them in a category. Josie was a case in point. She developed a reluctance to attend school shortly after starting secondary school. Sympathetic encouragement from her parents and teachers had no effect on her attendance so she was referred to a specialist educational service where she was quickly labelled as a school phobic and a behavioural programme was prescribed. Josie responded to this by retreating into her bedroom and becoming withdrawn. The adult experts pushed her further into the bedroom by sending home schoolwork, culminating in her father discovering a letter in a homework book in which she discussed her desire to die. This added to the pathological story of school phobia; like Steven, 'suicidal ideation' was added to her description. Her parents became worried that their daughter was very disturbed indeed and did not see how the caring adults had backed her into a very small space from which she could see no way forward.

Listening to Josie revealed that she had retreated into her bedroom as resistance against a therapeutic programme that was not only unhelpful but downright oppressive. I asked how she had coped when she had attended school earlier and she told a story of not fitting in socially; an insult vocabulary of 'snob' and 'swot' being frequently levelled at her. We explored this by talking about the Spice Girls (her favourite pop group), who I relabelled as Sad Spice, Snob Spice, Slag Spice, Success Spice and Shy Spice in order to cover the range of playground insults girls commonly receive. I anticipated her choosing Shy Spice but she had aspirations to be Success Spice, having coped with her shyness previously by shutting out the insults through what she could only describe as 'focusing': 'focusing is the way. That always works. They [her parents] sometimes push me into doing things. They think they're helping but it makes it worse. Pushing me into going out more. They push me too far.' Her parents were not particularly 'pushy' parents, they were simply applying the prescribed behavioural pro- gramme, but Josie could not cope with this. When asked what would help her get the 'focusing' back, she said if her parents backed off and gave her more space, that would help; as it would if they told her sister not to bring certain schoolfriends home for a while. These friends had been involved in the name-calling and, although Josie could cope with it at school until she fell out with her best friend, she found it intolera- ble at home. We had five sessions in which I struggled to get a clearer picture of how she did 'focusing', but Josie remained vague about this, apart from knowing that she needed peace and quiet in which to do it. After successfully explaining this to her parents, she returned to school.

Tim, similarly, did not attend school but he had the added burden of being entered into three different pathological stories. His secondary school teacher thought he had not made the social transition to secondary school and was developing a school phobia; his father saw his dyslexia, and the attendant academic difficulties, as the problem; and his mother worried that he stayed at home through anxiety about her panic attacks. Tim was resisting all these stories by withdrawing from social events as well as school. *His* story was one of a worried/sick feeling every day that started in his stomach and then moved up to his throat. This affected how good he felt about himself, making him feel 'split down the middle with one half smiling and one half raining and down'. Sometimes this stopped him getting to school or staying in school for a full day.

He felt 30 per cent in control of the sick feeling; this occurring when he knew he had achieved his goals for the day – mostly to do with how long he had predicted he could stay in school. Tim had plainly been attempting to supply his own solution to the problem, albeit unknown to the concerned adults because they hadn't asked him, so I asked him to tell me his ideal plan for coping with the sick feeling:

> I know I can cope with the worry and sick feeling. I stick with the sick feeling and think, I've got this far, I might as well do it. When the sick feeling comes back in the day, I can give myself bigger margins and by the time it's the last lesson, I will feel I've done it. Dinner time is a milestone. [I asked how he would cope with setbacks to this plan and if he needed any help.] By not thinking too much and spreading the time. I have been building up to doing a whole week. My science teacher says I can talk to him anytime ... I've got two good friends I can discuss it with ... If Mum and Dad say 'well done', that would help.

He rated the chance of the plan succeeding as about 80 per cent so I suggested he put it into operation on an experimental basis, not to be too disappointed if he came home some days as this would give us more material for our study. He was eager to do this, telling me that he would be motivated by achievement but his parents looked disappointed that this was all the advice I had to offer. I took the sheaves of reports about his school difficulties which his father had brought (concentrating on the '5 per cent' of problem behaviour) and promised to read them later, commenting that Tim sounded really good at solution finding and that I hoped they could support his plan. At the next session, Tim proudly reported that he had completed a full week in school. Eight weeks later, his mother reported that he had not missed a day's schooling but that he hadn't told his year head that counselling ceased after the second session because he had told Tim not to get discouraged as it would take a long time! Tim was also putting his new-found confidence in solution finding to good use with his mum's panic attacks. I consider him to be a much more talented solution finder than myself.

Sapphire, too, sorted out her Mum's problems as soon as she gained confidence in her solution finding. She was referred for assistance in coming to terms with her early experiences of sexual abuse which her social worker considered was the cause of her glue sniffing, persistent non-attendance at school, and aggressive behaviour towards her mother. Sapphire rated herself at 'about 15' on a 'happiness' scale but 10 on a 'satisfied with this score' scale because, 'I'm doing the best I can at the moment.' If she were sixteen years old and 70 on the happiness scale, she would be leaving college with a folder containing good exam results in her hand. She would have new friends, her hair would be down and she would not be wearing make-up. She would have done it with help and courage to do things; these would come from family and friends. Her first step would be to try to put the past behind her and get rid of the nightmares and flashbacks which make her angry so she throws things in her bedroom or fights with Mum or runs out of the house.

Sapphire chose a bedtime pampering programme for dealing with her intrusive thoughts, planned to the last detail:

I'll have a warm bath surrounded by blue candles which smell of blueberries ... lie in the bath with lots of bubble bath ... not scented, a sensitive one to make my skin nice and soft. I'll take my CD player in and listen to music and then dry myself on a green towel, put on my green, silky pyjamas ... read a romantic book, and then settle down to sleep.

Two weeks later Sapphire reported progress in every area of her life but what was most interesting was the effect she had had on her mum. They both benefited from the pampering:

> She explains things about her – all the family was abused – worse than what happened to me. And then we cry and she gets embarrassed and I say 'it's all right to cry a little sometimes'. It [the abuse] made her feel useless as a mum. We still have the odd argument about coming in on time. I got grounded but I said 'fair enough' and did it ... I still see my dad. My family's all right. No family's perfect but I like it the way it is, spend a weekend with Dad, gives Mum a break and come back to a better relationship. I feel better within myself as well. It's better than taking drugs.

No doubt her Mum and the social worker felt better within themselves too; I certainly did after this session, which showed her to have brains, guts and maturity. These qualities had been lost for a while under the burden of other people's stories about her problems. Nor does a child necessarily have to be present at sessions for their capacity for taking responsibility to have an effect on a whole family problem. I discovered that it is possible to access children's solutions 'by proxy' through working with Rita. She turned up at Northorpe Hall in a terribly distressed state after discovering a letter in her daughter's bedroom which confirmed all Rita's fears about Lauren getting involved with a 'crowd of wrong 'uns who all take drugs. She was lovely girl till she got in with that lot.' Rita had 'tried everything' to stop Lauren associating with the gang, resulting in increased family rows and Lauren staying out even later at night. Rita did not think that Lauren would agree to see anyone to talk about this.

I commented that Rita was obviously a caring Mum who had made a success of bringing up her daughter for many years but that as she had 'tried everything', how about doing something different? What would Lauren say needed to happen to reduce the rows and encourage her to stay at home more? Rita reeled off a long list of Lauren's wishes, all of which she saw as unreasonable and unsafe for such a young person. I suggested that they could be framed as reasonable responsibility taking; for example, Lauren could be asked what time she thought she ought to be home by and then asked to respect her own choice. Rita was dubious about this as she thought it would give Lauren carte blanche to stay out very late but was desperate enough to try anything so she set off home determined to engage Lauren in a discussion about what reasonable responsibility taking for a fourteen-year-old would look like.

We met at fortnightly intervals at which Rita reported steady progress; Lauren did not use the opportunity to demand to be allowed to stay out very late. There was one major row early on – 'I just blew it. I forgot and fuelled it' – for which we devised a competence cue strategy – she chose a symbol to represent strong, caring mothering which she kept on top of the microwave to remind herself of her strengths. Throughout the first four sessions, Rita remained dubious about the strategy, believing that I would have to meet Lauren eventually to help her 'get to the bottom of what caused this, why she behaved like this'; which she ascribed to Lauren losing contact with her natural father. At the fifth session she announced that she had decided that she didn't need to look into the past, things were fine at home now. Although I never met Lauren, I gained an impression of a competent, intelligent person who was capable of making choices and taking personal responsibility once her ideas were respected.

Neither is learning difficulty any barrier to utilising children's solutions; it merely makes it a little more difficult to access them. Despite extensive anger management training at a specialist educational unit, ten-year-old Darren had been excluded from school after kicking a teacher. His mother requested more 'anger management' as she was worried that Darren's inability to control his temper, combined with difficulties in communicating with adults, would lead to him being excluded from his new school. His 'communication difficulties' turned out to consist of not talking to adults at all; something of a barrier to my hopes of holding an externalising conversation with him.

After getting no response whatsoever from Darren, I asked him to change seats with his mum so that she could pretend to be him and answer his questions. I gave him two pieces of paper on which I had written CORRECT! and WRONG!, asking him to hold one up after each answer his mother gave:

*Me*: [to Mum as Darren] How long has the temper been in you?
*Mum*: [as Darren] About twelve months. CORRECT!
*Me*: [to Mum as Darren] Is it worse or better at the moment?
*Mum*: [as Darren] It's not as frequent. CORRECT!
*Me*: [to Mum as Darren] Are the episodes as bad as previously?
*Mum*: [forgetting her role] He's only had one really bad one. [Darren has difficulty deciding which paper to hold up, eventually proffering both.]
*Me*: [to Darren] Is Mum doing you well, Darren? [he nods]
*Me*: [to Mum as Darren] What is the temper like?
*Mum*: [as Darren] Like a volcano. Exploding! CORRECT!
*Me*: [to Mum as Darren] Is it a slow or sudden volcano?
*Mum*: [as Darren] Sudden. CORRECT!
*Me*: [to Mum as Darren] What does it make you do?
*Mum*: [as Darren] I don't know. [as herself] Here, Darren, you'll have to speak for yourself. [she changes places with him and takes the papers]

*Me*: [to Darren] What does the temper make you do?
*Darren*: Don't know.
*Me*: Have you got it blocked out?
*Darren*: No.
*Me*: Does the temper make you throw things?
*Darren*: No.
*Me*: Does it make you hit people?
*Darren*: Yes.
*Me*: Does it make you use your fists?
*Darren*: Yes.
*Me*: Does it make you kick?
*Darren*: Yes.
*Me*: Does it make you swear?
*Darren*: No. WRONG!
*Me*: Does it make you use the 'f' word?
*Darren*: No. WRONG!
*Me*: The 'b' word?
*Darren*: No. CORRECT!
*Me*: The 'c' word?
Darren: NO! CORRECT!
*Me*: Shout?
*Darren*: No. WRONG!
*Me*: Stamp about?
*Darren*: No. CORRECT!
*Me*: Break things?
*Darren*: No. CORRECT!

By this time both Darren and his Mum were laughing and thoroughly enjoying the 'game' and I was able to develop an externalising conversation which looked at what responsibilities an eleven-year-old could have (aiming for the future), with Darren being Mum; for example:

*Me*: [to Darren as Mum] How much control should an eleven-year-old have over his temper?
*Darren*: [as Mum] Don't know.
*Mum*: WRONG! [as herself] He should have some. Quite a lot, really.

I also looked at problem-free behaviour:

*Me*: [to Darren as Mum] I've asked you lots of things about the temper. Can I ask you something different? What makes you proud of Darren?
*Darren*: [as Mum] Don't know.
*Mum*: [as herself] WRONG! He's a happy child, very helpful when he wants to be. I'm proud of his swimming. Quite pleased with his

schoolwork. His temper only comes out at school ... once at home when it was really bad. And only once. [Darren is, again, unsure which paper to hold up]

By the end of the session, Darren had not only managed to talk about himself but he has worked out that he doesn't lose his temper when he is calm. As he could not say what 'calm' is like, I concluded the session by asking him to study how he does self-calming.

At the next session, Darren brought the CORRECT! and WRONG! papers with him and he and his mum changed places several times although they also negotiated between themselves for mutually agreed answers much more than they did in the first session. Darren reported two good weeks at school; he had been talking to one teacher in particular and had successfully resisted 'wind-ups' from other pupils. At home he had taken on more responsibility. I was unable to thicken the counterplot because he could not explain how he had gained control over his temper but he was confident that he had his temper under control. If he had a slip-back, he would ask for another session.

In this instance, I used the papers merely to facilitate talk between Darren and myself but Lisa Handley, a student social worker observing the session, commented that it also prompted increased talk between Darren and his mum as there were questions to which only Darren knew the answer. She wondered if they had not previously discussed matters in a way which involved Mum consulting with Darren. Since then I have found it a useful way of helping children talk with the adults in their lives; particularly about 'sensitive' issues. They overcome their reluctance to talk about these in their eagerness to correct an adult's wrong answer.

**Looked-after children**

In advocating that children's voices are listened to – on the grounds that they understand their problems best and devise the most effective solutions to them – I am not suggesting that adult voices should be ignored. An ethic of multiplicity honours *all* voices (Coale, 1998). This is not too difficult where it involves helping children and their parents and teachers listen to each other but the task becomes extremely complex where a child is looked after. Here the parental voice becomes fragmented between natural parents, field and residential social workers, the local authority as corporate parent, and dominant discourses about good practice in residential care. Some of these voices are more privileged than others, some collude to silence children, and some compete to confuse them and each other.

When working as a mentor for a demoralised children's reception centre, I found it very difficult to honour all these voices. Some of the professional voices were totally in opposition to one another in terms of both problem definition and solution finding. The field social workers complained that the residential workers did not sufficiently consider the children's individual needs; all of them wanting the children for whom they were responsible to have individual treatment plans which, although they frequently mentioned the child's need to learn about boundaries, still allowed for the child's antisocial behaviour to be both excused and exonerated. On the other hand, the residential social workers were concerned about how individual behaviour impacted on communal living, wanting much more support from field social workers in assisting individual children to accept responsibility for their behaviour and keep the rules of the home. For example, the residential staff reported two teenage girls to the police after they started a fire in their bedroom. The field social workers complained bitterly about the girls' 'disturbed' behaviour being 'criminalised' as this was 'only a very small fire'. To residential staff, concerned about the safety of all the children, there was no such thing as a small fire in a bedroom. The girls' voices were lost in the cacophony of adult argument and recrimination.

While the adult voices argue from differing professional positions about the meanings of looked-after children's antisocial behaviour, the children struggle to maintain some sense of control over their lives in a home where peer relationships are fraught with difficulty. Admitting teenagers to residential care, where they share a physical space with others of similar age, the same gender, and with shared experiences of adversity (and resistance), encourages relationships which are similar to those of high-access siblings (Kosonen, 1994). These quasi-sibling relationships in children's homes have the capacity for emotional intensity, both for nurturing and conflict. Iveson (1990, p. 75) argues that good relationships do not exist without a degree of conflict but, rather than help them learn to resolve conflict, warring children tend to be separated, thus losing fragile relationships which have the potential for nurturing (Horrocks & Milner, 1999). The volatile nature of peer relationships in children's homes is exacerbated in reception centres where the established social order is disrupted with every new admission. This means that looked-after children tend to be primarily concerned with their present lives; the very real difficulties of getting through any one unpredictable day. Robyn, for example, had been accommodated after a long period of family conflict. She was fearful about her future and had hopes for some sort of stability but could not carry through her plans because of the difficulties of daily living:

*Robyn*: I was tolerant for half an hour. Then I got wound up. Everyone knows I blow a gasket and go psycho. It didn't help that I'm not even in control of my socks. They have been thieved, four pairs! I only have one holey pair.

*Me*: And how did you do being tolerant for half an hour?

*Robyn*: Completely ignored everything that was said to me. With ordinary kids, they pack it in but these kids carry on till they get a reaction. Or do things like nicking your things and throwing them at you. Then you get annoyed and twat them one. They tried to put me in a wheelie bin last night. I jumped out and ran off. Stayed out all night. Cut myself.

*Me*: How much do you feel in control of your life at the moment? [She pointed to 15 on the scale I had drawn.]

*Robyn*: Not very. That's my pet hate. People running things for me. The kids, staff, my social worker. She says my options are go home, medium-stay unit or foster placement. And back home won't work.

*Me*: Where would you like your next placement to be?

*Robyn*: Foster, if I can. I don't want to be stuck in a long-term home. I'm poised at the end of a spiral, if you know what I mean. I don't want to go down it. But I can't take the other kids. I put in a complaint but nowt'll happen.

Iveson (1990) says that when people repeatedly shout about their complaints, or complain in other ways we find difficult to hear, they are almost invariably people who are not being heard; to hear them we must accept their language. Not being heard, Robyn was 'shouting louder' but the adults in her life made meaning of her self-destructive and antisocial behaviour by entering her into a psychiatric story. This story bolsters the loudest voice of all – the professional voice that says that looked-after children are the most 'disturbed' of all children. This story comes from cultural stories of loving family life, therefore the entry of an out-of-control teenager to residential care positions the natural parents initially as failed parents. However, adults have a greater capacity to resist such storying of their lives and do so by presenting their child for parenting by the local authority in a very particular way; one which will absolve mothers, especially, of both blame and shame. It is in the interests of the continuing integrity of the family that the ejected child is storied as a failed child, deficient in some way as a family member.

Social workers may collude with this story to some extent and, believing that children's best interests are served by living in families, devise elaborate individual therapy plans for the children in which they can come to terms with their past trauma and by 'getting in touch with their feelings' will become capable of making and sustaining family relationships. This is premised largely on the story of secure attachment formation; albeit that a child in residential care will be living in a social situation that promotes avoidant attachment formation, there being no point in making relationships as these will be severed at the first sign of conflict. Should a child successfully negotiate the minefield of peer relationships in residential care and 'improve', that child is highly likely to be returned home or placed with foster parents. Both outcomes highlight the deficiencies of natural parents, repositioning them as failures because someone else has managed to parent their difficult child. Therefore it is in the ejecting family's interests that the looked-after child remains sufficiently 'disturbed', not only to continue to require specialist residential care but also fail to settle in care.

As Durrant (1993) commented, the expectation that the residential home will assume responsibility for 'fixing' the child while maintaining the cooperation and involvement of the natural parents is fraught with tension. For example, Robyn was not only 'failing' to cope with peer relationships in the home but she was also expected to welcome her parent's weekend visits. These invariably degenerated into bitter accusations, with all parties becoming distressed; Robyn then being held responsible for upsetting her parents. When she decided to stop seeing her parents altogether and requested a foster placement, her natural parents suddenly offered to have her back. Six weeks later, the situation broke down again and she was returned to care, saying bitterly, 'what really hurts is that they all [family, social worker] seem so pleased about it'. Her second period in care was accompanied by further episodes of self-harm, confirming her psychiatric label. She attempted to assert her individuality and gain some sense of control over her life by eating peculiar mixtures of food but this, too, was seen as further evidence of the psychiatric story. A professionals' meeting was convened – to which she was not invited – where it was decided that she was not only unfosterable but in need of secure accommodation. Robyn's small, responsible voice had been so effectively silenced that she came to believe that she was, indeed, a failed child. As such she has nothing to gain from behaving responsibly.

The experience of repeatedly being sent home to 'fail' confirms the 'story' of looked-after children as disturbed – but at the expense of damaging children's identities. It would benefit these identities if children's voices were privileged in child care planning so that they could demonstrate their capacity to develop responsibility taking for their choices and thus undermine the pathological story. Equally, this would save social workers a lot of time spent in unfruitful and expensive professionals' meetings, providing them with more time to spend on direct work with children.

## SUMMARY

- Research shows that direct work with children is often not done well because social workers ask questions, listen to answers, and interpret these within an individual dependency-led model which is influenced by adult, white, Eurocentric norms and assumptions.
- Adults concentrate most on the emotional effects of past trauma whereas children often describe their problems largely in terms of their present and future functioning. They particularly talk about the misery of current unsatisfactory peer relationships and parental conflict.
- Dismissing children's descriptions of their current miseries as displacement and denial trivialises children's concerns and undermines their solution-finding capacities. Adults do not always know what is best for children.
- Children do not necessarily need to address individual emotional events in order to move forward. Rather they prefer to gain control over their everyday lives so that they can address such events from a position of competence.
- Casting children as inherently vulnerable denies them both competence in devising their own solutions to their problems and underestimates their willingness to exercise responsibility and make sensible choices.
- Where adult voices are not in harmony, children's voices go unheard. Fragmentation of the parental voice is particularly likely in work with looked-after children, making it even more difficult for children to exercise responsibility and make choices.

# 8

# Community care: interdependence in adult services

We know that care management was conceived as the means for the effective implementation of community care; thus social service departments were given the responsibility for improving coordination of both social and health care and for recognising and supporting individual carers (Sheppard, 1995). The current 'story' of community care was influenced by New Right ideology, which perhaps had more to do with reducing the spiralling costs of residential care for an increasingly ageing population, but how do people view 'community' and what is its capacity for caring? Supporting carers is a high cost-effective strategy as social care agencies only need to put in small amounts of formal resources to ensure extensive inputs from the informal sector (Malin *et al.*, 1999), most of whom are women (see, for example, Aitken & Griffin, 1996; Orme, 1998).

Williams (1993), for example, examines what community means to women in terms of 'space' and 'place'. Where a community offers opportunities for interconnectedness and mutual support, 'space' can be created but community policies, largely determined by men, also represent a restricted sense of community: 'community becomes women's *place*, the place to which they are relegated and belong: a place that represents not so much a bridge from the private to the public, but an extension of the private' (Williams, 1993, p. 34). And these restrictions are compounded by unequal opportunities for women in communities in terms of access to political groups, transport, and leisure facilities; all of which can be hostile to women with restricted mobility, such as being unable to go out without being attached to a pram. Added to this is the reality that the environment of a community is often dangerous for women, especially where there are badly lit streets at night and secluded areas during the day; notwithstanding the potential of the home for domestic violence.

Within such communities, women do not necessarily volunteer to be carers or are supported and valued by their communities. Read (2000), for example, makes the point that mothers of disabled children are mothers on the margin. Being the mother of a socially excluded child brings some degree of secondary exclusion while mothering becomes more public as the child's upbringing becomes professionalised 'with mothers under pressure to do the "right" thing at the "right" time according to the professional edicts of the time – these experts frequently change their minds quite fundamentally within a relatively short period. Consequently they make contradictory appraisals and demands on mothers within the life span of one disabled child' (Read, 2000, p. 108). All of which makes the social work task of creating wider spaces for service users and offering choices more difficult.

## The process of becoming a carer

Ungerson's (1987) study of informal care raised questions about how women are entered into a story that views them as natural carers. Although she found many 'joyful carers', most were 'negotiated' into care; what most determined who became a carer was a person's strength to say 'no' to caring. She was intrigued by the invisibility of non-carers in families; what determined their strength to say 'no' and why families accepted their reasons as legitimate. The answers to these questions are even more elusive as the coordination of services under the National Health Service and Community Care Act 1990 has led to care recipients and caregivers being separated into distinct groupings rather than recognising commonalties of class, race, age and gender. Ironically, it is only children's services which use the title 'children *and* families' services, reflecting perhaps assumptions that work with children is more skilled and important than work with adults, which is often viewed as routine and straightforward (Braye & Preston Shoot, 1995). Thompson (1998) points out that social work with adults is extremely diverse. Carers are not homogeneous, having unique relationships, needs and resources (Malin *et al.*, 1999) but unfortunately the Carers (Recognition and Services) Act 1995 'fixes' people as carers without questioning this positioning; further rendering non-carers invisible.

While useful in terms of identifying community care as a largely adult female activity, feminist analyses ignore the position of other, less assertive family members. Children are often carers too and are 'negotiated' into care in much the same way as women. Young carers are almost twice as likely to be female; many live in a family headed by a lone parent who is usually a mother, reflecting the fact that disabled women are considerably more likely to be divorced or separated. For example, 53 per cent of young carers attending the Northorpe Hall Trust Scheme live in single-parent families. In two-parent families, where the care recipient is most likely to be a man, his wife provides the bulk of the caring – even where she is working. Also young carers are as likely to young children as teenagers, the mean age being twelve (for an overview, see Blyth & Milner, 1997, Chapter 6). Although there are many 'joyful' young carers, like women carers, they lead 'double' lives with responsibilities at home and school/work. Where the 'invisible' non-carer is also an abuser, young carers' vulnerabilities are particularly acute.

As a seemingly mature teenager, Jackie was recognised by her family's social worker as the person most likely to provide responsible care for her wheelchair-bound mother and younger sister; especially as her alcoholic father had recently left home. Care management consisted of a package that provided some domestic help in the home and Jackie was enrolled at a young carers' scheme to give her some respite; a seemingly inexpensive and appropriate solution. The assumptions underlying this were that Jackie was a 'natural' carer on the grounds of her gender and age. The process by which she had been 'negotiated' into care was not questioned although it later emerged when Jackie turned up drunk at the young carers' scheme that her father had been violent towards her mother for many years. In attempting to defend her mother, Jackie had been beaten up in turn. As her mother was unable to protect her, Jackie attempted to hide her father's increasingly violent behaviour towards her. Barely able to stand up, her cardigan hanging off her shoulders, and reeking of cider, Jackie expressed her bewilderment at her predicament:

> You see, he had to beat me. He doesn't remember because he drank a lot, so I tried that. Not to get addicted, just to forget. It worked for five minutes and then I felt awful. I wanted to forget the flashbacks and nightmares. One night he came back from the pub, he smashed my face against the wall. There was blood all down the wall. I was whimpering on the floor like a puppy and he said, 'look at that mess you've made on the wall. Clean it up.' The next day, my face was all swollen and he put his hand on my face and he said, 'Oh my poor baby, what have you done? How did you get like that?' He took me to the hospital and he was being so nice. You see, he gets drunk and then he can't remember. What I want to know is, why? Not why me. I'm glad I got it and not my mum. Why did he do it? If he tells me why, I'd know it wasn't my fault. Maybe it is my fault? I've been giving

myself some reasons. Mum says there no reason... Wrong place, wrong time... He's not hitting me now, 'cos he's moved out. I saw him yesterday and he said he's coming round to see [younger sister]. I can't stop him. I can't stop her having a relationship with her dad. She likes him, she never saw him hitting. My mum had the locks changed but he says [younger sister] will tell him where we keep the key. When I saw him, it all came straight back, feeling the panic but he wasn't doing anything. I had a flashback because I actually felt it, physically... The nightmares are more emotional pain, not physical.

Jackie's situation demonstrates the complexities of caring and being cared for, and the problems inherent in constructing care management on the basis of discrete categories of service users. Whether she is storied as a victim of child abuse, an out-of-control teenager, or a caring daughter and sister, these stories all ignore the reality that it was an adult male who not only failed to provide care but also abused his family. Yet he remained invisible apart from the fact that caring is constructed around adult men as the norm; Doyal (1995) points out that even medical research is based on male samples and that treatments tested on men are given to women. As society is ruled by adults, particularly adult men, age and ageism affect both children and older people (Hearn, 1995). This means that all those who are not able-bodied men are cast as either vulnerable and needing care or competent and able to provide care. In reality they are often both.

For example, Tim's mother had many coping strategies for her panic attacks but found it difficult to operationalise them as she was determined to keep the attacks hidden from her children, who she viewed as vulnerable. Once she felt able to discuss this problem with her children, she was surprised at their competence:

I had to laugh. Tim sat me down for a serious chat and he asked me what was my biggest wish. I told him, having a happy family and all that, but he kept asking me for more. Then he said I hadn't mentioned panic attacks at all so they can't be all that serious. I should be firm with them, like he was about the school thing. He said grown-ups are a bit funny, they think they know everything so kids have to guide them a bit. Let them think they thought of it themselves. As panic attacks don't do you any harm, why waste your time worrying? He says what else can you expect from grown-ups, they always look for a deep explanation or a cure but looking wastes years. Just put up with them. He knows lots of mums who don't have panic attacks but he prefers me as I am ... Then Melissa chipped in: look after yourself and get on with life. Every magazine you pick up is full of panic attacks and how to cure them. People will come up with a cure for breathing soon and then you'll be looking for an explanation for breathing attacks. You'll be saying, 'Oh dear, why am I breathing? What can be done about it?'... Kids put a different emphasis on them. It's like the whole family owns the panic attacks and rallies round. Thinking I can give in to them means they don't build up so much. I feel quite cheated, really. I'm all geared up to enjoy one and I haven't had one at all.

I was struck not only with the fact that Tim and Melissa were much more effective in helping their mum than I had been but also by the invisibility of their father in all this. The family spoke very warmly of him but he seemed to play no prominent part in the caring process. The invisibility of male non-carers means that we do sometimes forget to ask male carers what caring means for them. Ungerson (1987), for example, asks what are the implications of the feminisation of caring on men: do men feel emasculated by caring and how do they feel about caring for women? Kenneth, for example, had been attending both group and individual person-centred counselling sessions for coming to terms with the deaths of his widowed mother and, later, his partner – both of whom he provided with intimate care over long periods. A year into counselling, Kenneth was disappointed that he didn't feel any better. This was hardly surprising as assumptions had been made about the nature of his problem, storying him as a feminised elderly man (on account of both his sexuality and history of caring) who had lost his purpose in life (a feminised version of the empty-nest syndrome). He explained that he was not grieving the loss of his mother and partner in terms of no longer having anyone to care for but in terms of a loss of interdependency; his balanced sense of his own vulnerability and competence: 'I propped them up physically but they propped me up emotionally.'

Community care is, therefore, not simply about some people caring and other people being cared for; of some people being competent and others dependent; it is about family relationships in which the weaker members, particularly, are interconnected and interdependent. To be more effective, community care needs to recognise this complexity but hold a common theme at the same time. Thompson (1998) sugests that this common theme is one of an adulthood in which people are empowered, supported constructively in their efforts to retain as much control as possible over their lives, and to enjoy a quality of life free from distress, disadvantage and oppression.

## Older people and disability

Older women are more likely than men to be marginalised in society which has an increasingly ageing population, a high proportion being women; many of whom live on their own and are mostly cared for by women who are coming into the young elderly age group themselves. They are more likely to be financially abused than men; compounding impoverishment due to lifelong economic disadvantage and the experience of having private lives only (Aitken & Griffin, 1996). However, this is not to say that older men retain their previous dominance as they lose power to younger men and are marginalised in that old age *per se* is feminised in society.

Although old people find old age to be a better experience than anticipated (for an overview, see O'Leary, 1996), they tend to be homogenized as automatically 'old', ill and deteriorating, inflexible, miserable, unproductive and dependent. Thus they are entered into a story which not only casts them as vulnerable and incompetent but also views them 'as an insidious menace threatening to overwhelm the rest of the population both in sheer numbers and in terms of the "drain" they are on resources' (Aitken & Griffin, 1996). In this sense they are seen as more 'dangerous' than children as a category; the latter having at least the potential to increase their autonomy and, perhaps, the vigour to protest. To be viewed as increasingly incompetent has serious implications for the delivery of services to older people as it not only denies the reality that what they have survived and achieved means that older people have many strengths but it also reduces their choices: 'Thinking, choosing and exercising that choice are three of the fundamental characteristics of being a human being ... once we treat someone as not having these qualities, we treat them as less than human' (Iveson, 1990, p. 82).

Both in their late seventies, Bill had been caring for Florence over a three-year period which saw her become increasingly dependent following a series of strokes and the onset of Parkinson's disease. Bill then suffered a heart attack and was admitted to hospital, only to cut his stay short when he heard that Florence was about to be admitted to a home. The community care manager provided a package of domiciliary and respite care which met the couple's needs until Florence was admitted to hospital after breaking her hip in a fall. As her mobility was then seriously restricted, the community care manager, concerned about Bill's health, again suggested that Florence be admitted to residential care. Bill strongly resisted this plan:

> She's [community care manager] always asking me how I'm coping but that's just to get her in a home. I do it [caring] 'cos I want to.

I do get tired but if she's at home, I won't be trotting up here every day. I still hurry home from the shops, I look in the room for her – even though I know she's in here … I can read her. If she gets unsettled, I know what she wants. I know what questions to ask her. Anyone else wouldn't realise this. She lets me know when she's had too much company. She still recognises her family, there's something there. When her sister comes, she talks a lot about nothing, and Florence closes her eyes. [Her] sister says, 'it's no good my coming, she's always asleep'. She thinks she should be in a home but she opens her eyes after she's gone. She's bored with her … but I can't tell her that.

He has also developed new skills during the previous period of caring (a counter-story to the 'deteriorating' story of his frail health). He has learned how to lift Florence without too much strain and how she can help him lift her; has managed her incontinence and is well equipped for accidents; has bought a microwave to ensure that he gets hot food even if his meal is disrupted by Florence having a shaking attack while he feeds her (he likes them to eat together); and has located a nurse at the respite care home whose advice and support be seeks with particular problems. The hospital nursing staff also have a great deal of respect for his caring abilities during visiting. The problem with the agency risk assessment form was that it only distinguised between independence and dependence. Thus it tended to reveal deficiencies; there being no space for competencies, interconnectedness or preferred choices. As Bill said:

If she's with me, I'm content. Looking after her is my pleasure. She's not an old boot to be thrown away. We've been married a long time. I was sixteen when we met, wasn't my seventeenth birthday for a week. I asked her friend how old she was and she said seventeen. I hoped and hoped she wouldn't ask me how old I was for another week. Young folk now, they'd think I was daft but we've been all right together. You see, it's one-to-one when she's with me. She wouldn't get that in a home. I can get some sense out of her. I'd like to have a go at having her home. [I offered to set things in motion.] I was going to see my doctor tonight about some sleeping tablets. I won't need to do that now, I've got something to look forward to. I miss her when she's not there.

Over one-third of the carers of severely disabled elderly women are men; mostly caring for spouses whom they have lived with most of their lives. Bill was a typical example of this group, whose main motivating factor is love (Arber & Gilbert, 1993), and who are slightly more likely to get additional support from formal services than other carers. Florence eventually returned home with support and the hospital bed was retained for a short period in case Bill could not cope. He also identified supportive people in his community network with whom he could talk honestly about any difficulties, despite his confidence in his abilities: 'My health's all right now, I haven't got to see the doctor again ... I know I'm not young but it's amazing what you can do when you want to.' He managed much better than anticipated, so perhaps Florence was motivated to 'help' him more when she was at home?

## Making choices about residential care

Being admitted to hospital for a second or third time as a result of increasing frailty often tips the balance in favour of a decision to admit a person to residential care; particularly when agency risk assessment checklists reveal a long list of self-care activities which the person is unable to perform. Braye and Preston-Shoot (1995) refer to this as incremental and reactive assessment so that admission to residential care becomes based on whim, chance and absence of choice (Sinclair *et al.*, 1998; Bywaters, 1991). Social workers at St James's University Hospital consider it important not to rush into arranging residential care before assessing both the service user's and carer's motivation to remain in the community. Much depends on the service user's feelings about themselves as a person with the determination to get home rather than as a patient entered into a story of dependence and the team (social worker, occupational therapist and physiotherapist) arrange home visits so that the person can join genuinely with them in an assessment of their coping abilities and plans for the future; what Thompson (1998) refers to as two-way helping to create the shared power of mutual definition.

For some people, a home visit reveals the need for a rethink of the original strategy; for example, more physiotherapy may be needed to optimise mobility or domiciliary care may need to be organised more flexibly. The team is prepared to arrange as many as three home visits before a final decision is made. This may seem an expensive use of scarce hospital and social work resources, but it pays off in terms of longer-term successful solutions. Where a service user eventually goes home, that person is appropriately supported and resources are most efficiently deployed. Neither are they wasted where they would be ineffective; failed home visits being also productive in that the service user makes the decision that remaining at home is not a viable option. It also serves as a ritual from which the mourning process for the loss of home can begin, enabling the person to begin planning for admission to residential care in a more positive manner, even though it is usually a second choice. For example, if Bill finds that he cannot cope, he has at least been given the opportunity to attempt his preferred solution. Having made the decision for themselves, service users can develop a sense of themselves as part of a residential community and exercise choice about the sort of home which will meet their future needs.

Where an elderly person also appears confused and, unlike Florence, has no partner who can 'read' her or speak for her, it is even more difficult to ensure that she is able to make choices. Iveson (1990) suggests that it can be helpful to reframe what seems like confusion as indecision about major changes in later life but Mrs Brown was perhaps a little too decisive about giving up her own home for residential care. When seen at her bedside in hospital, where she had been admitted after a fall, she had difficulty in remembering where she lived, where she was currently, and who had been to see her. For example, when I asked if I could sit on her bed while we talked, she was unsure whose bed it was. Although some memories were dim, the gaps did not divide easily into long- or short-term ones and it was possible that her 'confusion' was exacerbated by a long period of self-neglect when she had refused help and, perhaps, some underlying sadness as she made several comments about having 'lived long enough'. Asking her scaled and miracle questions only confused her further.

The hospital social workers find that a more discursive, narrative approach which aims to untangle 'confusion' is useful here, beginning a conversation which explores the different components of 'confusion'; such as forgetfulness, muddle, sadness and, possibly, weariness resulting from a pre-hospital period of struggle and difficulty with everyday living. The conversation also searches for exceptions to 'confusion' and attempts to work out what expectations the person has for the future and what is needed to help them keep going and overcome weariness. Detailed questions may be asked if the person is well enough to expand on their situation, but these are not just about gathering information. Rather they aim to get a feel of how a seemingly confused elderly person sees herself and whether her perception matches the presentation of herself to both ward and multidisciplinary team members.

After several conversations with Mrs Brown in hospital, it emerged that she did want a residential placement where she would not have to worry about cooking and managing her money. What continued to be important to her was the type and location of the residential home which she hoped would be lively, with friendly residents, and near enough to her old home so that she could resume social activities at her church as soon as her mobility improved and her pain eased. Pain, she said, caused her to worry more and this had probably prevented her from maintaining her links with the community in which she had lived most of her life and which centred on her local church. A visit was arranged so that Mrs Brown could spend some time in the home selected as most meeting her expressed needs and she became much more animated and less muddled as she left hospital and recognised familiar surroundings; even her mobility improved and it was easier to get her out of the wheelchair at the home than it had been to get her into it at the hospital.

The visit proved tiring for Mrs Brown, who greeted me on my arrival to collect her with a heartfelt 'Oh, I am glad you've come. I know you, don't I? I don't know where I am.' She was much more muddled on the return journey which took her past her old home; she thought someone else was living there, she had forgotten which of her two first names her husband had called her by, and she was unsure why she was going back to hospital – although she was keen to get to bed. Before visiting her on the ward next day, I wrote out a short account of our trip for her. I had given her notes of our conversations previously but she had immediately mislaid these and I wondered if she could make use of these notes as she was more muddled than earlier; confessing to no memory at all of her outing. How, then, could I ascertain her wishes about her future? I asked her to read the notes and then began a conversation about the outing. She replied with what seemed an incoherent account of talking to some women she didn't know about having their hair done and, at first, she seemed to talking about old memories. Looking at the notes again, she then said, 'I don't think I know them ... but if they can have their hair done, it must be a nice place. I think I'll be all right there. I can't remember their names ... but they were friendly.' After a period of rest in hospital, she was admitted to the home and settled in easily; she remained muddled about many things but had her hair permed immediately and was clearly enjoying the company of the other residents.

[Mrs Brown's interests lay more clearly in her own immediate situation and I hesitated to bore her too much with my need to check at length how freely she was giving me permission to use her story. If any reader has experience of how to ensure that such informed consent can be ensured in instances of muddle and forgetfulness, I would like to hear from them.]

Adopting a narrative approach with service users in hospital is made more difficult when they are storied as patients rather than persons.

People who are dependent on surgical expertise for their very lives have a vested interest in submitting to treatments which demand a high degree of compliance, even though chronically disabled people particularly need more assertiveness than most to cope with independent living (Lonsdale, 1990). Thompson (1998) says that the power vested in members of the medical profession is problematic as they do not necessarily have the appropriate training or expertise for dealing with complex psychological processes and the sociopolitical context in which they occur. The hospital social work context is particularly difficult in that is frequently an extreme example of gendered divisions, with the medical staff being mostly young males; the nursing staff mostly young females; and the social workers mostly rather older women. In picking up the emotional and social fallout from surgical stories, the social worker runs the risk of being storied as a sort of 'den mother' to both patients and staff.

Brook (1997) has developed a framework which enables children seriously ill with liver disease, many of whom will be offered transplantation, to participate actively in decision making about their treatment. This framework is based on the principles of talking *with* children not *to* them, sharing rather than giving information, privacy, time, and the development of a partnership based on honesty and respect. A vital part of this process is, she maintains, a whole-team belief in the ability and rights of children to contribute to decisions about treatment. Although children's competence to make decisions about treatment may be open to debate, adult competence, too, is often obscured by an illness story.

## Questioning psychiatric discourses

The application of solution-focused approaches to people with mental health problems has a long history; one of de Shazer's most cited examples being of a man who reported that he was always depressed (de Shazer *et al.*, 1986). Exceptions to the depression were found by asking him how he knew he was depressed if his state was unvarying; to which, of course, he answered that he knew he was depressed because he had 'up days'. Although it is usually possible to identify many exceptions to depression, I have found that people have difficulty in gaining control of their thoughts about the depression unless the 'voices' which induce the misery in the first place, and then others which 'diagnose' it as within the person, are undermined. Carol, for example, referred herself for help with understanding her depression. She reported that she got depressed for no reason at all and that her doctor prescribed Prozac on the grounds that her depression must be due to a chemical disorder of her brain.

He also told her that she would have to take Prozac all her life, a future which so alarmed her that she promptly stopped taking it. She was anxious to have a reason for her 'depression':

> It's like things are pulling on my hair, it's real. I get really angry, just wanting to clench my fists. The slightest thing, I'll burst into tears. It just sends me into despair. It seems so selfish. As though someone is poking at me, telling me I'm useless. And then I think, what do people think about me? Being a bum like my dad, my mum says. I will end up like my dad. A lot of panic and paranoia about that, it feeds on itself. I've been with my boyfriend for a year and a half and he's been through it before. He says it's not as bad as last time but it is getting as bad. It's like I'm possessed for some reason. I'll question why I'm feeling good. Like I'm monitoring myself all the time.

Carol's self-monitoring of her good days prevented her from building on her exceptions to what seemed a very miserable home life where she was constantly denigrated. She would need to be financially dependent on her family for another year and could not escape from a feeling that she was 'possessed' by the voices of her family; and the voice of her doctor, who told her the depression was in her brain:

> I didn't feel like crying, just six days … there was nothing to cry about. I don't feel six days not crying is much strength. More like six months. It's self-pity, that's all it is. Little things come into my head and bring me sadness … like I've dropped down a hole. All these things come from nowhere and push me in.

Carol's voices were critical and disqualifying, what White (1995, p. 127) refers to as rating highly on expectations of people and low on acknowledgement; and her doctor's diagnosis merely served to confirm her family's and her own low opinion of herself. If Carol had wanted to opt out of responsibility in her life, the psychiatric label would have been quite useful. It is, after all, one of the few ways in which over-stressed women can 'negotiate' themselves out of caring. The problem with psychiatric labels is that their benefits are gained at the expense of being declared mentally incompetent. White (1995) maintains that psychotic experience, particularly, rules people out of contention in the stakes of personhood as they are constructed as objects of psychiatric knowledge. Resistance to this story then becomes problematic as it is 'interpreted' as further evidence of the diagnosis (Epston, 1998, p. 129). They suggest that it is more helpful to question the purposes and motives of the 'voices'; whether these are actual auditory hallucinations or the more generalised voices of psychiatric expertise; for example:

- Are these voices for you having your own opinion or are they against you?
- These voices throw you into confusion. Whose interests are best served by this confusion?
- What is it like for the voices to have to listen to your thoughts for a change?
- What is it like for them to know that you are developing a disrespect and mistrust of them?

Using this approach with Carol proved to be the turning point; enabling her to use her existing competences – artistic skills – to undermine the disqualifying voices of her family and doctor. She literally painted her way out of misery and into hope and happiness. Work with Richard and Chrissy was to prove much more scary. Richard sought help with coming off heroin after two previous failed attempts. The first two sessions were encouraging but my heart sank as I saw him waiting for me on the third occasion. He was huddled in a chair with his head in his hands, looking scruffy and unkempt, and sweating profusely. As we sat down for the session, he began a long complaint about his life, not all of which I managed to record but it was all about despair:

*Richard*: I might as well tell you, I wasn't going to come to this. I don't know why I'm here really. I'm getting nowhere. There's more pressures. I feel like a grain of sand that's being pushed around. Every time television comes on, it's all Christmas things. It's doing my head in. I'm no better now than I was before. I have an all-right week when I get my Giro and then the next, well, I did a bottle of diazepam, drank a bottle of whisky and took all my methadone. My tolerance must be really high ... Heroin takes the pain away, makes me feel nice and warm ... I've not done it apart from three times. I just think, I can't cope with it. My little lad, he's eight years old. Christmas is coming up and I can't even cope with myself. He will be expecting to see me. He'll bring me something. I haven't been thieving for so long, not even a chocolate egg, but I'm going backwards. I can't survive ... I tried to get a job but I was knackered that night, I was sweating like I'd just come out of the bath, that's when I did the heroin. My friend's up for six years. And for four to five today, so he'll have to do the full six years. I don't know, I see myself doing something like that, doing a post office. Talk about non-support from my family. [this goes on for some considerable time]
*Me*: But you came here today ...
*Richard*: Yes. But the longer it goes on, the worse it is. I could really relapse.

*Me*: On one of my scales ...

*Richard*: [interrupting] Yeah, the one to ten thing. What's this one for? [leans over my paper and points to ten] There. No. Not likely to relapse. Top myself. Not tablets, hang myself. My flat has a wonderful drop. I've bottled that idea in the past ... It's got to be better than this twenty-four hours, seven days torture.

*Me*: How would being dead be better?

*Richard*: I don't think there's life after death. I'd have had a glimpse of my mother. When you're dead, you're dead. I'd be better off without this torture.

*Me*: There could be life after death and it might be full of heroin .... [he shakes his head] If you could speak to your mother, what would she say?

*Richard*: I don't think about that. I wouldn't have had these problems if she'd lived. [prompt] I would have had more opportunities.

*Me*: If she could speak to you, what would she say?

*Richard*: She'd say, come up here. I'll sort you out.

*Me*: If she said, I can't sort you out, what would she say would be your first step to doing it yourself?

*Richard*: I've a big addiction. You wouldn't believe how much I could take and it didn't really affect me. Some people do a £10 bag. That's nothing.

*Me*: But you only did heroin three times in a fortnight. How did you do that?

*Richard*: But I keep falling back and getting further and further into myself. And I'm still taking methadone. I don't feel particularly brilliant on methadone. [I continued searching for exceptions and he continued to talk about suicide] I don't mean to be rude but I've been through this a million times. Always back to the same reference point. I'm miserable. I'm cutting out heroin but it's worse. I've tried all sorts.

*Me*: What haven't you tried?

*Richard*: Hanging myself.

*Me*: What else?

*Richard*: I can't think. I've got no energy. This'll be the last time I come. You've been polite and listened to me but you can't relate to my life in your head. It's only an hour and when I'm back in my world, it's ten times worse.

*Me*: I've not been very helpful for you ...

*Richard*: You've done more than most.

*Me*: That's not good enough. How can I be more helpful?

*Richard*: This is me, not you.

*Me*: How could you be more helpful to yourself?

*Richard*: Putting myself out of my misery.

*Me*: That's one thing, what's another one?
*Richard*: I haven't got one.
*Me*: Are they all hard?
*Richard*: Impossible.

We continued for a while but he persisted with the suicide idea. After he had left, I wondered whether to inform his doctor and arrange for psychiatric treatment but he had 'been there, done that', and not found it helpful. I also hypothesised that he did not have the energy to kill himself. I still worried a great deal, as he was living alone in miserable surroundings, so I thought carefully about the notes I posted to him as I knew from his earlier comments that he read them over and over. In these I included an afterthought:

> I have been puzzling about how Richard can get his energy up so that he can use his survival skills and abilities and I remembered a young woman who came off heroin really easily but then couldn't do anything for two years. We all wasted a lot of time and energy trying to persuade her to get on with her life and got frustrated when she made no effort. Then it all came good for her – she did a back-to-work placement, which she enjoyed and then went to college. She is doing fine now. I wonder if it just that the post-detox period is one where the person needs to be sad and miserable and mourn for all the lost things, and that it simply takes ages for the energy to come back. Maybe Richard is handling it in exactly the right way and this period of misery just has to be lived through? It seems hard to me – and frustrating that there is so little other people can do to help reduce that misery. Does Richard know of any people who have turned their lives round after heroin? Maybe they might have more ideas about how long this utter misery will last? Richard does not want another appointment but I will keep [date and time] free for him, in case he changes his mind. He can ring and cancel it if necessary.

Richard kept the appointment and was full of plans for his future. He had consulted with people who had got heroin out of their lives and they all told him that if he had a job he wouldn't spend hard-earned money on heroin. To get a job, he had arranged a further period of supported detoxification (mainly so that he would not be alone in his flat over the Christmas period); stopped taking his methadone (as this stays in the system longer than heroin and makes detox harder); taken small amounts of heroin (smoked not injected) to make the week before detox bearable; and obtained details of a return-to-work programme. Ten weeks on he was busy redecorating his flat, had become houseproud, learning to shop and cook, enrolled on the return-to-work programme, become reconciled with his father, and begun having his son to stay at weekends. I have no idea whether or not the notes had any influence on Richard's thinking as I didn't ask but I was highly relieved, as well as delighted, to see his successes.

Chrissy was referred by her employer after an unspecified crisis at work. She told me that she was having difficulties at work and wanted 'to get things sorted out' before going abroad with her partner. I struggled to make sense of Chrissy's story, which was rambling, with abrupt changes of topic and full of one-off statements such as 'I've been struggling with myself; I've come to a block; I'm rebelling against myself; I find it difficult to have an ending'; none of which she could elaborate on at all. She hinted at some sort of breakdown at work but, apart from feeling vaguely unsupported and lacking organisational skills, she did not seem capable of either giving detail or what I could recognise as an emotional response. Conscious on my part that here was someone in the early stages of schizophrenia, I made a deliberate effort not to pathologise her, becoming more puzzled as a means of helping her explain herself to me. This was not productive so I ended the session by saying that she was an interesting enigma to me and that I would need to think about her some more. I also suggested an experiment to help her get through her last few weeks at work: to borrow from a life she admired and pretend to be that person on days when the coin toss came up tails; have a normal day when the coin came up heads.

I felt most uneasy after the session. All my previous training indicated that I was possibly dealing with someone in the early stages of a major mental illness. Should I refer her to a psychiatrist, especially as she was due to leave the country shortly and would be in an extremely vulnerable position? I discussed the situation with my line manager and supervisor and was encouraged to have at least one more session with her. The main reason I could go along with this was my conviction that the traditional treatments available locally might keep her safe but would involve psychotropic drugs which would not help her develop a sense of reality about herself.

Writing up my notes proved difficult; after I edited out all questions and answers that did not lead to a useful narrative line, there was nothing left at all! After much thought, I took what few *words* were useful for constructing a scenario with as much hope for the future as possible; for example, as part of the 'problem' section I wrote:

At the moment Chrissy lacks confidence in her ability at work and home; this is affecting her health, motivation and thoughts – which tend to be negative. Chrissy has experienced a good deal of well-meant, but confidence-sapping, criticism in her life. She is a sensitive person who does not shrug off criticism easily. Although she has no idea what she will be like in the future, she does know that she will be more balanced. Chrissy values peace more than ambition.

Under 'thoughts on solutions', I included:

> Chrissy is a very interesting person who can cope with her own company. She may just not be a management person – I see her as more footloose and fancy-free, probably very creative and relaxed in these circumstances. My only criticism of Chrissy's coping strategies to date is that they have focused more on what she is doing wrong; not enough on what she can do well and what she *wants* to do. This is bound to get in the way of being 'balanced'.

A fortnight later, Chrissy reported several successes at work and was able to discuss her emotional responses. Again I sent her a copy of the session notes; carefully phrased in tentative language and identifying more potential. She cancelled the third session on the grounds that she was too busy wrapping up work before leaving for her trip abroad. Two days later, her employer called in to say that she was 'a new person'. I am not sure what sort of person that is but I am glad that I did not refer her to traditional mental health services. Questioning traditional psychiatry is not just something I do to help women restory their lives, it is a way of questioning my own thinking. My thoughts on Chrissy's possible schizophrenia had more to do with keeping me safe than Chrissy:

> Therapeutic interaction is a two-way phenomenon. We get together with people for a period of time over a range of issues, and all our lives are changed for this. On some occasions these therapeutic interactions change our lives more significantly than on other occasions ... In being privy to the performance of this radical responsibility for choices in life, we cannot be so resigned to the 'received' versions of our own lives. (White, 1995, p. 8)

Once I was able to get out of my 'received' version of schizophrenia, I began to be able to recognise the person inside the label and how that label pushed the person further inside themselves. For example, Lorna's behaviour had become increasingly strange:

> My son thinks I'm strange. He says, 'please, please don't embarrass me'. My husband says I come out with strange things ... wear

strange things. He says I look like a witch. Martin says 'well, you know how you are, Mum'. He's stopped bringing his friends home now. Linda's the same, says I'm not like other mums ... I find people difficult to deal with. You give them an inch and they take a mile. I don't want to be bothered with friends any more. I just don't understand people, that's why I don't want to be near them.

Her not being 'near them', consisted of staying in bed at weekends, eating takeaways she had ordered by phone. During the week she sent her children shopping and stayed in the house: 'I say I'm decorating but nothing gets done.'

Rather than presuming that she is strange, or mentally ill, and her family 'normal', we talked more about how she feels alienated from (conventional) people in a small village. I suggested that she might be a beautiful cuckoo in a village full of sparrows and that maybe she should allow herself one cuckoo day each week to balance the sparrow days her family want so that she can avoid being mobbed and see what personality suits her best. Giving her permission to be herself, however strange (even though my 'old' knowledge still makes me alarmed about her withdrawal from life), was obviously important to her; she commented that it is 'a relief to be understood'. To my surprise, she reported at the next session that she had resisted definitions of her strange behaviour: 'I made a determined effort to dress how I wanted. It didn't go down well. A couple of friends said, "oh, you look awful". I had no make-up and some trainers with paint on them. I found it quite amusing. I dressed up for a Hallowe'en party with dark eye make-up and black nail varnish. I got compliments.' She was still not sure who she is or what she will be like but agreed to continue with her 'experiments'.

At the third session Lorna was animated (and wearing a brand new 'classical' sweater). She reported that she 'is getting there'. She had started shopping again at quiet times, volunteered to help out at school one day a week, and signed on at a local college for pottery classes: 'I can find my way about the place now. I'm really pleased with myself ... I found out with [husband]'s friends, it's play, it's role acting. They've become more friendly ... if you're humorous, friendly, it goes a long way. It's not me but it's been quite good. We've been out a bit.' Lorna was still not sure who she was but she enjoyed finding out so much that she was no longer spending long periods avoiding people and her family were finding her less 'strange'.

Chrissy and Lorna, perhaps more than anyone, have taught me to distrust my 'expert' knowledge. Beresford and Croft (1993) suggest that the knowledge of service users, what they refer to as 'citizen involvement', is preferable to 'participation', which locates service users in terms of the services they use rather than the services they want. Indeed, it is likely that both services and community would need to change and adapt to accommodate everyone's 'personhood': 'We can make it our business to work collaboratively with people in identifying those ways of speaking about their lives that contribute to a sense of personal agency, and that contribute to the experience of being an authority on one's own life' (White, 1995, p. 122).

Making a distinction between caregiving and care receiving, vulnerability and productiveness, normality and abnormality, leads to a patronising 'rights' stance which ignores the interconnectedness of most people's lives and how their competencies can be discovered and utilised. Placing responsibility for community care management in social rather than health services is vital here. As long as social work is concerned primarily with context and community, and remains centred around complex relationships, it has the capacity to recognise the diverse experience of all service users and 'transform policy, practice and the organisation of service delivery which constrains people in gender-specific roles or oppresses them by the inappropriate exercise of power' (Orme, 1998).

### SUMMARY

- The notion of community care ignores the reality that women and children are more likely to be negotiated into caring than men.
- Community care is not simply about some people caring and some others being cared for, of some people being competent and others dependent. It is about family relationships in which members are interconnected and interdependent.
- Viewing older people as increasingly incompetent ignores their competencies and reduces their choices. Even muddled older people are capable of participating in decisions about residential care.
- Psychiatric narratives disqualify personal narratives, deny personhood, and diminish people's problem-solving capacities.
- Narrative approaches to people troubled by hearing voices focus on the critical and disqualifying elements of the voices, encouraging the person to question the purposes of the voices.
- Recognising the interconnectedness of people's lives enables social workers to discover and utilise people's competencies.

# 9

# Serious gossip as method

When I talk social workers about solution-focused and narrative approaches to social work, they often protest that it can't be that easy; surely people cannot solve long-standing problems or recover from extreme trauma so quickly? I usually say that it is simple but not particularly easy. Recognising the uniqueness of each individual's life experiences, abilities and solutions means that there can be no short cuts through the use of categorisations and diagnoses. There can never be a sense of having 'been here before' and this means that the approach cannot be adopted half-heartedly. It demands complete concentration on what is being said and a constant search for each service user's unique way of cooperating and possible solutions. Both can seem frustratingly elusive at times. It seems hardest when people have no vision of what a happier future would look like. People who have been abused from a very early age often have no experience of joy at all and some young men, particularly, find that giving up violence or addiction leaves them with a very bleak future as they have not developed any qualities to offer the world. The smallest and oddest of things become important in these instances – if any reader has any ideas about how shoplifting skills can be transferred to more socially acceptable situations, I would be delighted to hear from them. It is also hard where people are unable to say 'how they did that' as you are left worrying about whether or not the counterplot has been thickened sufficiently; although follow-up checks have not proved this to be an issue.

It is definitely not easy as long as social workers cling to their own explanations about the nature of people and retain the role of expert in problem solving. Being an expert leads to talk about boundaries and it then becomes difficult for service users to challenge these boundaries without being storied as difficult and resistant. Davis and Ellis (1995), for example, found that where social workers were responsible for allocating scarce resources, they labelled people who appeared knowledgeable about their entitlements as 'demanding' and those who tried to exercise choice or challenge workers' judgements as 'fussy' or 'manipulative'. These rationalisations are not available to the solution-focused or narrative worker, who has to take responsibility for not having discovered the service user's unique way of cooperating.

Furman and Ahola (1992) suggest that resistance can be more aptly described as 'discontent with the agenda' but experts resist changes to their agenda. The solution-focused or narrative social worker who is influential in assisting service users to take responsibility for their own life inevitably increases the number of service users who are more politicised; who will question the agenda. This too can be seen as an assault on professional boundaries and may be restoried as social worker transference or unprofessionalism. Most of all, the establishment and defence of expert boundaries limits social workers and their service users to the expectations and knowledge of the social worker. With a stressed, burnt-out social worker these expectations can be very low indeed. For any of us, our knowledge is always a limiting factor. I find that I am so often wrong about people; my gloomy hypotheses (they will persist in popping unasked into my mind) are fortunately mostly proved to be completely inaccurate.

Through really listening to people, I have also found that the major themes of their lives are rarely those most frequently cited in textbooks. For example, friendship often turns out to be more central to recovery than family; having a supportive friend who laughs as well as sympathises, being able to accept the limitations of purely 'social' friends, and acknowledging the very real misery of unrequited love. I have also learned that service users are talented, creative and incredibly resourceful when provided with the opportunity to concentrate on their successes rather than their failings. Dolan (1998b) asserts that an unwavering belief in service users' capacities has not only to be held but also consistently and implicitly communicated.

Another frequent question is 'does it really work?', with social workers suspecting that the effects are superficial and the questions mechanical and patronising. In its emphasis on a problem-free future, the approach does not ignore past events and emotions. Simply, the service user sets the agenda in terms of subjects discussed and goals chosen and these do not necessarily coincide with social worker's ideas of what are important. The social worker asks questions patiently and persistently to reveal competence and encourage reasonable responsibility taking. Providing written feedback is an important element as change occurs between sessions and service users report that they find this aid to reflection on their capabilities and preferred solutions very helpful. Written feedback also greatly reduces the number of sessions needed – and the possibility of misunderstandings and conflict. How well 'it works' can only be evaluated through the satisfaction service users express about their solutions. For example, a colleague returned delightedly from one session of solution-focused brief therapy saying: 'I came out of that session intact, whole. I went back to work after, felt positive. I thought, there's a solution out of this. Counselling can be painless! When I had counselling before, it was like an operation without an anaesthetic. That helped but I was only a survivor, someone clinging on to wreckage.'

An overview of the evaluation research can be found in Parton & O'Byrne (2000). The examples in this book provide only limited information about how well it works as they represent only the more straightforward problems I encounter. The more complex situations are too distinctive to be included, particularly some hospital and prison examples, and the people who opt not to continue sessions, approximately 2 per cent of all referrals, have not given me permission to include their stories. However, in terms of consumer feedback, service users tell me not only when it works but also often let me know when I am getting it wrong, giving me another opportunity. I also know that it works for me, both on a personal and work level. The basic philosophy is a good one for living as well as helping other people restory their lives.

I still wonder a little what to call the way I work; a combined solution-focused/narrative approach is a bit of a mouthful and rather 'expert' sounding. I would prefer to call it 'serious gossip' on the grounds that lives are restoried through talk which provides the opportunity for emotional speculation, to reflect about oneself as well as others, and to reflect on how others construct what we should be like:

> [gossip] embodies an alternative discourse to that of public life, and a discourse potentially challenging to public assumptions; it provides language for an alternative culture. Gossip's way of telling can project a different understanding of reality from that of society at large ... gossip epitomizes a way of *knowing* as well as telling. (Spacks, 1986, p. 46, my emphasis)

A final few words – for those of you who are not satisfied with the outcomes of your social work practice (try a scaled question), what would *you* be doing differently if your service users found solutions to their problems? Is any of this happening already? How can you do more of it? Is there anything you can do instead? Have you any skills which are not being used? How will you know that the outcomes of your practice are more satisfactory? And, if the service users you meet have any good ideas, please broadcast them.

# Appendix 1

# Survival of poor parenting chart

Name: _ _ _ _ _ _ _ _ _ _ _ _ _ _ _ _ _ _ _ _ _ _ _ _ _ _ _ _ _ _ _ Date: _ _ _ _ _ _ _ _ _ _ _ _

| please answer with a tick | not at all | just a little | pretty much | very much |
|---|---|---|---|---|
| 1   able to talk about what happened | | | | |
| 2   able to talk about other things | | | | |
| 3   able to grieve about what happened | | | | |
| 4   able to cope with guilt about what happened | | | | |
| 5   able to express anger about what happened | | | | |
| 6   feels part of a new family | | | | |
| 7   stands up for self | | | | |
| 8   sleeps OK | | | | |
| 9   eats well | | | | |
| 10  keeps smart | | | | |
| 11  goes to social events | | | | |
| 12  copes with new situations | | | | |
| 13  meets new friends | | | | |
| 14  laughs | | | | |
| 15  interested in the future | | | | |
| 16  able to choose supportive relationships | | | | |
| 17  able to relax | | | | |
| 18  able to tolerate criticism | | | | |
| 19  able to accept praise | | | | |
| 20  likes self | | | | |

Comments:........................................................................................................................

................................................................................................................................................

# Appendix 2

# Counselling by post: sample homework sheets

Using ideas developed by Berg and Reuss (1998), Dolan (1998a) and Denborough (1996), these were designed for a young prisoner who requested assistance for resisting heroin use, temper outbursts in prison, and angry feelings about his father's previous domestic violence. This young man enjoyed working out in the gym so the homework was explained as complementary emotional keep-fit exercises. Each stage was developed from the responses to the earlier homework responses and where these were not discussed in the monthly sessions, a letter accompanied them in which the dialogue was developed.

The homework on the range and effects of violence helped the young man to make links between his angry responses to perceived unfairness at school and in prison, enabling him to learn how to back down from confrontations without losing his self-pride.

The impact of the family differentiation exercises is more difficult to assess but his family are now visiting regularly, he will be welcomed home on release, and his father has promised him work.

Over a four-month period, he moved from being a category B to a category D prisoner and was accepted for transfer to an open prison with work training and group counselling facilities. These would give him an opportunity to strengthen his resistance to heroin use; he had already volunteered for random drug-testing.

## Homework sheet A1

When families work well they help young people to grow into confident people who know who they are and where they stand with their families. When families work less well, it is not unusual for the young person to feel torn between love and hate, one parent and another. This homework sheet is designed to help you sort these feelings out.

1   In what ways are you similar to your Mum? (e.g. looks, temperament, good and bad qualities, etc.)

2   In what ways are you similar to your Dad? (e.g. as above, and does anyone ever say "you're just like your Dad"? and what do they mean when they say this?)

3   In what ways are you different from your Mum? (as above)

4   In what ways are you different from your Dad? (as above)

5   Of all the ways that you are like your parents, which do you like most and want to keep?

6   Of all the ways you are like your parents, which do you least like and want to get rid of?

## Homework sheet A2

If you manage to complete the first sheet, try this one which makes a start on handling anger. Only do this if you feel comfortable and ready for it:

1    Make a list of everything you resent about your Dad:

2    Make a list of everything you resent about your Mum:

3    Make a list of everything you appreciate about your Dad (including what you learned from him):

4    Make a list of everything you appreciate about your Mum (including what you learned from her):

5    Look at your list and decide which of these things have been most important in your life:

*Appendix 2*

## Homework sheet B1

Now that you have written down the things you resent and appreciate about your dad and these showed that your dad does care for you (not that he has always shown it very well!) write these things on separate sheets. Keep the one with things you appreciate about your dad and tear up the sheet with things you resent.

This is to give you both a chance of a fresh start. You will see how well this is working by how you are with him on his next visit. If you find it difficult to tear the sheet up, tell Mum and Dad what you are doing and ask them to help you.

(Sheet 1: things appreciated about Dad)

(Sheet 2: things resented about Dad)

## Homework sheet C1

As you would like to change your dad's behaviour to your mum, perhaps the best way will be by example; if you can be a considerate tough person maybe Dad might be able to learn this too. So – concentrate on the ways you want to be different to your dad and the ways you want to continue being like your parents: being good towards Mum, keeping kind, and caring about your family. How will you show this for your mum? Will it be to do with how you talk to her, how you behave, or what?

You can ask your mum for her ideas on this. For example, how does she feel about you being angry with your dad? Would she prefer that you got on better, even if you were pretending a bit? Would she rate stopping taking drugs more than kind words? What would you be doing if she was bursting with pride for you? Make a list below:

## Homework sheet C2 (keeping a steady girlfriend)

You have no difficulty getting girlfriends but say that you can't always keep them as long as you would like. You know that giving up drugs will help but to help with the sort of things you can do instead of drugs, ask your sisters what qualities they look for in a man.

[As a starter for this exercise, Judith asked all the young women at Northorpe Hall what they looked for in a man and they came up with quite a list – see attached sheet (comments about neat bottoms and such like were edited out!).]

Add any other qualities your sisters suggest and then see how you score on the sheet.

## Qualities women look for in men

|  | not at all | just a little | pretty much | very much |
|---|---|---|---|---|
| Keep clean and smart | | | | |
| Take her out (walks are fine) | | | | |
| Hold hands | | | | |
| Speak *to*, not *at* | | | | |
| Make her feel special (good manners, small presents) | | | | |
| Cuddles (not necessarily leading to sex) | | | | |
| Joint responsibility for contraception | | | | |
| Make her laugh | | | | |
| Show you are interested in her | | | | |
| Not looking at other women when out together | | | | |
| Not expecting sex when drunk | | | | |
| Treat her as an equal | | | | |
| Shared decision making | | | | |
| Give compliments | | | | |

## Homework sheet D1

In what specific ways have you made changes that you can consider yourself fully recovered from heroin use?

1


2


3


4


5

## Homework sheet D2

Imagine it is two years from today. You are completely clean. What have you done to prevent a backslide?

## Homework sheet D3

This is a repeat of one you did recently but with a twist to make it harder. Imagine it is two years from today. Life has been much harder than you thought it would be. Although you were tempted to give up trying, you are still completely clean. How did you stay confident and prevent a backslide?

## Homework sheet E1

This is the first part of an exercise for increasing temper control. Lots of men have become tough guys because of earlier violence in their lives – no one wants to be a wimp. Being tough can lead to a lot of trouble so most people prefer to develop a tough, cool personality. It seems to help to look at the range of violence and then ask if any of it is good for your life and if any of it needs to stop. List the different sorts of violence in your life:

1  Violence in the family (fathers and sons, husbands and wives, etc.)

2  Violence at school (playground bullying, queer bashing, insulting girls, teachers' sarcasm, hitting, etc.)

3  Violence from the police (what happens when arrested, etc.)

4  Prison violence (fighting, being tough, not backing down, etc.)

5  Violence with mates (fighting at football matches, settling scores, criminal violence, etc.)

## Homework sheet E2

Increasing temper control, part two.

1   When you were violent towards your dad, who won and who lost? And in what ways?

2   When you had fights with teachers, who won and who lost? And in what ways?

3   When you were bullied at school or people tried to take advantage of you in prison, can you think of any other ways in which you could have stood up for yourself without actually fighting? (This is a really hard question, so don't worry if you can't think of anything).

4   If your mates start fighting when you are out drinking, how could you avoid this without being a wimp? (Another hard question – half the England football fans couldn't answer this one).

# References

Aitken, L. & Griffin, A. *Gender Issues: Elder Abuse*. London: Sage, 1996.

AHA (American Humane Association). *The Cycle of Violence to Children and Animals*. Englewood, CO: American Humane Society, 1995.

Arber, S. & Gilbert, N. 'Men: the forgotten carers', in: *Community Care. A Reader*, ed. Bornat, J., Pereira, C., Pilgrim, D. & Williams, F. Basingstoke: Macmillan Press – now Palgrave, 1993.

Aronsson, K. 'Social interaction and the recycling of evidence', in: *(Mis)Communication and Problematic Talk*, ed. Coupland, M., Giles, H. & Weiman, J. H. London: Sage, 1991.

Ascione, F. R. 'Children who are cruel to animals: a review of the research and implications for development and psychopathology'. *Anthrozoos* 6 (4): 226–47, 1993.

Barber, J. G. *Beyond Casework*. Basingstoke: Macmillan Press – now Palgrave, 1991.

Beresford, P. & Croft, S. *Citizen Involvement. A Practical Guide for Change*. Basingstoke: BASW/Macmillan Press – now Palgrave, 1993.

Berg, I. K. *Family Preservation. A Brief Therapy Workbook*. London: B. T. Press, 1991.

Berg, I. K. & Miller, S. D. *Working with Problem Drinkers: A Solution-Focused Approach*. New York: W. W. Norton, 1992.

Berg, I. K. & Reuss, N. H. *Solutions, Step by Step. A Substance Abuse Treatment Manual*. New York: W. W. Norton, 1998.

Bertolino, B. & O'Hanlon, B. *Invitation to Possibility-Land. An Intensive Teaching Seminar with Bill O'Hanlon*. Philadelphia, PA: Brunner/Mazel, 1998.

Biestek, F. *The Casework Relationship*. London: Unwin, 1957.

Blyth, E. & Milner, J. *Social Work with Children. The Educational Perspective*, London: Longman, 1997.

Blyth, E., Saleem, T. & Scott, M. *Kirklees Young Carers Project*. Huddersfield: Kirklees Metropolitan Council and the University of Huddersfield, 1995.

Braye, S. & Preston-Shoot, M. *Empowering Practice in Social Care*. Buckingham: Open University Press, 1995.

Brod, H. (ed.) *The Making of Maculinities: The New Men's Studies*. New York: Allen & Unwin, 1987.

Brook, G. 'Help me make choices too!' *Action for Sick Children* 26: 10–11, 1997

Brown, G. & Harris, T. *Social Origins of Depression. A Study of Psychiatric Disorder in Women*. London: Tavistock, 1978.

Bywaters, P. 'Case finding and screening for social work in acute general hospitals.' *British Journal of Social Work* 21 (1): 19–39, 1991.

Cavanagh, K. & Cree, V. E. 'Moving on', in: *Working With Men. Feminism and Social Work*, ed. Cavanagh, K. & Cree, V. E. London: Routledge, 1996.

Challis, D. & Davies, B. *Care Management in Community Care*. PSSRU: University of Kent at Canterbury, 1986.

Chanter, T. 'On not reading Derrida's texts. Distancing hermeneutics, misreading sexual difference, and neutralising narration', in: *Derrida and Feminism. Recasting the*

*Question of Woman*, ed. Feder, E. K., Rawlinson, M. C. & Zakin, E. New York and London: Routledge, 1997.

Cleaver, H. & Freeman, P. *Parental Perspectives in Cases of Suspected Child Abuse*. London: HMSO, 1995.

Coale, H. W. *The Vulnerable Therapist. Practising Pyschotherapy in an Age of Uncertainty*. New York and London: The Haworth Press, 1998.

Collinson, D. L. & Collinson, M. 'Sexuality in the workplace: the domination of men's sexuality', in: *The Sexuality of Organisation*, ed. Hearn, J., Sheppard, D. L., Tancred-Sheriff, P. & Burrell, G. London: Sage, 1989.

Cordery, J. & Whitehead, A. 'Boys don't cry: empathy, collusion and crime', in: *Gender, Crime and Probation Practice*, ed. Senior, P. & Woodhill, B., Sheffield: Pavic Publications, Sheffield City Polytechnic, 1992.

Culley, S. *Integrative Counselling Skills in Action*. London: Sage, 1991.

Dalrymple, J. & Burke, B. *Anti-oppressive Practice. Social Care and the Law*. Buckingham: Open University Press, 1995.

Davis, A. & Ellis, K. 'Enforced altruism or community care', in: *Ethical Issues in Social Work*, ed. Hugman, R. & Smith, D. London: Routledge, 1995.

Dearden, C. & Becker, S. *Young Carers: The Facts*. Sutton: Community Care, 1996.

Denborough, D. 'Step by step: developing respectful and effective ways of working with young men to reduce violence', in: *Mens' Ways of Being*, ed. McLean, C., Carey, M. & White, C. Boulder, CO and Oxford: Westview Press, 1996.

Denney, D. *Racism and Anti-Racism in Probation*. London: Routledge, 1992.

Dermer, S. B., Hemesath, C. W. & Russell, C. S. 'A feminist critique of solution-focused therapy'. *American Journal of Family Therapy* 26: 239–50, 1998.

de Shazer, S. 'The death of resistance'. *Family Process* 23: 79–221, 1984.

de Shazer, S. *Clues: Investigating Solutions in Brief Therapy*. New York: W. W. Norton, 1988.

de Shazer, S., Berg, I. K., Lipchik, E., Nunally, E., Molnar, A., Gingerich, W. & Weiner-Davis, M. 'Brief therapy: focused solution development'. *Family Process* 5: 207–21, 1986.

DeViney, E., Dickert, J. & Lockwood, R. 'The care of pets within child abusing families'. *International Journal for the Study of Animal Problems* 4: 321–9, 1983.

Digby, T. (ed.) *Men Doing Feminism*. New York and London: Routledge, 1998.

Dingwall, R., Eckelaar, J. M. & Murray, T. *The Protection of Children*. Oxford: Blackwell, 1983.

Di Stephano, C. 'Dilemmas of difference: feminism, modernity, and postmodernism', in: *Feminism/Postmodernism*, ed. Nicholson, L. J. New York, London: Routledge, 1990.

Dobash, R., Dobash, R., Cavanagh, K. & Lewis, R. *Research Evaluation of Programmes for Violent Men*. Edinburgh: Scottish Office Research Unit, 1996.

DoH (Department of Health). *Protecting Children. A Guide for Social Workers Undertaking a Comprehensive Assessment*. London: HMSO, 1998.

DoH (Department of Health). *Framework for the Assessment of Children in Need and their Families. Consultation Draft*. London: HMSO, 1999.

DoH (Department of Health). *Framework for the Assessment of Children in Need and their Families*. London: HMSO, 2000.

DHSS (Department of Health and Social Security). *Protecting Children. A Guide for Social Workers Undertaking a Comprehensive Assessment*. London: HMSO, 1988.

Dolan, Y. *Resolving Sexual Abuse. Solution-Focused Therapy and Eriksonian Hypnosis for Adult Survivors*. New York: W. W. Norton, 1991.

Dolan, Y. *One Small Step. Moving Beyond Trauma and Therapy to a Life of Joy.* Watsonville, CA: Papier Mâché Press, 1998a.

Dolan, Y. *Beyond Survival. Living Well is the Best Revenge.* Workshop held in London: the Brief Therapy Practice, 2–3 July, 1998b.

Dominelli, L. 'Masculinity, sex offenders and probation practice', in: *Gender, Crime and Probation Practice*, ed. Senior, P. & Woodhill, D. Sheffield: Pavic Publications, Sheffield City Polytechnic, 1991.

Dominelli, L. & McLeod, E. *Feminist Social Work.* Basingstoke: Macmillan Press – now Palgrave, 1989.

Doyal, L. *What Makes Women Sick. Gender and the Political Economy of Health.* Basingstoke: Macmillan Press – now Palgrave, 1995.

Dryden, W. & Fletham, C. *Developing the Practice of Counselling.* London: Sage, 1994.

Durrant, M. *Residential Treatment. A Cooperative, Competency-Based Approach to Therapy and Program Design.* New York: W. W. Norton, 1993.

Elliott, H. 'En-gendering distinction: postmodernism, feminism and narrative therapy'. *Gecko, Journal of Deconstruction and Narrative Ideas in Therapeutic Practice* 1: 52–71, 1997.

Epston, D. *Catching Up with David Epston: A Collection of Narrative Practice-based Papers. 1991–1996.* Adelaide: Dulwich Centre Publications, 1998.

Epston, D. & White, M. *Experience, Contradiction, Narrative and Imagination.* Adelaide: Dulwich Centre Publications, 1992.

Essex, S. & Gumbleton, J. 'Conversations in the "similar but different": working with denial in cases of severe child abuse'. *Australia and New Zealand Journal of Family Therapy*, forthcoming.

Essex, S., Gumbleton, J. & Luger, C. 'Resolutions: working with families where responsibility for abuse is denied'. *Child Abuse Review* 5: 191–201, 1996.

Evans, J. *Feminist Theory Today. An Introduction to Second-Wave Feminism.* London: Sage, 1995.

Fahlberg, V. *Putting the Pieces Together.* London: BAAF, 1988.

Fahlberg, V. *A Child's Journey Through Placement.* London: BAAF, 1991.

Farmer, E. & Owen, M. *Child Protection Practice: Private Risks and Public Remedies.* London: HMSO, 1995.

Fransella, F. & Dalton, P. *Personal Construct Counselling in Action.* London: Sage, 1990.

Freeman, J., Epston, D. & Lebovits, D. *Playful Approaches to Serious Problems.* New York: W. W. Norton, 1997.

Freer, M. 'Taking a defiant stand against sexual abuse and the mother-blaming discourse'. *Gecko, Journal of Deconstruction and Narrative Ideas in Therapeutic Practice* 1: 5–28, 1997.

Furman, B. & Ahola, T. *Solution Talk. Hosting Therapeutic Conversations.* New York: W. W. Norton, 1992.

Gardiner, J. K. 'Feminism and the future of fathering', in: *Men Doing Feminism*, ed. Digby, T. New York and London: Routledge, 1998.

George, E., Iveson, C. & Ratner, H. *Problem to Solution. Brief Therapy with Individuals and Familes.* London: B. T. Press, 1990.

Gilbert, S. M. & Gubar, S. *The Madwoman in the Attic. The Woman Writer and the Nineteenth Century Imagination.* New Haven and London: Yale University Press, 1979.

Gilgun, J. F. 'Mapping resilience as process among adults with childhood adversities', in: *The Dynamics of Resilient Families*, ed. McCubbin, H. I., Thompson, E. A., Thompson, A. I. & Futrell, J. A. London: Sage, 1999.

Gilligan, C. *In A Different Voice*. Cambridge, MA: Harvard University Press, 1982.

Gilligan, R. 'Beyond permanence: the importance of resilience in child placement and planning'. *Adoption and Fostering* 21 (1): 12–20, 1997.

Gilligan, R. 'Promoting positive outcomes for children in need: the assessment of protective factors', in: *The Child's World. Assessing Children in Need*, ed. Horwath, J. London: Department of Health/NSPCC/University of Sheffield, 2000.

Graddol, D. & Swann, J. *Gender Voices*. Oxford: Blackwell, 1989.

Hanmer, J. & Statham, D. *Women and Social Work. Towards a Women-centred Practice*. Basingstoke: Macmillan Press – now Palgrave, 1998.

Harding, S. 'Can men be subjects of feminist thought?', in: *Men Doing Feminism*, ed. Digby, T. New York, London: Routledge, 1998.

Harris, T. 'Getting off the conveyor belt from childhood adversity: what can we learn from naturalistic studies?', in: *Surviving Childhood Adversity*, ed. Gilligan, R., Ferguson, H. & Torode, R. Dublin: Social Studies Press, 1993.

Harrison, H. 'Child assessment and family support'. Conference paper given at *Assessing the Needs of Children*. London: National Children's Bureau, 1995.

Hearn, J. 'Imaging the aging of men', in: *Images of Aging: Cultural Representations of Later Life*, ed. Featherstone, M. & Wernick, A. London: Routledge, 1995.

Hearn, J. 'Ageism, violence and abuse – theoretical and practical perspectives on the links between "child abuse" and "elder abuse"', in: *Children, Child Abuse and Child Protection. Placing Children Centrally*, ed. Violence Against Children Study Group. Chichester: Wiley, 1999.

Herrenkohl, E. C., Herrenkohl, R. C., Rupert, L. J., Egolf, B. P. & Lutz, J. G. 'Risk factors for behavioural dysfunction: the relative impact of maltreatment, SES, physical health problems, cognitive ability, and the quality of parent–child interaction'. *Child Abuse and Neglect* 19 (2): 191–204, 1995.

Herrenkohl, R. C., Herrenkohl, E. C., Egolf, B. & Seech, M. 'The repetition of child abuse. How frequently does it occur?' *Child Abuse and Neglect* 3 (1): 67–72, 1979.

Hester, M., Pearson, C. & Harwin, N. *Making an Impact. Children and Domestic Violence. A Reader.* London: Department of Health, School for Policy Studies, University of Bristol, NSPCC and Barnados, 1998.

Hollis, F. *Social Casework: A Psychosocial Therapy*. New York: Random House, 1964.

hooks, b. 'Third World diva girls', in: *Yearning: Race, Gender, Cultural Politics*, ed. hooks, b. Boston, MA: South End Press, 1990.

Horne, M. 'Is it social work?' In: *Taking Child Abuse Seriously*, ed. Violence Against Children Study Group. London: Routledge, 1990, reprinted 1993.

Horrocks, C. & Milner, J. 'The residential home as serial step-family: acknowledging quasi-sibling relationships in local authority residential care', in: *We Are Family. Sibling Relationships in Placement and Beyond*, ed. Mullender, A. London: BAAF, 1999.

Hudson, A. 'The child sexual abuse "industry" and gender relations in social work', in: *Women, Oppression and Social Work: Issues in Anti-Discriminatory Practice*, ed. Langan, M. & Day, L. London: Routledge, 1992.

Hudson, P. *The Solution-Oriented Woman. Creating the Life You Want.* New York and London: W. W. Norton, 1996.

Humm, M. *Practising Feminist Criticism. An Introduction.* London: Prentice Hall/Harvester Wheatsheaf, 1995.

Ingleby, D. 'Professionals as socialisers: the "psy complex"', in: *Research in Law, Deviance, and Social Control*, ed. Spitzer, S. & Scull, A. T. New York: Jai Press, 1985.

Iveson, C. *Whose Life? Community Care of Older People and their Families*. London: B. T. Press, 1990.

Jack, G. 'An ecological approach to social work with children and familes'. *Child and Family Social Work* 2: 109–20, 1997.

Jenkins, A. *Invitations to Responsibility. The Therapeutic Engagement of Men Who Are Violent and Abusive.* Adelaide: Dulwich Centre Publications, 1990.

Jenkins, A. ' Moving towards respect: a quest for balance', in: *Men's Ways of Being*, ed. McLean, C., Carey, M. & White, C. Boulder, CO and Oxford: Westview Press, 1996.

Kagle, J. D. *Social Work Records.* Belmont, CA: Wadsworth, 1991.

Katz, M. *On Playing a Poor Hand Well.* New York, London: W. W. Norton, 1997.

Kelly, N. 'An Analysis of Decision Making in Child Protection Practice'. Ph.D. thesis, School of Human and Health Sciences, University of Huddersfield, 2000.

Korman, H. 'On the ethics of constructing realities'. *Contemporary Family Therapy* 19: 105–16, 1997.

Kosonen, M. 'Sibling relationships for children in the care system'. *Adoption and Fostering* 18 (3): 30–5, 1994.

Law, I. & Madigan, S. 'Power and politics. Introduction'. Adelaide: *Dulwich Centre Newsletter* 1: 3–7, 1994.

Lees, S. *Losing Out. Sexuality and Adolescent Girls.* London: Hutchinson, 1986.

Lees, S. *Ruling Passions. Sexual Violence, Reputation and the Law.* Buckingham: Open University Press, 1997.

Lethem, J. *Moved to Tears, Moved to Action. Solution Focused Brief Therapy with Women and Children.* London: B. T. Press, 1994.

Lockwood, R. & Ascione, F. R. (eds) *Cruelty to Animals and Interpersonal Violence. Readings in Research and Application.* West Lafayette, IN: Purdue University Press, 1998.

Lonsdale, S. *Women and Disability. The Experience of Physical Disability among Women.* London: Macmillan, 1990.

Lyotard, J-F. *The Postmodern Condition: A Report on Knowledge.* Minneapolis: University of Minnesota Press, 1984.

Mac an Ghaill, M. *The Making of Men,* Milton Keynes: Open University Press, 1994.

Madge, N. *Abuse and Survival. A Fact File.* London: The Prince's Trust (in association with NCB), 1997.

Madigan, S. & Epston, D. 'From "spy-chiatric gaze" to communities of concern. From professional monologue to dialogue', in: *The Reflecting Team in Action*, ed. Freidman, S. New York: Guilford, 1995.

Malin, N., Manthorpe, J., Race, D. & Wilmot, S. *Community Care for Nurses and the Caring Professions.* Buckingham: Open University Press, 1999.

Marsh, P. 'Social work with fathers', in: *The Children Act 1989: Working in Partnership with Families.* London: Family Rights Group, HMSO, 1991.

May, L. 'A progressive male standpoint', in: *Men Doing Feminism*, ed. Digby, T. New York and London: Routledge, 1998.

Mayer, J. E. & Timms, N. *The Client Speaks: Working Class Impressions of Casework.* London: Routledge & Kegan Paul, 1970.

Maynard, M. & Purvis, J. *Researching Womens' Lives from a Feminist Perspective.* London: Taylor & Francis, 1995.

McLean, C. 'The politics of men's pain', in: *Men's Ways of Being*, ed. McLean, C., Carey, M. & White, C. Boulder, CO and Oxford: Westview Press, 1996a.

McLean, C. 'Boys and education in Australia', in: *Mens' Ways of Being*, ed. McLean, C., Carey, M. & White, C. Boulder, CO and Oxford: Westview Press, 1996b.

Messerschmidt, J. W. *Nine Lives. Adolescent Masculinities, the Body, and Violence.* Boulder, CO: Westview Press, 2000.

Miller, G. *Becoming Miracle Workers. Language and Meaning in Brief Therapy.* New York: Aldine De Gruyter, 1997a.

Miller, G. 'Systems and solutions: the discourses of brief therapy'. *Contemporary Family Therapy* 19: 5–22, 1997b.

Miller, G. & de Shazer, S. 'Have you heard the latest rumour about ... ? Solution-focused therapy as rumour'. *Family Process* 37 (3): 363–77, 1998.

Milner, J. 'A disappearing act: the differing career paths of fathers and mothers in child protection investigations'. *Critical Social Policy* 38: 48–63, 1993a.

Milner, J. 'The gendered nature of child protection policy and practice', in: *Surviving Childhood Adversity*, ed. Ferguson, H., Gilligan, R. & Torode, R. Dublin: Social Studies Press, 1993b.

Milner, J. 'Men's resistance to social workers', in: *Violence and Gender Relations*, ed. Fawcett, B., Featherstone, B., Hearn, J. & Toft, C. London: Sage, 1996.

Milner, J. & Blyth, E. 'Theoretical debates and legislative framework', in: *Improving School Attendance*, ed. Blyth, E. & Milner, J. London: Routledge, 1999.

Milner, J. & O'Byrne, P. *Assessment in Social Work.* Basingstoke: Macmillan Press – now Palgrave, 1998.

Mirza, H. S. *Young, Female and Black.* London: Routledge, 1992.

Morrison, T., Erooga, M. & Beckett, R. *Sexual Offending Against Children. Assessment and Treatment of Male Abusers.* London: Routledge, 1994.

Mullender, A. 'Sketching in the background', in: *We Are Family. Sibling Relationships in Placement and Beyond*, ed. Mullender, A. London: BAAF, 1999a.

Mullender, A. 'Drawing out messages for policy and practice', in: *We Are Family. Sibling Relationships in Placement and Beyond*, ed. Mullender, A. London: BAAF, 1999b.

Mylam, T. & Lethem, J. *Searching for Strengths in Child Protection Assessment: From Guidelines to Practice.* London: B. T. Press, 1999.

Newburn, T. & Mair, G. *Working with Men.* Lyme Regis: Russell House Publishing, 1996.

Nicholson, L. J. *Feminism/Postmodernism.* New York and London: Routledge, 1990.

O'Hanlon, B. 'Possibility therapy: from iatrogenic injury to iatrogenic healing' in: *Therapeutic Conversations*, ed. Gilligan, S. & Price, R. New York: W. W. Norton, 1993.

O'Hanlon, W. & Weiner-Davis, M. *In Search of Solutions. A New Direction in Psychotherapy.* New York and London: W. W. Norton, 1989.

O'Leary, E. *Counselling Older Adults. Perspectives, Approaches and Research.* London: Chapman & Hall, 1996.

Orme, J. 'Feminist social work', in: *Social Work: Themes, Issues and Crtical Debates*, ed. Adams, R., Dominelli, L. & Payne, M. Basingstoke: Macmillan Press – now Palgrave, 1998.

Packman, J. with Randall, J. & Jacques, N. *Who Needs Care? Social Work Decisions about Children.* Oxford: Blackwell, 1986.

Parton, N. & O'Byrne, P. *Constructive Social Work. Towards a New Practice.* Basingstoke: Macmillan Press – now Palgrave, 2000.

Peake, A. & Fletcher, M. *Strong Mothers. A Resource for Mothers and Carers of Children Who Have Been Sexually Abused.* Lyme Regis: Russell House Publishing, 1997.

Perry, L. 'Against the grain', in: *The Personal is the Professional. Therapists Reflect on Their Families, Lives and Work*, ed. White, C. & Hales, J. Adelaide: Dulwich Centre Publications, 1997.

Phoenix, A. *Young Mothers.* London: Polity Press, 1991.

Prince, K. *Boring Records? Communication, Speech and Writing in Social Work*. London and Bristol, PA: Jessica Kingsley, 1996.

Pringle, K. *Men, Masculinities and Social Welfare*. London: University College London Press, 1995.

Read, J. *Disability, the Family and Society. Listening to Mothers*. Buckingham: Open University Press, 2000.

Rich, A. *Of Woman Born: Motherhood as Institution and Experience*. London: Virago, 1977.

Richmond, M. E. *Social Diagnosis*. New York: Russell Sage Foundation, 1917.

Richmond, M. E. *What is Social Casework? An Introductory Description*. New York: Russell Sage Foundation, 1922.

Rowbotham, S. *Woman's Consciousness, Man's World*. Harmondsworth: Penguin, 1973.

Rowbotham, S. *Dreams and Dilemmas*. London: Virago, 1983.

Roth, S. & Epston, D. 'Consulting the problem about the problematic relationship: An exercise for experiencing a relationship with an externalised problem', in: *Constructive Therapies 2*, ed. Hoyt, M. F. New York: Guilford Publications, 1996.

Ryan, T. & Walker, R. *Making Life Story Books*. London: BAAF, 1985.

Segal, L. *Slow Motion. Changing Masculinities. Changing Men*. London: Virago, revised edition 1997.

Selwyn, J. 'A "for ever and ever family": siblings' views as represented in reports for adoption hearings', in: *We Are Family. Sibling Relationships in Placement and Beyond*, ed. Mullender, A. London: BAAF, 1999.

Shafi, S. 'A study of Muslim Asian women's experiences of counselling and the necessity for a racially similar counsellor.' *Counselling Psychology Quarterly* 11 (3): 301–14, 1998.

Sheldon, B. *Cognitive-Behavioural Therapy. Research, Practice, and Philosophy*. London: Whiting & Birch, 1995.

Sheppard, M. *Care Management and the New Social Work. A Critical Analysis*. London: Whiting & Birch, 1995.

Sinclair, I., Standforth, L. & O'Connor, P. 'Factors predicting admission of elderly people to local authority residential care'. *British Journal of Social Work* 18 (3): 251–68, 1998.

Sinclair, R., Garrett, L. & Berridge, D. *Social Work and Assessment with Adolescents*, London: National Children's Bureau, 1995.

Smith, G. 'Dichotomies in the Making of Men', in: *Mens' Ways of Being*, ed. McLean, C., Carey, M. & White, C. Boulder, CO and Oxford: Westview Press, 1996.

Smith, G., Cox, D. & Saradjian, J. *Women and Self-Harm*. London: The Womens' Press, 1998.

Smith, P. (ed.) *Boys. Masculinities in Contemporary Culture*. Boulder, CO and Oxford: Westview Press, 1996.

Spacks, P. M. *Gossip*. Chicago, London: University of Chicago Press, 1986.

Spender, D. *Man Made Language*. London: Routledge & Kegan Paul, 1985, 2nd edition.

Stacey, K. 'Alternative metaphors for externalising conversations'. *Gecko, Journal of Deconstruction and Narrative Ideas in Therapeutic Practice* 1: 29–51, 1997.

Tamasese, K. & Waldegrave, C. 'Cultural and gender accountability in the "just therapy" approach', in: *Men's Ways of Being*, ed. McLean, C., Carey, M. & White, C. Boulder, CO and Oxford: Westview Press, 1996.

Teft, P. 'Work with men who are violent to their partners: time to re-assert a radical pro-feminist analysis'. *Probation Journal* 46 (1): 11–18, 1999.

Thomas, G. *Travels in the Trench between Child Welfare Theory and Practice*. New York: Haworth, 1995.

188     *References*

Thompson, N. *Anti-Discriminatory Practice*. London: Macmillan Press – now Palgrave, 1993.

Thompson, N. 'Social work with adults', in: *Social Work: Themes, Issues and Critical Debates*, ed. Adams, R., Dominelli, L. & Payne, M. Basingstoke: Macmillan Press – now Palgrave, 1998.

Turnell, A. & Edwards, S. *Signs of Safety. A Solution and Safety Oriented Approach to Child Protection Casework*. New York and London: W. W. Norton, 1999.

Turnell, A. & Lipchik, E. 'The role of empathy in brief therapy: the overlooked but vital context'. *Australian and New Zealand Journal of Family Therapy* 20 (4): 177–82, 1999.

Ungerson, C. *Policy is Personal. Sex, Gender and Informal Care*. London and New York: Tavistock Publications, 1987.

Waldegrave, C. 'Mono-cultural, mono-class, and so-called non-political family therapy'. *Australian and New Zealand Journal of Family Therapy* 6 (4): 197–200, 1985.

Walsh, T. (ed.) *Solution Focused Child Protection – Towards a Positive Frame for Social Work Practice*. Dublin: University of Dublin, Trinity College, Department of Social Studies. Occasional Paper No. 6, 1997.

Weingarten, K. 'The small and the ordinary: the daily practice of a postmodern narrative therapy'. *Family Process* 37: 3–15, 1998.

White, M. *Re-Authoring Lives: Interviews and Essays*. Adelaide: Dulwich Centre Publications, 1995.

White, M. *Narrative Therapy*. Brief Therapy Practice Workshop, London, 10–11 June 1999.

White, M. & Epston, D. *Narrative Means to Therapeutic Ends*. New York: W. W. Norton, 1990.

Williams, F. 'Women and community', in: *Community Care. A Reader*, ed. Bornat, J., Pereira, C., Pilgrim, D. & Williams, F. Basingstoke: Macmillan Press – now Palgrave, 1993.

Wise, S. 'Feminist ethics in practice', in *Ethical Issues in Social Work*, ed. Hugman, R. & Smith, D. London: Sage, 1995.

# Index